1995

Traditionally, critics of the English Renaissance have viewed pastoral as a static, idealizing genre aimed at the recreation of an idyllic past. More recently, these idealizing humanist approaches have been forcefully challenged by studies written from historicist perspectives. In *Pastoral and the poetics of self-contradiction* Judith Haber complicates the conventional opposition between humanist and historicist criticism by examining the ways in which pastoral poets themselves interrogate the contradictory relations inherent in their genre. Haber explores problems of representation, self-representation, and imitation in classical and Renaissance pastoral, focusing on texts by Theocritus, Virgil, Sidney, and Marvell. Her original approach revises current understanding of pastoral as a genre, and raises wider questions about the place of literature in society and the difficulties involved in constituting literary traditions.

PASTORAL AND THE POETICS OF SELF-CONTRADICTION

PASTORAL AND THE POETICS OF SELF-CONTRADICTION

Theocritus to Marvell

JUDITH HABER

Tufts University

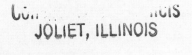
CAMBRIDGE
UNIVERSITY PRESS

Published by the Press Syndicate of the University of Cambridge
The Pitt Building, Trumpington Street, Cambridge, CB2 1RP
40 West 20th Street, New York, NY 10011-4211, USA
10 Stamford Road, Oakleigh, Melbourne 3166, Australia

First published 1994

Printed in Great Britain at the University Press, Cambridge

A catalogue record for this book is available from the British Library

Library of Congress cataloguing in publication data

Haber, Judith.
Pastoral and the poetics of self-contradiction: Theocritus to Marvell / Judith
Haber.
p. cm.
Includes bibliographical references and index.
ISBN 0 521 44206 0 (hardback)
1. English poetry – Early modern, 1500–1700 – History and criticism.   2. Marvell,
Andrew, 1621–1678 – Criticism and interpretation.   3. Pastoral poetry, English –
History and criticism.   4. Pastoral poetry, Latin – History and criticism.
5. Pastoral poetry, English – Roman influences.   6. Sidney, Philip, Sir, 1554–1586.
Arcadia.   7. Theocritus – Criticism and interpretation.   8. Contradiction in
literature.   9. Self in literature.   10. Virgil. Bucolica.   I. Title.
PR539.P3H33   1994
821'.309321734–dc20   93-46826   CIP

ISBN 0 521 44206 0 hardback

TAG

To the memory of my parents,
Stanley Bernard Haber
and
Bernice Kraditor Haber

Contents

Acknowledgments

This book was completed with the aid of a Mellon grant from Tufts University. It would never have been finished, however, without the aid and encouragement of my teachers, students, colleagues, and friends. My debt to Paul Alpers is evident on every page. The book had its origin in his seminar on pastoral at the University of California, Berkeley; it began to take shape as a dissertation under his direction, and it continued to benefit from his generous advice in its later stages. I am also indebted to Donald Friedman and Thomas Rosenmeyer for their many careful readings and challenging questions. The faculty and students at Tufts University made numerous contributions; I am particularly grateful to Carol Flynn, who read almost everything I wrote, and to Lee Edelman, John Fyler, and Sonia Hofkosh for their advice, encouragement, and support. I would like to thank my editor, Kevin Taylor, and the two readers for Cambridge University Press: both Michael Schoenfeldt and the anonymous reader provided me with detailed comments and helpful criticism. Richard Burt and Marshall Grossman also read large portions of the manuscript and offered many useful suggestions; and Charles Trocano prepared the bibliography in record time. William Batstone, Michelle Elkin, Jeffrey Knapp, Suzanne Qualls, and Deborah Willis all provided much-needed aid at significant times. And I am forever grateful to Julia Genster: I thank her for her friendship, her advice, her patience, and her puns.

Texts and abbreviations

The following abbreviations refer to Philip Sidney's major texts:

Apology   *An Apology for Poetry; or, The Defence of Poesy*, ed. Geoffrey Shepherd (London: Thomas Nelson and Sons, 1965).

AS   *Astrophil and Stella*, cited in *The Poems of Sir Philip Sidney*, ed. William A. Ringler, Jr. (Oxford: Clarendon Press, 1962); all references to Ringler's commentary in this edition will be credited to Ringler, *Poems*.

NA   *New Arcadia*, cited in *The Prose Works of Sir Philip Sidney*, ed. Albert Feuillerat, 4 vols. (1912; Cambridge: Cambridge University Press, 1962), I–II.

OA   *Old Arcadia*, cited in *The Countess of Pembroke's Arcadia (The Old Arcadia)*, ed. Jean Robertson (Oxford: Clarendon Press, 1979).

When references follow logically, I have simply given page and line numbers.

I also use the following texts throughout:
For Theocritus' *Idylls*, I cite the text of A. S. F. Gow, ed., *Theocritus*, 2nd edn., 2 vols. (Cambridge: Cambridge University Press, 1952), and the translations of R. C. Trevelyan, *The Idylls of Theocritus* (Cambridge: Cambridge University Press, 1947). For Virgil's *Eclogues*, I follow Paul Alpers' modernization of R. A. B. Mynors' text (Oxford: Oxford University Press, 1969), in *The Singer of the Eclogues: A Study Of Virgilian Pastoral*

(Berkeley: University of California Press, 1979); translations are Alpers' unless otherwise noted (I have occasionally supplied more literal, prose translations). For Marvell's poetry, I cite the text of *The Poems and Letters of Andrew Marvell*, ed. H. M. Margoliouth, rev. P. Legouis and E. E. Duncan-Jones, 3rd edn., 2 vols. (Oxford: Clarendon Press, 1952), 1. Unless otherwise noted, my text for Shakespeare's plays is *The Riverside Shakespeare*, ed. G. Blakemore Evans (Boston: Houghton Mifflin, 1974).

"Remedies themselves complain": pastoral poetry, pastoral criticism

> Alas! I look for Ease in vain,
> When Remedies themselves complain.
> Marvell, "Damon the Mower"

This study had a dual genesis: I wished to account for the persistence of the "antipastoral" in pastoral poetry and to arrive at an interpretation of the Renaissance texts that seemed to me to exemplify the problems signaled by that term – the lyrics of Andrew Marvell. Traditionally, the dominant practice among critics of Renaissance poetry has been to view pastoral as a static, idealizing genre, whose goal was the recovery of an Edenic past – a goal that pastoral poets pursued by creating images of idyllicism within their works, and by imitating their predecessors as closely as possible. Poets who failed to meet these criteria – and the list could include every canonical Renaissance poet – were regularly exempted from the genre, and characterized as "antipastoral."[1] In looking back at classical pastoral, however, I found not a stable origin from which later works deviated, but a mode that worked insistently against itself, problematizing both its own definition and stable definitions within its texts: from the beginning of the genre, presence, continuity, and consolation have been seen as related to – indeed as dependent on – absence, discontinuity, and loss. While the term "antipastoral" seemed, therefore, to be clearly reductive from one perspective, it also clearly answered to a fundamental self-contradictoriness within the genre – a contradictoriness that is frequently registered self-consciously in pastoral poems: the quotation from Marvell that I have chosen for the title of this section could apply to any of the texts I examine, although its paradoxical implications would resonate differently with every one.

In recent years, many of the most interesting and vital studies of pastoral have been written from historicist perspectives (new or otherwise).[2] Critics such as Louis Adrian Montrose, Annabel Patterson, and Leah Marcus have made major contributions to our understanding of the genre – not the least of which is their general movement away from prescriptive, idealizing definitions. Almost universally, however, historicist critics underestimate the self-consciousness of Renaissance and classical poets about precisely those assumptions upon which their own criticism is based; they ignore or downplay, that is, the extent to which pastoral texts problematize relations between the literary and the "real," the aesthetic and the material, and the present and the past, creating neither a simple union of contraries nor an equally simple discontinuity. As a result, they reproduce, in different ways, the idealist assumptions they wish to eschew.

This is most obviously true of the leading historicist critic of the genre, Louis Montrose.[3] In a series of illuminating articles, Montrose persuasively demonstrates that even the "simplest" Renaissance pastoral is never wholly simple. He investigates how it "busily negotiat[es] by coulor of otiation,"[4] making play a form of work, and wielding power by acknowledging limitation; he argues that its exclusions are significant, and that its simplifying forms can effectively efface and displace contradictions. But Montrose's perspective causes him to overemphasize both the idealizing force of Renaissance pastoral and its discontinuity from earlier pastoral. He focuses primarily on texts or portions of texts that lay claim to simplicity, purity, and presence;[5] simultaneously, his synchronic approach allows him to posit an ideally "impure" origin in earlier pastoral and in material reality, while his theoretical beliefs call the existence of such an origin into question. Commenting on a court entertainment, he makes it clear that he regards "pastoral's metaphorizing process" as a "process of purification"; he continues:

The shepherd's assertion demonstrates that the creation of figurative pastoral discourse involves a distortion, a selective exclusion, of the material pastoral world. One of the most remarkable features of this appropriation of pastoral forms by Renaissance court culture is its transformation of what in other contexts was a vehicle of agrarian complaint, rustic celebration, and popular religion into a vehicle of social mystification.[6]

Elsewhere, he maintains that "pastoral itself progresses from the literal pastoralism of the countryside to the metaphorical pastoralism of the court by means of verbal formalization."[7] Such statements underestimate both the extent to which "pastoral's metaphorizing process" has always been a problem in the genre, and the complexity with which that process is presented by pastoral poets.

Montrose's emphasis on the paradoxically impure "purifying" force of pastoral metaphors contrasts strikingly with his own stance: in a series of disclaimers that have become the hallmark of new historicist criticism, he freely admits the impurity of his own representations, and manages to turn this admission into a virtue – into an assertion of a kind of purity.[8] The self-consciousness implicit in this strategy is felt to mark a distance between the critic and the texts he analyzes, a distance made explicit in his formulation of intent, "If the poet's task was to celebrate, the critic's task is to understand the uses of celebration."[9] But Montrose's strategies could, themselves, be characterized as versions of pastoral; they are anticipated in numerous pastoral texts. On the one hand, pastoral poets often thematize his perception that their exclusions signify – that their "purity" depends upon and recreates what it excludes – thus problematizing the distinction between text and context that new historicists simultaneously deny and rely upon. On the other hand (and frequently on the same hand), they often see their own metaphorizing process directly as a mark of impurity – an impurity that consists precisely in a felt distance from "simpler" material and literary realities; and this direct acknowledgment of separation, absence, and lack can become a means of connection to more innocent "simpler" realities that are now seen as not completely innocent. Moreover, the question – much debated today – of whether this strategy is legitimate, whether this sort of self-consciousness has "consequences,"[10] is itself a subject of investigation and debate in the texts I consider. Their various responses suggest that the answer will depend on what one means by "consequences" (and on what one means by "answers"). None of them implies that acknowledging one's limitations actually allows one to escape them; attempts to achieve this end invariably recreate what they seek to elude. The one poet I examine for whom absolute freedom from limitation is the only result that would count as "consequential" is Sidney – and he is forced to answer, in effect, that the pastoral strategy has absolutely no consequences; the difficulties inherent in self-consciously assuming this position are, as we shall see, paradoxically demonstrated by his inability to bring his pastoral romance to an effective conclusion.

In contrast to Montrose, Annabel Patterson does emphasize the self-consciousness of most pastoral poetry. She provides a diachronic perspective in her impressive study of Virgil's influence, *Pastoral and Ideology*, and she makes it clear that literary referentiality and poetic utility have been explicit problems in pastoral at least since the *Eclogues*.[11] But Patterson's general approach – and her understanding of literary self-consciousness, in particular – are quite different from my own. To a certain extent, her work reproduces Sidney's uncompromising approach to pastoral (if not his self-critical perspective on that approach). Her study is structured around a series of oppositions – between Virgil and Theocritus, between Virgil's first and second eclogues, between the real and the ideal, the political and the aesthetic, the complex and the simple, content and form. She presents these oppositions as easily separable, and their separation has clear ideological force.

This is perhaps most evident towards the beginning of her book, when she sets up a programmatic distinction between different versions of Virgilian pastoral. After pointing to the presence in the *Eclogues* of an implied "argument ... as to whether poetry has a social function," she declares:

At one end of the argument stand the lovelorn, idle Corydon of Eclogue 2 and his counterpart Gallus in Eclogue 10, the former

defined by his opening quality, *formosus*, the lovely one, as belonging
to a pastoral in which formal and aesthetic properties count for almost
everything, provided the mirror of art does not lie.[12]

A little later, she speaks of a reader for whom "the 'formosum
pastor'" represents Cornelius Gallus, and she implicitly associates this phrase with Corydon's scornful beloved, Alexis.[13] The
fundamental difficulty with both these interpretations is that
there is no "formosum pastor"; neither is there any simply
"beautiful" pastoral in Virgil or (even more clearly) in
Theocritus. The juxtaposition of the first two words in the
opening line of *Eclogue* 2 – *Formosum pastor Corydon ardebat Alexin*
("The shepherd Corydon burned for the beautiful Alexis" [my
trans.]) – points, first of all, to their logical as well as their
grammatical incompatibility, and to the analogous incompatibility of great and small, of sophisticated urban artifice and
simple "realistic" rusticity. The associations Patterson makes
are not, of course, unjustified: Corydon *is* an aesthetician, and
he becomes a more self-conscious one as the eclogue continues;
we are thus forced to rethink the simple oppositions with which
we began. By seeing him simply as the embodiment of formal
beauty, however, she forecloses the questions that the eclogue
foregrounds – questions about the efficacy and the accuracy of
poetic representation – and she simultaneously distances the
poem from Virgil's explicitly political eclogues.[14] What is
occurring here is a kind of aesthetic scapegoating: the creation
of a stable category of pure, "empty" idyllic formalism allows
for the simultaneous creation of a category of pure, "full"
political meaning, of an unmediated real uncontaminated by
"the mirror of art."[15]

I dwell upon this reading not to impugn Patterson's scholarship, which is considerable, but because the assumptions that
motivate it are operable throughout her book, and are
discernible behind much current political criticism. Whereas
Montrose repeatedly demonstrates that form has ideological
implications, the ideological force of Patterson's work is to assert
the primacy and priority of the ideational. The divisions that
she effects among and within texts are clearly reflected in her
critical methodology. The formal properties of a text are viewed

as fundamentally non-signifying: form is seen either as emptily self-reflexive, or as a simple veil placed over a real and separable truth – a veil that is consciously assumed in response to external constraints. She thus credits the poets she examines with both too much control over and too little self-consciousness about problems of referentiality, representation, and imitation.

If Patterson settles the question of referentiality too quickly, most thematic political criticism treats it as already settled. The difficulties inherent in this position are particularly obvious in discussions of Marvell, because Marvell thematizes the problematics of earlier pastoral in a particularly radical way; arguments about his poetry tend therefore to revolve – even more frequently than in other cases – around the question of their reference. Ann Berthoff, attempting to remove *Upon Appleton House* from the realm of politics, inadvertently poses the right question when she asks rhetorically, "Would Marvell refer to a somber allegory of the Civil War as 'these pleasant Acts'?"[16] The answer to this question is emphatically "yes" – but to say this is not to say that Marvell's pleasantries, his displacements, his formal exclusions are extrinsic to the real, serious meaning of his poems; it is rather to assert that they are inseparable from anything that may be construed as meaning. By viewing them as dispensable defense mechanisms, even a fine critic like Leah Marcus necessarily reproduces Berthoff in another key,[17] creating a mirror image of the idealist position that views all serious "antipastoral" elements as extrinsic to the genre. What is at stake here – and that stake is, itself, political – is precisely the logical, hierarchical separation between seriousness and play, form and meaning, inside and out, text and context. And while a focus on political thematics is both useful and illuminating, it inevitably obscures this fact. It seems significant that Berthoff is just as – if not more – eager to exclude serious theology from *Upon Appleton House*;[18] and another like-minded critic gestures, despite himself, toward an extreme form of the problem when he attempts to separate the Mower poems from all associations with the Fall: commenting on the frequent appearance of the word "fall" in the poems, he remarks, "the similarity is verbal, not real."[19] Any thematic criticism necessarily assents to this opposition. Marvell's poetry does not – or more precisely, like the best new historicism, it simultaneously assents and problematizes, criticizes while making it clear that it cannot avoid reproducing what it criticizes, "celebrates" and uncovers "the uses of celebration."

I am not, of course, attempting to declare specific political readings out of bounds; in fact, I am suggesting that they are inescapably relevant even to poems that appear to erect boundaries around them. Even less would I care to deny the relevance of specific material circumstances to the different texts I examine, although my focus in the following chapters prevents me from considering them in detail. That focus is "literary" in a number of respects – in my choice of exemplary poets and poems, in my methodology, and in my interest in examining the creation (and continual recreation) of a literary tradition. My emphasis in the preceding pages on Virgil's second eclogue is not arbitrary; this study as a whole could be subtitled "some versions of Corydon": it examines the most self-reflexive strain of a self-reflexive genre. In so doing, however, it repeatedly calls the fixity of its own limits into question – and it raises similar questions about the self-consciously limited mode of pastoral and about the category of "literature" in general. I foreground the literary, in other words, not to assert its lack of connection to the social and the historical, but to address the complexity with which those contradictory relations are constructed, understood, and interrogated by pastoral poets themselves. And because my purpose here is to explore contradictions (rather than to "explain" them by appealing to a stable notion of literature or of history), my own account will often reproduce (and emphasize) the terms, the structures, and the problems that I am locating in the poems I examine.

I begin by considering the origins of pastoral in the poetry of Theocritus and Virgil. I would insist on the importance of reexamining Theocritus: the common tendency among critics of English pastoral to ignore or oversimplify his poetry inevitably limits their view of the genre. His position as the originator of pastoral is, of course, largely the creation of later poets: he writes, as David Halperin has shown, within the epic tradition.[20] His bucolicism is not, therefore, the expression of a longing for simplicity, but a means of acknowledging his limitations, of ironically distancing himself and his contemporaries from the epic poets and heroes that had preceded them. Theocritus' ironies are, however, quite consciously two-edged. Throughout the *Idylls*, both the poet and his characters repeatedly recreate, in diminished forms, the heroism they leave behind. Attempts to evade this dilemma, moreover, merely succeed in reinforcing it: at its most extreme, the bucolic perspective becomes identified with and indistinguishable from the heroic. While Theocritus' poetry insistently denies any originary force, then, it simultaneously evidences an awareness of the ways in which this diffidence constitutes an assertion, and it anticipates many of the paradoxes of power recent critics have seen in Renaissance pastoral.

When the *Idylls* became a model of poetic practice, the contradictions at their center provided Theocritus' successors with a means of affirming connections to the pastoral tradition while simultaneously acknowledging their distance from it. I trace this development in the chapter on Virgil's *Eclogues*, and I discuss Virgil's transformation of pastoral into the extremely self-conscious, insistently self-reflexive form that the poets of the Renaissance inherited. In the *Eclogues*, the paradoxical ironies of the *Idylls* are rationalized and made explicit, and the oppositions that Theocritus had conflated are suspended or (to invoke the image Virgil uses) "interwoven." Simultaneously, Theocritus' focus on the problematic relation between the limited man and his heroic models is supplemented (and frequently supplanted) by a focus on the parallel relation between the literary image and the literal reality it represents. Virgil's emphasis on the intertwined powers and limits of art is clearly coextensive with his social concerns: it is precisely because he places so much pressure on his poetry to "work" in the world that he is so deeply aware of its insufficiencies. While I concentrate my analysis of his pastoral on the Theocritean poems, I therefore attempt to suggest how the questions raised here are related to those in the contemporary eclogues.

In the second part of this study, I focus on Sidney's *Old Arcadia* and Marvell's lyrics (the Mower poems and *Upon Appleton House*), using these texts to address the problems and possibilities that the Theocritean/Virgilian model offered to English poets of the sixteenth and seventeenth centuries. My emphasis on the *Old Arcadia* may strike some as idiosyncratic. I believe, however, that Sidney's romance presents us with a particularly acute expression of the difficulties confronting Renaissance pastoralists – difficulties that many of his contemporaries (most obviously Spenser and Shakespeare, whom I consider briefly) are repeatedly attempting to resolve. The romance is the quintessential Elizabethan form of pastoral: its structure throws into high relief Renaissance humanist concerns about the persuasive power of poetry and the relation of "fiction" to "history."[21] We are forced to move beyond the self-imposed limits of the eclogue here, to consider the motives for and the consequences of action. As a result, the suspensions that had characterized the *Eclogues* are both anatomized and disrupted, and Virgil's questions about the efficacy of art in the external world become even more pressing. In the *Old Arcadia*, Sidney deliberately heightens the disjunctions that were implicit in earlier pastoral romances, repeatedly presenting us with two mutually exclusive, reflecting alternatives, variously figured as pastime and passion, a lack of discharge and an uncontrollable flood, self-enclosure and public exposure. As he pursues the conflicting implications of his own ideals to their logical conclusions, the paradoxical processes of pastoral recoil upon themselves: traditional consolations are disabled, and self-contradiction becomes self-cancellation.

Marvell's lyrics are frequently seen as a further movement away from the origins of pastoral. In the final chapter of this study, I argue that they also represent a movement back. Marvell sees distance itself as means of connection – indeed, as the only means available to him. Throughout his lyrics, he creates literal reality out of self-reflexive metaphor, enclosure out of violation, innocence out of desire, and continuity out of disjunction and displacement. His extreme self-consciousness about the problems Sidney had faced (problems, themselves, of self-consciousness) simultaneously exacerbates those problems and presents itself as their solution. And, by explicitly inverting the ironies with which pastoral began, Marvell effectively reaches beyond his more recent predecessors, and cements his connection to Theocritus.

"Remedies themselves complain" is itself, I believe, one of Marvell's many homages to Theocritus: it translates into English the contradictory meanings of the term *pharmakon* ("remedy," "poison"),[22] which appears prominently in several of Theocritus' idylls (including *Idyll* 11, a source of "Damon the Mower").[23] When Virgil imitated Theocritus' second idyll, he rendered *pharmaka* as *carmina* ("songs," "charms"), characteristically emphasizing his self-reflexive concern with the powers and limits of art. In the Mower poems, Marvell retains (and redoubles) the self-reflexivity that was Virgil's legacy: in so doing, however, he returns to Theocritus' paradoxes, insisting, on many levels, on the coincidence of distance and identity, bucolic and heroic, remedy and complaint. In *Upon Appleton House*, he more directly confronts the dilemmas that were posed by the pastoral romance: he explores the connections that exist between his creations and the greater world, and he acknowledges that his fictions are subject to external constraints; he makes this acknowledgment, however, from a perspective that is itself represented as fictional. He does not abandon his self-enclosed ironies; instead, he unpacks their implications, making explicit the ways in which "greater [is] in less contain'd" (*Upon Appleton House*, 44).

The neat (if paradoxical) narrative structure of the story I am telling is quite clearly dependent on its end. I include an epilogue focusing on John Gay's mock-pastoral, *The Shepherd's Week*, in which I address both the general question of pastoral "endings" – which have been centrally important to the genre since its inception – and my particular reasons for ending with the Renaissance: although Theocritus' ironies continue to exert considerable force after the Restoration, the relation between "pastoral" poets and their classical predecessors undergoes a significant change. Even within the parameters of this study, of course, one could easily construct another narrative: a history of pastoral that concluded with Milton rather than Marvell would, undoubtedly, seem more expansive. But the very limitations and exclusions that mark my exemplary texts serve effectively to foreground the paradoxes that underlie the pastoral tradition. Most obviously, the "end" that I have chosen (like the "origin" it recalls) radically questions such temporal limits even as it invokes them; and the questions that it raises reappear, in less extreme forms, in less self-consciously limited examples of the mode.

Indeed, the self-critical perspective that Marvell's lyrics epitomize seems to be peculiarly at home in pastoral poetry. It is not surprising that, as Montrose remarks, "theories of pastoral have a way of turning into theories of literature."[24] Not only is this an extremely self-reflexive mode, explicitly concerned with constructing representations of representations, it is also a supremely self-correcting mode: each of the poets I consider demonstrates an acute awareness of the problems inherent in his own strategies and assumptions. For that reason, these texts are particularly worth examining, on their own terms, at a time when we are ourselves struggling with the problem of "placing" literature within society and the difficulties involved in constituting literary traditions.

CHAPTER I

Bringing it all back home: bucolic and heroic in Theocritus' Idylls

Too often, Theocritus' poetry has been oversimplified or simply overlooked by readers of English pastoral; the *Idylls* have regularly been dismissed as a naive point of origin from which Virgil and later poets deviated.[1] Such an approach does a clear disservice to Theocritus himself, and it inevitably limits our view of the genre: by allowing critics to treat as entirely new themes and techniques that are indebted to earlier texts, it helps to obscure not only specific allusions, but one of the primary concerns of much pastoral – the self-conscious focus on the interrelations that exist between "new" poets and their literary models, between present exigencies and the pressures and promises of the past.

That focus is, in fact, central to the *Idylls* themselves. One of the most important literary debates of Theocritus' day was the disagreement between Callimachus and the Homeric poets over whether contemporary writers should attempt to duplicate the epic scope and style of their predecessors.[2] Theocritus' paradoxical approach to this question exerted a profound influence – both directly and through Virgil's *Eclogues* – on the poetry of his successors. It is therefore instructive and ultimately necessary for students of later pastoral to return to the *Idylls*, to consider carefully the problems they pose.

Theocritus' "pastoral"[3] does, of course, differ from that of his successors in at least one major respect. Later poets must come to terms with their distance from earlier pastoral poetry – a distance that may be imaged in their works by their characters' loss of a simpler, more innocent bucolic existence. For Theocritus, however, what has been lost is not pastoral, but the heroic – the great Homeric epics and the attitudes toward life they represent.[4] Bucolic simplicity is not, therefore, an object of longing in the *Idylls*; it is a mode of acceptance.

This aspect of Theocritus' poetry is emphasized by Thomas Rosenmeyer in his influential study, *The Green Cabinet*. Rosenmeyer focuses on Theocritus' Epicurean acceptance of the present; the *Idylls*, in his view, celebrate the joys of "a minuscule life fully lived"[5] – a life characterized by humor, freedom, equanimity, simplicity, and *otium*. The pleasures of that life, he repeatedly demonstrates, are inextricably tied to its limitations.

I have found Rosenmeyer's work extremely illuminating, and I would agree that the qualities he identifies are characteristic of Theocritean pastoral – are, indeed, a large part of what makes us want to identify it as "pastoral." But Rosenmeyer's Epicurean emphasis causes him to undervalue other elements in the *Idylls*. He sees pain and loss as fundamentally alien to Theocritus' vision; they are introduced, in small quantities, into the bucolic world only to provide it with some much-needed backbone: `

> Theocritean pastoral ... cannot do without intimations of a sterner and more hurtful life ostensibly excluded from the arbor ... Without these subtle reminders of a disavowed order, the pastoral becomes sweet and cloying.
>
> But, in contrast to Hesiodic poetry, the pastoral has such reminders lightly etched in. They furnish muscle and tone; they do not attract our ideological attention.[6]

He similarly maintains that heroic modes of expression appear only infrequently in the *Idylls*, and that they are therefore immediately recognizable as "foreign element[s]."[7] Generally, heroism is excluded from the bower: "The noon peace is an imperious master; it brooks no rivals. *Hasychia* is all."[8]

The consequence of this stance is that Rosenmeyer is forced to declare, at different points in his book, that almost every pastoral idyll is in some way atypical.[9] For the *Idylls* focus not only on the limits of the present, but on the relationship that exists between a limited present and a heroic past. Theocritus repeatedly calls our attention to this relationship by presenting us with ordinary men and women who are singing about, comparing themselves to, and attempting to substitute for absent heroes. This situation provides the basic "plot" for many of the *Idylls*; and even when it is not made explicit, it is implied by the recurrent spectacle of shepherds mouthing heroic words and assuming heroic postures.

The constant juxtaposition of high and low throughout the *Idylls* creates a series of tensions that have been noted by many critics, and analyzed most fully by Charles Segal. Segal views Theocritus' poetry as an ongoing dialectic between two opposed perspectives, which one could term "heroic" and "bucolic." He comments, for example, on *Idyll* 1:

The contrast between Thyrsis and Daphnis ... expresses an aspect of the same dialectic that binds together Lycidas and Simichidas in VII, Corydon and Battus in IV, Lacon and Comatas in V, Milo and Bucaeus in X: a dialectic between sentiment and factuality, between hopeless passion and the continuities of work, between dreamlike aspiration and practical acceptance, between imagination and reality ... Each side needs the other to anchor it to the wholeness of reality. And each stands in perpetual oscillation with the other.[10]

Segal performs a valuable service by demonstrating at length that while bucolic acceptance may be the hallmark of Theocritus' pastoral, it never exists alone. The easy separation that he effects between the conflicting perspectives he identifies, however, prevents him from making their relation quite clear: in all of his essays, he assigns one perspective to each of the characters in a poem and then reconciles the two by appealing to an abstract, unifying ideal (e.g., "the wholeness of reality"[11]). This critical procedure becomes particularly unhelpful when he is attempting to define Theocritus' attitude toward the heroic: he will sometimes maintain that the qualities he associates with heroic aspiration are fundamentally "non-bucolic," and at other times declare that they represent "the essence of [Theocritus'] bucolic world,"[12] without adequately explaining how both assertions can be true. His criticism has been accurately characterized as suggesting that Theocritus' perspective on heroic poetry is fundamentally "nostalgic":[13] he feels that the *Idylls* are motivated by a desire "to recover, in a sceptical and self-conscious age, something of the power and range of myth available to earlier poets."[14] But he never fully reconciles this claim with his clear awareness of the anti-heroic impulses that Rosenmeyer finds in the *Idylls*, and that Theocritus' ironies repeatedly imply.

Similar difficulties with Segal's approach have led other critics to conclude that Theocritus' attitude toward both his characters and his predecessors is primarily "ironic."[15] I would suggest, however, that the contradictions apparent in Segal's analysis are, in fact, reflective of paradoxes that are central to the *Idylls* – paradoxes that derive not from a "cleavage in the nature of reality,"[16] but from contradictions inherent in the attempt to recognize and accept one's own limitations, to acknowledge one's distance from the texts and assumptions of the past. The problems that these paradoxes pose for critics of classical literature reappear throughout pastoral criticism: the absolute separation that Segal attempts to create between the "bucolic" and the "heroic" resurfaces, in somewhat different forms, in analyses of the opposition between Virgil and Theocritus, between "hard" (serious) and "soft" (escapist) pastoral, between antipastoral and pastoral itself.[17] From its inception, however, pastoral has been a self-consciously self-contradictory mode. The "bucolic" perspective in the *Idylls* is repeatedly implicated in its opposite: even when a poem appears to present us with two clearly contrasting characters, the positions those characters espouse are interrelated. I would like to begin examining their relation through a brief analysis of the poem in which it appears in its most crystallized form: the programmatic first idyll.

In *Idyll* 1, Theocritus presents us with his most serious picture of heroic aspiration. Daphnis the neatherd, whose mysterious death for love the shepherd Thyrsis enacts and mourns in song, is the only herdsman in the *Idylls* who could accurately be considered a hero. As we have seen, Segal views him almost exclusively in this light, contrasting his tragic self-assertion with the bucolic diffidence and joy that is exemplified by Thyrsis. I would agree with much of this analysis: Daphnis is, I believe, a figure for the absent hero, with whom the ordinary man of the

present must come to terms. But he is also himself an ordinary
man when compared to the epic heroes of the past. And he is
presented as acutely aware of his own limitations: throughout
his speech, he implicitly concedes his distance from his epic
predecessors, at the same time that he claims identity with
them. This dual perspective is especially evident in his dismissal
of Aphrodite. After telling the goddess to return to her shepherd-
lovers Anchises and Adonis,[18] Daphnis declares:

> And then I'ld have thee go encounter Diomed, and say
> "The herdsman Daphnis have I conquered; now fight *thou* with
>   me."   (112–13)

These lines have sometimes been read as an "ironic" commentary on the herdsman's heroic pretensions.[19] But Daphnis is
himself acknowledging here that he is vastly inferior to
Diomedes, who triumphed over Aphrodite in the *Iliad* (5.330
ff.); he is saying, in essence, "Now that you've defeated a poor
herdsman, let's see how you fare with a real hero." At the same
time, of course, his statement is fundamentally self-assertive;
like all such statements, it naturally suggests its opposite – that
this herdsman is, in fact, the heroic warrior's equal. And, as
several readers have noted, his challenge insistently evokes those
in the *Iliad*, not simply in its content, but in its "epic" language
and style.[20]

In the lines that follow (115–18), Daphnis similarly juxta-
poses his status as a cowherd with his familiarity with the wild
beasts "that sleep in mountain caves." And he pulls us in
opposite directions once more in his address to Pan:

> O Pan, Pan, whether thou art on the high hills of Lykaios,
> Or whether o'er great Mainalos thou roamest, hither come
> To the Sicilian isle, and leave the tomb of Helike,
> And Lykaonides' lofty cairn, which even the Gods revere.
>
>   (123–26)

By characterizing Pan's habitual haunts as "high," "lofty,"
and "great," the herdsman suggests their superiority to his own
lowly dwelling; by insisting that Pan leave the mountains to
come "hither," he implies that his home is at least as important
as the blessed heights that "even the Gods revere." These
contradictory impulses are, of course, implicit in the very act of

commanding a god, as his next words – "Come, lord" (128) – make clear.

The tension that is apparent in all these lines revolves around and reaches a climax in Daphnis' central statement – his self-definition:

> I am that Daphnis, he who drove the kine to pasture here,
> Daphnis who led the bulls and calves to water at these springs.
>
> (120–21)

This is usually seen as a moment of pure heroic self-assertion. What is truly remarkable about Daphnis' statement, however, is its extraordinary ordinariness. Daphnis is not boasting of any heroic accomplishments here; he is, in fact, making no special claims for himself at all: he is professing only to be an ordinary herdsman. In this respect, his self-definition differs from Virgil's imitation of it in *Eclogue* 5 – *Daphnis ego in silvis, hinc usque ad sidera notus, / formosi pecoris custos formosior ipse* (43–44, "I woodland Daphnis, blazoned among stars, / Guarded a lovely flock, still lovelier I")[21] – and seems closer in spirit to Marvell's much later version in "Damon the Mower":

> I am the Mower *Damon*, known
> Through all the Meadows I have mown.   (41–42)

Marvell, of course, intensifies the self-enclosure of Theocritus' lines; in so doing, however, he makes their essential mechanism more clear. Daphnis is saying, "I am important because – and only because – I am I; this place is important because it is my place."[22] He is shrinking the world to "I" and "here," and, at the same time, claiming that his "I" is heroic, his "here," everywhere.[23] His diffidence thus only heightens his self-assertiveness. The paradoxical nature of his statement reminds us that William Empson's formulation, "In pastoral you take a limited life and pretend it is the full and normal one,"[24] is necessarily two-edged: it is potentially both "bucolic" and "heroic" in force.

By collapsing the two sides of Empson's equation, Daphnis is, in effect, bringing heroism back home. No other speaker in the *Idylls* does this so completely; no other speaker so entirely conflates the bucolic and the heroic, and makes distance

equivalent to identity. But the conflicting perspectives that
Daphnis fuses are common to them all.

Thyrsis, for example, is no more purely "bucolic" than
Daphnis is purely "heroic." As Daphnis is and is not Diomedes,
so Thyrsis is and is not Daphnis. The self-assertiveness of
Daphnis' central statement finds its ultimate source in Thyrsis'
introductory celebration of his powers as a singer: "Thyrsis am
I of Etna; and sweet is the voice of Thyrsis" (65). And it is
precisely Thyrsis' ability to identify with Daphnis' death-bent,
"heroic" individualism that allows him to affirm the ongoing,
communal life of pastoral song.

Thyrsis does, of course, distance himself from the hero whose
death he performs. His self-proclamation is considerably less
assertive than Daphnis'; and it is balanced by a diffident
acknowledgment of his own lack of artistic autonomy: "Lead
now, I pray, dear Muses, lead you the pastoral song" (64). The
distance from Daphnis' perspective that Thyrsis' prayer suggests
is, moreover, widened when this line becomes a refrain. Like the
ivy on the cup described by Thyrsis' goatherd companion
(27–56),[25] the refrain of the Daphnis-song serves to remove us
from the events being portrayed, to foreground the formal
qualities of the artist's performance, and to affirm the primacy
of stasis and continuity over movement, disruption, and death.
Any refrain, simply by being repeated, will perform a similar
function; for this reason, refrains eventually become regular
features of pastoral poems: they are, in effect, the poetic
equivalent of the limits of the bower.[26]

Like the limits they embody, however, pastoral refrains
usually function in a paradoxical manner. And this refrain –
originary despite its refusal to see itself as such – is no exception.
Its content as well as its form seems to remove us from Daphnis,
by calling attention to the artifice of Thyrsis' performance. But
the refrain is not simply static and repetitive: it changes with the
movement of the song; and, as it does so, the gap between living
singer and dead hero – between pleasing performance and
disturbing "reality" – begins to close. When Daphnis prepares
to hand his pipe back to Pan (127), it becomes "Break off, dear
Muses, break off the pastoral song," and it continues in this

form through his death (142). Until its final appearance, this
line could be appropriately assigned to Daphnis as well as to
Thyrsis; it seems to mean not simply "Thyrsis' pastoral song is
now ending," but "All pastoral song is now ending with
Daphnis' death." And that meaning asserts itself most strongly
when Daphnis asks that the harmonies of the pastoral world be
disrupted by his passing:

> Let all things be confounded; let the pine-tree put forth figs,
> Since Daphnis lies dying! Let the stag tear the hounds,
> And screech-owls from the hills contend in song with nightingales.
> Break off, I pray, ye Muses, break off the pastoral song.
> These words he spoke, then said no more.   (134–38)[27]

The intermingling of speakers here points to an intermingling of
ideas; pastoral song will continue, Theocritus suggests, because
Thyrsis can participate in Daphnis' self-aggrandizing view that
is dying with his death.

A similar paradox is suggested by Thyrsis' final words: "O
Muses, fare you well, / And again farewell. Another day a
sweeter song I'll sing you" (144–45). These lines echo Daphnis'
earlier valedictions:

> O wolves, O jackals, O ye bears that sleep in mountain caves,
> Farewell! The herdsman Daphnis you shall never meet with more.
> Never in forest, glade or grove. Fare thee well, Arethusa.
> And all you streams that down the vale of Thymbris flow so fair.
>
> (115–18)

The echoes clearly serve, as Segal claims, to contrast "the death
of the embittered individual" with "the creative life of art," to
"oppose ... continuity and finality, hope and despair."[28] But
once again, hope, community, and continuity are dependent
upon an ability to feel and to reproduce isolation, despair, and
finality. It is no coincidence that all these passages are – and
contain – repetitions: the continuity that exists here is created
by repetition; but what is being repeated is the fact of
discontinuity itself.

The two opposed perspectives that we have been tracing are
thus continually interrelated in *Idyll* 1; they are not, however,
perfectly balanced. When Thyrsis speaks in his own voice, the
qualities I have called "bucolic" seem much more prominent

than their opposites; and the voices of Thyrsis and the even more diffident goatherd contain that of Daphnis. Bucolic community, harmony, and acceptance seem, then, to triumph over heroic isolation, aspiration, and despair. Insofar as this is true, however, the idyll, like all of the *Idylls*, merely recreates the paradox that Daphnis represents in another form.

That paradox resurfaces quite clearly in *Idyll* 4. This idyll is a conversation between two herdsmen – Korydon, who is minding the cows of his friend Aigon, and Battos, a goatherd; to a certain extent, it may be seen as a lower, more comic version of *Idyll* 1. Once again, we are presented with an ordinary man attempting to substitute for an absent hero. Aigon, who has "vanished" (5) to perform heroic endeavors, whose cows mourn his departure (according to Korydon, 12 ff.), and without whom song will die (according to Battos, 28), is clearly a latter-day Daphnis; and even more obviously than Daphnis, he is himself an ordinary man when compared to his models: his "heroism" appears to consist primarily in feats of wrestling and gluttony.

In the course of their discussion, the two herdsmen adopt contrasting attitudes towards what is absent: Korydon may be identified with the bucolic perspective, Battos with the (pseudo-) heroic.[29] We can see this contrast quite clearly when Battos begins to grieve for his dead beloved:

> O beautiful Amaryllis, thee alone, though thou be dead,
> I'll ne'er forget. Dear are my goats: so dear in death art thou.
> Ah me, too cruel was the daemon that disposed my fate. (38–40)

The goatherd's obsession with one irreplaceable human being, his unrequited love, his concern with death, and his despairing acceptance of a "cruel...fate" all recall Daphnis; and his words serve, perhaps, as an ironic commentary on that herdsman's "fated end" (1.93).[30] Korydon, on the other hand, puts his faith in the ongoing rhythms of life; he responds:

> Take heart, dear Battos. Better luck will come tomorrow.
> While there is life there's hope. Without hope are the dead alone.
> Zeus one day shows a clear and cloudless sky, the next he rains.

> (41–43)

Life's continual changes, he implies, render any one person or event unimportant. And his non-hierarchical, communal perspective is emphasized by the form of his remarks: his aphorisms, by their very nature, suggest that the same basic truths hold for all human beings, and his final maxim, by moving from better to worse (rather than vice-versa, as we might expect), implies that accepted hierarchies are meaningless:[31] all things are finally equal.

But neither man's stance is as simple as this static comparison suggests. The idyll itself moves more or less steadily toward the present: after a brief introduction, the herdsmen's conversation centers first on Aigon, then on Korydon's ability to replace his friend, then on increasingly attenuated forms of heroic aspiration (e.g., romantic love). As this progress occurs, the complexity of both perspectives becomes apparent. Battos, who always wants what he doesn't have, repeatedly sees the past as special and irreplaceable; and the more distant that past is, the larger it looms in his imagination. He therefore initially dismisses Aigon as ridiculously inferior to the great mythic heroes (7–9); but he finds Korydon, in turn, completely incapable of replacing Aigon as a herdsman (12 ff.) or a singer. Aigon now becomes, in Battos' mind, the indispensable human being upon whom the physical and spiritual well-being of the pastoral world depends:

> Alackaday, poor Aigon! your very kine will go
> To Hades, while you are thus in love with a luckless victory;
> And mildewed is the pipe which once you fashioned for yourself.
>
> (26–28)

Battos' position inevitably involves him in a contradiction: he reproduces, in himself, the heroic longings he criticizes in Aigon; the absent herdsman is clearly not the only one "in love with a luckless victory."

Korydon's stance is even more pointedly paradoxical. Unlike Battos – or Daphnis – he never yearns for what is out of reach; he accepts and celebrates the present, the ordinary, and the concrete. In so doing, however, he repeatedly makes the present a version of the past, and the ordinary man a version of the hero. Thus, he maintains that Aigon "rivals Herakles in lustiness and strength" (8), and sees him as exerting a Daphnis-like influence over his herd. When Battos laments that all is lost without Aigon, however, Korydon affirms his own ability to carry on. He first asserts his prowess as a herdsman: he praises the beauty and lushness of the pastures he frequents in such convincing detail (17–19, 23–25) that it is difficult to remember, while he is speaking, that the cows in his care are supposedly wasting away. He then answers Battos' charge that Aigon's pipe is mouldering in his absence:

> Not his pipe, by the Nymphs, not so; for when he went to Pisa,
> He left it me to keep; and I am something of a minstrel.   (29–30)

Korydon's remarks here are not as naive as his earlier equation of Aigon with Herakles. Like Thyrsis, he diffidently acknowledges his indebtedness to others: his song is enabled by Aigon's gift of the pipe. But like Thyrsis, he also displays the self-assertiveness necessary to make that gift bear fruit. Song will not die, he says in effect, because "I, too, am something of a singer." This statement itself recapitulates, in miniature, the balance of diffidence and self-assertiveness that is evident in the passage as a whole. It is a weaker version of Daphnis' self-definition: Korydon simultaneously acknowledges his limitations, and maintains that a limited man is equal to a task that he perceives as heroic. While he does not entirely conflate these ideas, he does manage to hold them in tension: he sees himself as a diminished hero, but as a hero nonetheless.

In the same way that the ordinary man and the hero come together here, so, too, do ordinary speech and song, diffident repetition and self-assertive originality. Korydon continues:

> Right well can I strike up the songs of Glauke and of Pyrrhos;
> And I sing the praise of Croton, and "A fair town is Zakynthos,"
> And "Fair too is Lakinion that fronts the dawn," where Aigon,
> The boxer, by himself alone devoured eighty cakes.
> And there he caught the bull by the hoof, and dragged him from
>   the mountain,
> And gave him to Amaryllis, while the women shrieked aloud
> For terror; but the herdsman burst into a mighty laugh.   (31–37)

As the widespread disagreement among editors and translators testifies, it is impossible to tell here precisely when Korydon is speaking and when he is singing, when he is quoting the words of others and when he is choosing words of his own.[32] And these ambiguities are mirrored in the content of his song. Once more, an ordinary man proves his ability to replace a departed hero by celebrating that hero's uniqueness: Korydon memorializes Aigon's prowess in devouring eighty cakes "by himself alone"; and his joyous vision of heroic singularity leads naturally into Battos' more mournful view of it: "O beautiful Amaryllis, *thee alone*, though thou be dead, / I'll ne'er forget" (emphasis mine).

After Battos has grieved for Amaryllis and Korydon has uttered his maxims, the idyll moves more noticeably to the present – to Korydon's position. As it does so, it reproduces some of the paradoxes that position implies. Battos agrees to "take heart," and, at the same time, he notices that the starving cows are now happily eating – in fact, they are eating too much (44–45). He is forced to chase after an errant heifer in the hills, where he is pricked by a spindle-thorn (50–53). Korydon then extracts the thorn, and gives him some friendly advice:

> When you walk in hilly places, never go barefoot, Battos;
> For on these hillsides everywhere brambles and thorns grow thick.
>
> (56–57)

Readers have often remarked on the change of tone here, noting, for example, that "after nostalgic recollection of the past and feeble generalities, the concrete presentness of the pastoral world seems to consolidate and reassert itself."[33] But the change is not quite so complete as this formulation implies. This episode very clearly replays, on a more realistic level, the preceding conversation concerning Amaryllis: the concrete hills, "brambles," and "thorns" here are not simply opposed to nostalgic yearnings and the pains of love; they also suggest these ideas.[34] It is quite important, as Rosenmeyer points out, that these connections are not made explicit;[35] symbolic figures, which subordinate concrete particulars to larger, more abstract ideas, are out of keeping with the bucolic perspective. But while symbolism is not exactly present here, it is not completely absent either. Both in the themes that it suggests, and in the very fact that it does suggest these themes, this "realistic" portion of the idyll remains in touch with modes of thought it seems to have abandoned.[36]

Korydon's advice to Battos both explains and reproduces what is occurring here. In light of the frequent association of hills with heroism throughout the *Idylls*, it is difficult to avoid paraphrasing his admonition along the following lines: "You should protect yourself against the inevitable dangers of the heroic perspective by keeping it at a distance" (*not*, significantly, by doing away with it altogether). But Korydon, of course, is actually saying nothing of the kind; he is merely offering his friend "a bit of practical advice about wearing shoes on brambly mountains."[37] His statement – like the idyll as a whole – is itself "wearing shoes"; but it remains in contact with "hilly places."

The governing structure of the idyll – and it is one that recurs throughout the *Idylls*[38] – could be described as a series of diminishing mirrors. As we progress from Herakles to Aigon to Korydon, from heroic yearnings to bucolic acceptance, from abstract generalities to concrete particulars, we are continually confronted with diminished versions of what we have left behind. We are thus asked repeatedly to contemplate how great things are – and are not – comparable to small: how shepherds are – and are not – similar to heroes, and how we ourselves are – and are not – similar to either. Theocritus' urbane contemporaries are asked to recognize both their distance from and their connection to his naive subjects – a dual recognition that Theocritus suggests most succinctly in *Idyll* 11, when he calls Polyphemus "our countryman, the Cyclops" (8).[39] And they are forced, finally, to admit that these conflicting perspectives are intertwined: any attempt to insist on one alone inevitably recreates the other.

This final recognition is made inescapable by the end of the idyll. Once Battos has recovered from his wound, the two herdsmen turn their attention to the sexual exploits of the old man who is overseeing Korydon's work:

BATTOS. Pray tell me, Korydon, is it true that the silly old gaffer still

Sports with that black-browed darling, whom once he used to dote on?

KORYDON. Aye, just as much as ever, friend. But two days gone I
    chanced
  To catch them at the very byre, when he had her in his arms.
(58–61)

Here, heroic aspiration appears finally to be forgotten. Absent,
heroic Aigon and beautiful, dead Amaryllis are now replaced
by the nameless, sexual, and very much extant "silly old gaffer"
and his "black-browed darling." We seem, at last, to be firmly
ensconced in the concrete bucolic present; John Van Sickle
comments wryly, "The old man's in his barton, all's right on the
hill."[40] But at this very moment, the heroic perspective reasserts
itself quite strongly; Battos exclaims:

Well done, lusty old lecher! 'Tis plain you are near akin
Both to the Satyrs and the slim-shanked Pans, whose feats you rival.
(62–63)

His words recall not only his own apostrophes of Aigon and
Amaryllis (25–26, 38–40), but also Korydon's praise of Aigon:
"They say he rivals Herakles in lustiness and strength" (8).
Like Aigon, the old man is seen as capable of "rivaling" – and
perhaps ultimately displacing – figures from legends and
myths;[41] he is a hero of bestiality, to be sure, but he is a hero all
the same.

The ending of *Idyll* 4 is by no means unique. We may compare
Idyll 7, which progresses generally from movement, striving,
and tales of the mythic past, to songs in which these themes are
presented and contained, to concrete rusticity, stasis, and
contentment.[42] Once more, when the bucolic perspective seems
to have triumphed, the heroic returns. The narrator celebrates
the virtues of the wine at the harvest festival by comparing it
favorably to the drinks consumed – with notoriously painful
consequences – in two heroic myths:

Ye Nymphs of Castaly, that haunt the steep Parnassian hill,
Did ever aged Cheiron in Pholos' rocky cave
Set before Herakles a bowl with such a vintage filled?
Did ever such a draught of nectar beguile that shepherd lout
Who dwelt beside Anapos, and pelted ships with crags,
Strong Polypheme, and set his feet capering about his folds?[43]
(148–53)

We might also consider *Idyll* 11, in which Polyphemus wrestles with his desire for Galateia. Here – as always – Theocritus presents love-longing as a diminished version of heroic endeavor;[44] and Polyphemus' unwitting evocations of Odysseus make both the differences and the similarities between these two experiences particularly clear. He exclaims at one point:

> But if my body seem too rough and shaggy for your taste,
> Well, neath the ashes on my hearth oak-logs are ever smouldering,
> And gladly would I suffer you to singe my very soul,
> And this one eye of mine, the dearest treasure I possess.   (50–53)

His burning desire is seen here both as essentially innocent and comic, and as a precursor of his famous heroic agony.

Towards the end of the idyll, however, Polyphemus turns away from even the limited heroism of love to focus on present obligations and pleasures:

> O Cyclops, Cyclops, whither are your wits gone wandering?
> Nay go and weave your baskets, and gather tender shoots
> To feed your lambs. If you did that, far wiser would you be.
> Milk the ewe that's beneath your hand. Why pursue one who shuns
> you?   (72–75)

Rosenmeyer aptly characterizes the first half of line 75 as "a really brutal phrase," and maintains that here, as in all the *Idylls*, sexual desire effectively "neutraliz[es] ... the claims of the romantic passion."[45] But even this brutal expression of sexuality turns, before our eyes, into a form of romantic aspiration; in the next line, Polyphemus comforts himself with the thought that his anonymous ewe will be another beloved – and a better one: "You'll find perchance another and a fairer Galateia" (76). The resolution to his song fulfills the ambiguities implicit in the narrator's early description of it as a *pharmakon* ("remedy," "poison," 1, 17);[46] and his wistful projection of the future both recalls and illuminates Thyrsis' parting statement in *Idyll* 1, "Another day a sweeter song I'll sing you" (145): "sweeter" (*hadion*) here seems to connote not only "less bitter," but also "superior" – or more precisely, "superior *because* less bitter."

Each of these moments, I believe, thematizes the central paradox of Theocritus' pastoral. Throughout the *Idylls*, bucolic

values contain, mock, and triumph over heroic ones. Their triumph, however, is perforce incomplete: insofar as the bucolic perspective threatens to displace the heroic completely, it necessarily becomes a version of what it defeats. If no man is special, then every shepherd is potentially heroic; if no woman is a true-love, then any ewe will do. If "a limited life" is unequivocally substituted for "a full and normal one," then it is no longer truly limited. If, as Rosenmeyer claims, "the noon peace is an imperious master [which] brooks no rivals," if "*hasychia* is all," then *hasychia* itself has effectively become heroic.

Thus, all of Theocritus' characters, regardless of their attitude towards the heroes and poets of the past, end up saying with Korydon, "I, too, am something of a singer; I, too, am something of a hero." Versions of this statement recur throughout the *Idylls*. When Simichidas, in *Idyll* 7, challenges Lycidas to a song-contest, he declares, "I too serve the Muses; their clear-voiced mouth am I" (37). When Polyphemus finally accepts his place on land, he proclaims, "It's plain enough, I too on land seem to be somebody" (11.78). And behind each of these assertions, we can hear the voice of Daphnis – the one ordinary man who did truly "defeat" heroism – declaring his "I" heroic and his "here" everywhere.

Characters who try to exempt themselves from this chorus join in even more strongly. Milon, in *Idyll* 10, is the most communally minded of all Theocritus' rustics. More openly than any other character, he identifies and censures the heroic element in pastoral;[47] he takes his lovelorn partner Bucaeus[48] to task for being childishly self-assertive, for desiring what is absent and neglecting present duties, and for falling out of step with his neighbors, "like a ewe that straggles from the flock, when a thorn has pricked her foot" (4). Such behavior, he feels, is ridiculously inappropriate to men of their station. His criticisms are, of course, completely justified; heroic individualism reaches a new low in this idyll when Bucaeus celebrates his unique ability to love an ugly girl: "Charming Bombyka, Syrian do they call thee everywhere, / ... it is *I alone* that call thee honey-fair" (26–27; emphasis mine). But Milon's attempts to excise the heroic element from his own character prove fruitless, as the following exchange makes clear:

[BUCAEUS]. Milon, you who can reap so late, true chip of stubborn
    stone,
  Has it never been your lot to long for one that was away?
MILON. Never. What right has a labouring man to long for what's
    not there?
[BUCAEUS]. Then has it never been your lot to lie awake for love?
MILON. Nay, God forbid! It's ill to let a dog once taste of pudding.
                                        (7–11)

By insisting on seeing himself as a type ("a labouring man," "a dog"), rather than an individual, Milon is effectively denying all his personal limitations. And when he claims to be immune to the pains of love, he is – as Bucaeus later asserts – really "talk[ing] big" (20). His rigidly communal stance here paradoxically prevents him from participating fully in his community: he is unable to empathize with Bucaeus' plight; it has "never been [his] lot." His attitude toward song is similarly self-defeating. Bucaeus, like Thyrsis, begins singing by attributing his verses to both the Muses and himself (24–25); he then proceeds to praise his beloved in a series of somewhat unusual – and generally laughable – images. When he has finished, Milon mocks his pathetic creative efforts, and declares that he himself is satisfied simply to repeat the song of a greater singer:

Truly, we had no notion what fine songs [Bucaeus] could make.
How cunningly he measured out and shaped his melody!
Alas for this man's beard, which to no purpose I have grown!
Yet hear these too, these couplets of Lityerses the divine.   (38–41)

Once again, however, in attempting to be completely diffident, Milon becomes completely self-assertive. By maintaining that he adds nothing to the songs he sings, he is implying that he is capable of producing an unmediated version of Lityerses' poetry; he is claiming, in effect, that he can become "Lityerses the divine."

Theocritus' attitude toward the inevitable recurrence of the heroic perspective is difficult to describe. He clearly does not view it as a recovery to be celebrated with unallayed delight; quite frequently, he communicates something closer to an amused recognition that "you can't get rid of the damn thing." But if Theocritus' relation to his heroic predecessors is not, therefore, primarily "nostalgic," it is not purely "ironic" either: if Theocritus realizes that heroic longings must always be distanced by irony – because they are, at best, ludicrously out of place in a limited age, and, at worst, extremely hazardous to your health – he simultaneously realizes that his irony inevitably reproduces what it distances. A new poet adding his voice to an established tradition cannot hope to recreate the past, but neither can he hope to escape it; he can only acknowledge, as fully as possible, the puzzles and paradoxes that are necessarily involved in saying, "I, too, am something of a singer."

Idyll 7 is, among other things, an exploration of what it means to make this statement with a self-conscious awareness of its implications. Lycidas the goatherd is presented as possessing such an awareness; and the idyll as a whole self-consciously explores the paradoxes involved in the creation of a "new" form of poetry. While it implicitly denies its own originary force, it simultaneously evidences an awareness of the ways in which such a denial constitutes an assertion, and it provides us with an (appropriately self-contradictory) myth of origin for bucolic song.[49]

When Simichidas, the urban narrator of the poem,[50] challenges Lycidas to a song-contest (27–41), his words betray his city-bred pride and aggressiveness. He attempts to balance the various oppositions we have been examining: he alternates between self-assertion and diffidence, "rival[ry]" and "shar[ing]" (31, 35), his own opinion and that of others. But he does so in a somewhat clumsy fashion: his diffidence is rather transparently assumed in an effort to entice Lycidas to compete. While he prides himself on the cleverness of this maneuver (42), he seems remarkably unselfaware. Lycidas responds by gently mocking his pretensions. He does not, however, simply recite

aphorisms or attempt to erase his own assertiveness. Rather, he
takes Simichidas' assumed modesty at face-value, and compli-
ments him on his truthfulness:

> I offer you this crook, because I know
> You are a sapling Zeus has moulded wholly in truth's mould.
> Even as I loathe your builder who strives to raise a house
> As lofty as the topmost peak of Mount Oromedon,
> So all birds of the Muses do I loathe, that croak and cackle
> Against the Chian minstrel, wasting their toil in vain.
> But come let us begin forthwith our pastoral melodies,
> Simichidas: and I first – well, friend, see if this chance to please
>   you,
> This ditty which I worked out not long since on the hills.   (43–51)

This speech is ostensibly a paean to humility, and it appears to
establish a clear distinction between the two competitors.
Lycidas begins by completely repudiating heroic aspirations: he
condemns the arrogance of those "mountain-building" poets
who attempt to compete with Homer, and places himself on
Callimachus' side in the controversy over the scale and style
appropriate to contemporary literary efforts. As he continues,
however, he balances his diffidence with some subtle touches of
self-assertion ("I first" is set against "see if this chance to please
you," "worked out" against "ditty").[51] And the heroic striving
he had renounced at the beginning returns full-force at the end,
when he announces his place of composition (51): he uses
exactly the same word here (nom. *oros*, "mountain" or "hill")
that he had earlier used to designate the unreachable "Mount
[*oros*] Oromedon." Like Theocritus, he seems to be acknowledging – with an amused smile – that bucolic humility necessarily recreates the heroism it eschews.

Lycidas is, himself, a walking embodiment of this paradox.
He is presented to us simultaneously as a goatherd – the lowliest
herdsman in the bucolic community – and as a god.[52] He is
clearly the more bucolic character in this encounter, but he is
also the more heroic: he is the absent hero whose staff is given
to and whose words are repeated by the more ordinary man
who narrates the poem. His bucolic song provides the frame of
reference within which Simichidas competes, and the standard

against which he is judged: it replaces the standard of the heroic poets and becomes "heroic" itself in the process.

In this song, Lycidas continues to play with paradoxes of distance and identity, and to explore the relationship between bucolic and heroic modes of perception. Like the idyll as a whole (which recounts a journey from the city to a country harvest festival), the song deals with the theme of coming home – from heroic passions and desires to bucolic ease, rest, and contentment; and, like the idyll as a whole, as it moves homeward, it repeatedly reinscribes heroic modes of thought in the humble, the familiar, and the bucolic. The song thus clearly parallels and comments upon the ways in which Lycidas himself is criticizing heroic aspiration – and, simultaneously, bringing it all back home.

Lycidas begins by invoking Ageanax's journey by sea to Mitylene. The faraway places and stormy seas that he associates with this voyage quite obviously parallel his own "burning... love" for the voyager (56): if Ageanax will requite his desire, Lycidas predicts, "the halcyons will calm the ocean waves" (57) so that "his ship [may] come safely home to port" (62). With this wish, Lycidas himself "comes home": he pictures himself safely ensconced in an indoor version of the bucolic *locus amoenus*, "drink[ing] luxuriously with Ageanax in [his] thoughts" (69). After this moment, Ageanax disappears from the song; having imagined his love fulfilled, Lycidas appears to forget it.

The feelings and images associated with this experience, are, however, not forgotten. They reappear, in diminished forms, in the songs that Lycidas imagines Tityrus singing at his celebration. When Tityrus sings of Daphnis, we are again confronted with the pain of unrequited love. Daphnis' pain is then turned into – and, to a certain extent, contained by – song: Tityrus recounts how untamed nature itself sang the dying herdsman's dirge (74–75). Lycidas thus creates an image of what he is both doing for himself here, and imagining that Tityrus is doing for him. Tityrus' song does not, however, end on this note: he concludes by describing Daphnis' death and evoking the faraway, forbidding mountain ranges that are

associated with heroic emotions (76–77). He then proceeds to
recount the more benign tale of the goatherd Komatas, who
"was enclosed alive / In a great coffer by his lord's outrage and
cruel spite" (78–79). Here again, pain is transformed into song;
Tityrus sings

> how the blunt-faced bees, as from the meadows they flew home
> To the fragrant chest of cedar-wood, fed him with dainty flowers
> Because with sweet nectar the Muse had steeped his lips.   (80–82)

The bees' flight does not only relieve Komatas' suffering; it also
serves to bring us "home" (80) from Daphnis' mountains.
These mountains reappear one more time, however, in Lycidas'
address to Komatas; and their return seems to signal a final
return of the heroic perspective:

> O fortunate Komatas, such joys indeed were thine;
> Yea, prisoned in the coffer, by the bees thou wast fed
> With honey-comb, and didst endure thy bondage a whole year.
> Would that thou had been numbered with the living in my days,
> That I might have grazed thy pretty she-goats on the hills,
> Listening to thy voice, whilst thou under the oaks or pines
> Hadst lain, divine Komatas, singing sweet melodies.   (83–89)

Unfulfilled desire – with which Lycidas had begun – is still
present at the end of his song. And while Lycidas' longing for
Komatas is less disruptive than his desire for Ageanax, it is also
less realizable: companionship and song may be readily
available to Lycidas, but Komatas himself is not.

As the above summary makes clear, while Lycidas is singing,
he is simultaneously reflecting self-consciously on the project in
which he is engaged. The figure of Komatas is central to this
project: he is the absent bucolic hero in relation to whom
Lycidas himself is an ordinary man. And Lycidas' address
makes us aware of the extent to which the living singer can –
and cannot – replace his model. Harry Berger comments that
Komatas "is brought closer to us"[53] when Lycidas expresses the
wish that he "hadst been numbered with the living in [these]
days." And so he is: both the fact and the content of Lycidas'
address serve to bring the mythic hero home. But Lycidas
secures Komatas' presence only by simultaneously acknowledging his absence; he unites his own time with that of his

predecessor by recognizing the gulf that divides them. Lycidas'
wish is, moreover, an acknowledgment of inferiority to and
dependence upon past singers: he desires to listen silently to the
"divine" Komatas, while he himself tends their goats, as befits
a lesser singer. But Lycidas can achieve this diffident silence
only by actively creating it with his own voice.[54] This situation
is further complicated, of course, by the fact that Lycidas' voice
comes out of that of another singer: his address is a response to
the song of Tityrus, which he has, in turn, created and imagined
himself hearing. Berger feels that this complex series of singers
and listeners sets up "an ideal of easy song" only to undercut
it.[55] But the mutually exclusive antitheses that he posits seem
foreign to Theocritus' vision. Rather than championing either
communal inspiration or individual authorship, Lycidas is
demonstrating here that the two are intertwined: he is
acknowledging both that the songs we sing are indebted to those
we have heard, and that the songs we listen to are inevitably our
own creations.

Simichidas confirms his own status as both a listener and a
singer in the lines that follow; he responds to Lycidas' longing
for a friend's song by repeating the goatherd's own words:

> Dear Lycidas, many things else the Nymphs
> Have taught me too, while I was pasturing kine among the hills.
> Good songs, that fame perchance has brought even to the throne of
>   Zeus.
> But one there is, the best of all, which now to do you honour
> I'll sing. Do you then listen, since the Muses love you well.   (91–95)

In these lines, Simichidas imitates Lycidas' prelude to song, and
draws as well upon his address to Komatas, while simultaneously expressing his own situation and temperament. He
seems to be aware of the paradox that Lycidas' mountains
imply: he calls attention to it by emphasizing the even greater
heights his own songs have attained, and by implicitly connecting the "hills" where he was instructed with those on which an
illustrious predecessor – Hesiod – received his inspiration.[56] He
has not, of course, gotten rid of his penchant for self-
aggrandizement; but he is now able to view it self-consciously,
within a context provided by another.

Simichidas also incorporates elements of Lycidas' song into
his own composition. Lycidas had transformed his desire for
Ageanax into a desire for friendship and song – first from
Tityrus and then from Komatas; and Simichidas now transforms his passion for Myrto into compassion for his friend Aratos
(96–98). His delight in the godlike song of another friend further
serves to deflect his pride in his own talents (99–101), as
Lycidas' admiration for other singers had allowed him to
participate in a community while singing by himself. The series
of addresses in his song, moreover, clearly parallels the series of
songs in Lycidas': like his model, Simichidas moves back and
forth between visions of centered contentment and increasingly
attenuated evocations of faraway places, mountains, and heroic
emotions. He first asks Pan, "lord of the pleasant pastures of
Mount Homole" (103), to bring Aratos' beloved "unbidden to
[his] friend's longing arms" (104). If Pan will comply,
Simichidas promises him freedom from pain (106–08); but if he
should refuse, he will be bitten, scratched, and pierced by
thorns, exiled from his homeland, and forever cursed (109–34).
Then, as Lycidas had moved from Daphnis to Komatas,
Simichidas turns from Pan to the more benevolent Loves,
asking them to leave "Oikeus' hill, the lofty shrine of golden-
tressed Dione," and come "hither" (115–17). And, once more,
the pain that has been left behind reappears in a more benign
context:

> O ye winged Loves, rosy as blushing apples, hither come,
> Pierce, I pray, with your arrows Philinos the desired,
> Pierce him, that miserable wretch, who pities not my friend.
> And yet he's but a pear that's over-ripe, and the girls cry,
> "Ah welaway Philinos! fading is thy fair bloom!"   (117–21)

Finally, Simichidas addresses his friend directly for the first
time, and attempts to bring him home:

> Come then, Aratos, let's no more stand watching at his gates,
> Nor wear our feet away; but let the cock that crows at dawn
> Give others over to be chilled by numbing misery.
> Alone let Molon wrestle, friend, with anguish such as that.
> But our concern be peace of mind: some old crone let us seek,
> To spit on us for luck and keep unlovely things afar.   (122–27)

Like Lycidas, Simichidas finds his voice here by listening to the speech of others: his address is a response to the cry of the girls, which he has just imagined. And like Lycidas, he ends by expressing a longing for content.[57]

While he has learned from Lycidas' song, Simichidas does not, of course, simply imitate it. His own composition is aggressively witty and distinctly urban. Critics have frequently faulted him for his urban perspective;[58] for Simichidas to deny this, however, would be to deny his own limitations: he can become "bucolic" only by acknowledging his unbucolic qualities. Lycidas may laugh when Simichidas has finished singing, but he also gives him the staff:[59] the city poet has demonstrated that he can both "rival" and "share" the verses of the country singer.

Because *Idyll* 7 introduces an urban figure as a central character, it differs somewhat from the rest of Theocritus' pastoral poems. It is the only idyll in which the bucolic perspective is presented as a point of departure as well as a mode of acceptance. And Simichidas is the only character who acknowledges his limitations by self-consciously accepting his portion of urban wit, sophistication, and pride: through a double irony that seems quintessentially Theocritean, he effectively brings Lycidas' bucolic heroism back home. He thus provides Theocritus' readers – and Theocritus himself – with a (necessarily ironized and distanced) model for recognizing the limitations of their own perspectives. And he may also serve as a model for later pastoralists, who are writing at a time when Theocritus' pastoral has itself become part of what has been lost, part of what each poet must confront and contend with in attempting to say, "I, too, am something of a singer."

CHAPTER 2

Si numquam fallit imago: *Virgil's revision of Theocritus*

Virgil clearly understood the paradoxical irony at the heart of the *Idylls*; he invokes it, for example, at the end of *Eclogue* 7. Corydon, the more perfectly "bucolic" of a pair of herdsmen competing in a song-contest, triumphs over his pseudo-heroic partner; he becomes, as a result, the self-defining hero of pastoral song:

> ex illo Corydon Corydon est tempore nobis. (70)
>
> From then on, it's been Corin, Corin with us.[1]

There are, however, several important differences between Virgil's poetry and that of his predecessor, and these helped shape the course of Renaissance pastoral. The most important – arising in part from the simple fact that Theocritus was Virgil's predecessor – becomes immediately apparent when we read the first lines of the *Eclogues*:

> Tityre, tu patulae recubans sub tegmine fagi
> silvestrem tenui musam meditaris avena;
> nos patriae finis et dulcia linquimus arva.
> nos patriam fugimus; tu, Tityre, lentus in umbra
> formosam resonare doces Amaryllida silvas. (1–5)
>
> You, Tityrus, under the spreading, sheltering beech,
> Tune woodland musings on a delicate reed;
> We flee our country's borders, our sweet fields,
> Abandon home; you, lazing in the shade,
> Make woods resound with lovely Amaryllis.

If Theocritus, throughout his *Idylls*, was bringing heroism back home, Virgil is now confronting us with the loss of home and all that it represents. The Roman poet clearly views his own era not only as more limited than that of his model, but also as more turbulent and unsettled. The qualities that I have termed "bucolic" – stasis, limitation, community, etc. – are therefore no longer simply means of acceptance (however paradoxical); they are also objects of longing. Throughout the *Eclogues*, we still encounter those who long for "greater things"; but we also hear the voices of shepherds – sometimes the same shepherds – who feel displaced from a simpler mode of existence, whose primary limitation consists in their relative lack of limitations.

We encounter these displaced rustics not only in the contemporary eclogues, but also in the more conventionally Theocritean pieces like *Eclogue* 2. Like Polyphemus, his model, Corydon bewails his distance from his beloved (here, significantly, associated not with the tempestuous sea – the heroic "world elsewhere" – but with the sophisticated city). Unlike Polyphemus, however, he is also troubled, throughout the eclogue, by his alienation from simpler pastoral pleasures. He characterizes his own condition in words modeled on the rebuke given by a countryman to a citydweller in *Idyll* 7:[2]

> nunc etiam pecudes umbras et frigora captant,
> nunc viridis etiam occultant spineta lacertos,
> Thestylis et rapido fessis messoribus aestu
> alia serpyllumque herbas contundit olentis.
> at mecum raucis, tua dum vestigia lustro,
> sole sub ardenti resonant arbusta cicadis. (8–13)

> Now even cattle seek out shade and coolness,
> Green lizards hunt for shelter in a thornbush;
> Thestylis pounds thyme, garlic, and pungent herbs
> For reapers weary in the consuming heat.
> But with me shrill crickets, as I trace your steps
> Under the burning sun, sound through the trees.

And he regrets his inability to be satisfied with a more conventional rustic love:

> nonne fuit satius tristis Amaryllidis iras
> atque superba pati fastidia? nonne Menalcan,
> quamvis ille niger, quamvis tu candidus esses? (14–16)

> Better put up with [Amaryllis'] moody rages
> Or haughty whims – better Menalcas,
> Tanned though he was and you all gleaming white.

As Paul Alpers has commented, "Corydon is aware that both the intensities and the divisions of his feelings put him on the border between his familiar world and the world of woods and passions to which his love has driven him."[3]

Corydon's position "on the border" is paradigmatic for the *Eclogues*. Virgil's rustics are, on the whole, much more conscious of borders and boundaries than their counterparts in the *Idylls*,[4] and they (and their creator) are more concerned to bring together the different worlds these boundaries separate. Virgil's primary impulse is, in other words, more connective than Theocritus'. Whereas Theocritus begins, I believe, by attempting to acknowledge his distance from his heroic predecessors, Virgil seeks to bring different eras, styles, and emotions into a relation of simultaneous connection and separation, to suspend oppositions through a poetic process that he regularly images as "interweaving."[5]

Despite the differences between the two poets, Theocritus' ironies gave Virgil a means of accomplishing his goal. In the *Eclogues*, as in the *Idylls*, heroic aspirations that have been abandoned tend to reappear in diminished forms.[6] But Virgil also reverses this process: the fact that the more stable and innocent perspective from which he is separated was not, itself, entirely idyllic enables him to establish connections with it.

We can see these connections being forged in the lines that I have already quoted from *Eclogue* 2. We should note, first of all, that Corydon's alienation is not presented in a wholly static fashion. He seems, initially, to be completely cut off from the normal pastoral routine; and Virgil allows us to sustain this impression through the beginning of line 12:

> nunc etiam pecudes umbras et frigora captant,
> nunc viridis etiam occultant spineta lacertos,
> Thestylis et rapido fessis messoribus aestu
> alia serpyllumque herbas contundit olentis.
> at me...   (8–12)

> Now even cattle seek out shade and coolness,
> Green lizards hunt for shelter in a thornbush;
> Thestylis pounds thyme, garlic, and pungent herbs

> For reapers weary in the consuming heat.
> But [me] …

When *me* becomes *mecum*, we may assume that the speaker is not altogether alone;[7] whatever is accompanying him, however, seems relatively unpleasant and unbucolic (*raucis*). We are then forced to revise this impression at the end of the following line, as Virgil gradually places Corydon's song in a conventional, benign pastoral context:

> at mecum raucis, tua dum vestigia lustro,
> sole sub ardenti *resonant arbusta cicadis*.[8]
>
> (12–13; emphasis mine)

> But with me shrill *crickets*, as I trace your steps
> Under the burning sun, *sound through the trees*.

If the resounding chatter of the cicadas here reminds us of the songs in *Eclogue* 1 (see particularly 1.5; also 1.54–58), we may also be forced to alter our perception of *raucis*, as we remember the *raucae palumbes* (1.57, "throaty pigeons") that the displaced herdsman Meliboeus longed to hear.

Corydon's isolated lament, which is first presented as fundamentally alien to pastoral, is thus reimagined as a conventional pastoral song. This reinterpretation is, of course, partially justified by the very fact that these lines do recall a speech from *Idyll* 7 (as the entire eclogue recalls *Idyll* 11). It is further validated by the following lines. When Corydon offers two examples of ordinary rustic love, one is immediately struck by the similarities between the "innocence" he has abandoned and his present experience; the rustic simplicity he describes seems to contain, in a diminished form, all the pain, desire, and isolation he currently feels. The likeness between Amaryllis, whose scorn (*fastidia*, 15) he has suffered, and the disdainful Alexis is sealed by the final line of the poem:

> invenies alium, si te hic fastidit, Alexin. (73)

> You'll find another Alexis, if this one scorns you.
>
> (my trans.)

And the allusion to Polyphemus' ambiguous acceptance of his
own rusticity – "You'll find perchance another and a fairer
Galateia" (*Id.* 11.76) – takes on added resonance as a result.
Corydon's second example is even more telling:

> nonne Menalcan,
> quamvis ille niger, quamvis tu candidus esses?
> o formose puer, nimium ne crede colori:
> alba ligustra cadunt, vaccinia nigra leguntur.   (15–18)

> better Menalcas,
> Tanned though he was and you all gleaming white.
> Don't, lovely boy, stake too much on complexion:
> White privets fade, dark blueberries are picked.

Here, Virgil is pointedly recalling a passage from *Idyll* 10; the
reaper Bucaeus, having been criticized for his foolish, destructive passion, first celebrates its uniqueness, and then
justifies his preference by appealing to communal values:

> Charming Bombyka, Syrian they do call thee everywhere,
> Lean, sunburnt: it is I alone that call thee honey-fair.
> Dark is the violet, and dark the scriptured iris grows;
> Yet when we're making garlands, the first we choose are those.

> (26–29)

We are thus reminded that self-assertive impulses had existed in
Theocritus' poetry, that they were problematic even there, and
that they were ultimately seen as essential elements in the
pastoral community.

The process of connection through separation that Virgil is
invoking here is taken one step further in *Eclogue* 10, when the
poet Gallus, after wishing that he had been born a shepherd,
reworks Corydon's lines:

> certe sive mihi Phyllis sive esset Amyntas
> seu quicumque furor (quid tum, si fuscus Amyntas?
> et nigrae violae sunt et vaccinia nigra) ...   (37–39)

> Whether its Phyllis or Amyntas by me
> Or someone else I'm mad for – what if he's dusky?
> Violets too are dark, and blueberries ...

And the mad passion that he imagines himself feeling finds its enlarged reflection in the irremediable madness that is, in fact, his lot (*tamquam haec sit nostri medicina furoris*, 60, "as if this could salve my madness").

In *Eclogue* 9, Virgil thematizes this technique. Here, he explicitly confronts the problem of the absent master singer, and he alludes to both *Idylls* 4 and 7.[9] Like Korydon in *Idyll* 4, Lycidas and Moeris sing quotations from their master, two of which recall Theocritus' poems (23–25, 39–43; cf. *Idd.* 3, 11), and two of which reimagine the substance of the others in contemporary terms (26–29, 46–50).[10] Virgil does not, of course, answer the questions that he raises, but neither, really, did Theocritus. The two poets are connected because they are both concerned with problems of continuity. And the fact that Virgil's vision is considerably bleaker than Theocritus' reinforces their connection at the same time that it makes their separation clear: the problematic that exists in both poets' works is reproduced in the distance between them.

Virgil's understanding of Theocritus thus enables him to reimagine pastoral in increasingly darker forms, and, conversely, to view seemingly "antipastoral" situations and emotions as essentially pastoral. The reinterpretation of a singer's isolation that we observed in 2.8–13 is, for example, repeated in a more serious vein in *Eclogue* 9, when Lycidas exclaims: *Quid, quae te pura solum sub nocte canentem / audieram?* (44–45, "There was one I heard you sing [alone] one cloudless night"). The solitary, nocturnal song of line 44 is placed in a pastoral context by *audieram* ("I had heard") in the next line, and by Lycidas' repetition of it in the lines that follow.[11]

Once more, this process is taken to its limit in *Eclogue* 10. Here, Virgil reverses the characteristic movement of Theocritus' *Idylls* – the movement that is typified by the songs in *Idyll* 7. Simichidas and Lycidas had progressed from expressions of "heroic" passions, to visions of "home" and contentment, to increasingly attenuated evocations of the emotions they had left behind. Gallus now repeatedly imagines himself in a pastoral context, is moved by the limitations of his visions to confront the emotions they exclude, and then returns to the bower to incorporate these emotions into increasingly "heroic" versions of pastoral. Finally, he bids farewell to pastoral song in a pastoral manner; he expresses its ultimate inadequacy by imaging himself as a displaced and ineffective herdsman (62–67). And his paradoxical valediction is matched, a few lines later, by Virgil's conclusion to the *Eclogues*:[12]

> surgamus: solet esse gravis cantantibus umbra,
> iuniperi gravis umbra; nocent et frugibus umbrae.
> ite domum saturae, venit Hesperus, ite capellae.   (75–77)

> Arise: the shade weighs heavily on singers,
> The shade of junipers, and shade harms crops.
> Go home well fed, my goats: go: Vesper comes.

It is important to emphasize that the distance between different modes of perception is never entirely bridged in the *Eclogues*. As we have seen, this distance is itself an important element in the connections being established. And, as the example of Gallus suggests, when any character becomes wholly involved in the connections he is creating, he is inevitably brought up against their limitations. One might say that the ideas of connection through separation and separation through connection are themselves "interwoven" and suspended.

This suspension is intimately related to the self-reflexive focus on the problems of poetic representation in Virgil's pastoral. In the *Idylls*, Theocritus had placed considerable emphasis on the powers and limits of song. In the *Eclogues*, however, there is much more pressure on art to reflect, contain, and control the external world, and there is a correspondingly more acute awareness of its limitations. This difference is clearly attributable to Virgil's situation as well as his temperament: he is forced to consider his pastoral songs both as the diminished reflections of a complex and threatening world and as the sophisticated reimaginings of a simpler reality. As a result, his relation to his own fictions is significantly different from Theocritus'. The herdsmen in the *Idylls* had functioned primarily as the ironical images of the limitations experienced by the poet and his audience. The reader's sense of kinship with these simple characters was invariably intertwined with an awareness of distance from them, but, since simplicity was not a longed-for quality in the *Idylls*, that distance was not especially problematic. In the *Eclogues*, it necessarily becomes so. The relationship that exists between the sophisticated poet and his simpler creations parallels, to a certain extent, the one that Virgil perceives between himself and his more "naive"[13] predecessor. He therefore repeatedly focuses on the puzzles and paradoxes that relationship entails.

He calls these to our attention in *Eclogue* 2 when he describes Corydon's utterances as *incondita* ("rude, disordered [words]," "ramblings," 4).[14] In some respects, the song that follows merits this description: it is a representation of uncontrolled passion, and it contains appropriately abrupt shifts in mood and style. But it is also – particularly when compared with its model – extremely artful and pointedly artificial, a sentimental tour de force "interwoven with allusions to literature no herdsman could know."[15] Virgil is self-consciously "graft[ing] upon the Wild the Tame"[16] here, and he is asking us to consider to what extent this can be done: to what extent, that is, can his "sentimental" pastoral connect with and reflect Theocritus' more "naive" version, to what extent did Theocritus' pastoral itself really represent simple human beings and their passions and, more generally, to what extent can any artistic representation claim to image and contain "pure" emotion and concrete reality?

These questions are, inevitably, mirrored in the problems Corydon himself faces. Throughout the eclogue, he is attempting to bring together the "wild" and the "tame":[17] he is trying to unite Alexis with himself (perceived as rustic) and, simultaneously, trying to unite himself (perceived as sophisticated) with simpler rustics; he is attempting to reconcile his conflicting desires and wishes, to bring together the contradictory pieces of his own identity.

Corydon's primary means of effecting these unions – like Virgil's – is his poetic imagination, here aptly symbolized by the "well-joined pipe of hemlock stalks" that Damoetas gave him (36–37). Corydon has frequently been criticized for the unreality of his imaginings;[18] and indeed, the narrator begins

by speaking of his *studium inane* ("pointless passion," "empty
art," 5).[19] But he himself is not entirely unaware of their
limitations. Early in the eclogue, he gives naive voice to the
poet's anxieties; he tells Alexis:

> nec sum adeo informis: nuper me in litore vidi,
> cum placidum ventis staret mare. non ego Daphnin
> iudice te metuam, si numquam fallit imago.   (25–27)

> Nor am I ugly: once by the shore I saw
> Myself in the wind-calmed sea. I would not fear to
> Compete for you with Daphnis: mirrors don't lie.

[26b-27, *lit.*: I would not fear Daphnis, with you as the judge, if the
image never lies.]

The difference between these lines and their model in *Idyll* 6 is
instructive. Polyphemus had simply referred the question of his
attractiveness to his own limited judgment:

> For truly not ill-favoured is my face, as they pretend.
> Not long ago I looked into the sea, when it was calm,
> And beautiful my beard seemed, beautiful my one eye,
> If I have any judgment.   (35–37)

Not only is Corydon more self-consciously constrained by the
values of others (he compares himself to the established standard
of pastoral excellence,[20] and he imagines Alexis as the "judge"),
he also ultimately founds his faith in himself on his belief in the
accuracy of reflections. And his "if" implies a questioning of
that faith that Polyphemus' parallel qualification does not.[21]

Corydon's judgment is quite clearly at fault here; his self-
assessment is ludicrously inflated. But his final line resonates
beyond its context: all of Virgil's creations are fully adequate to
the realities they reflect, *si numquam fallit imago*.[22] And as
Corydon continues to reflect upon his self-definition,[23] and
proceeds to define himself primarily as an artist (a self-conscious
creator of reflections), he gradually develops a more sophisticated awareness of the ways in which images do – and do
not – lie.

His celebration of the powers of art reaches a climax in his
catalogue of flowers. Once again, comparison with Polyphemus
is illuminating. In *Idyll* 11, the Cyclops had rejected out of hand

the possibility of bringing Galateia both "white snowdrops"
and "the soft, scarlet-petalled poppy" (57):

> Nay, but these blow in summer, those in winter months.
> So I never could bring you both these kinds at the same time.
>
> (58–59)

His comment had clearly functioned as an implicit criticism of
his romantic aspirations: we were left to contemplate the
hopeless naiveté of a character who would join himself with a
sea-nymph – and who has just wistfully imagined adorning his
monstrous body with gills (54–56) – and yet cannot conceive of
uniting the flowers of different seasons.

For Corydon, by contrast, the awareness that his floral
offering is necessarily imaginary is liberating: it enables him to
construct a powerful vision of the union of those "good
qualities," which, in William Empson's words, "are so hard to
bring together in life."[24] And, unlike Polyphemus, Corydon
clearly sees the imaginative connections he is creating as
reflecting the actual unions he wishes to effect.

The passage preceding the catalogue had encapsulated the
oppositions – between country and city, homely simplicity and
sophisticated beauty, Corydon and Alexis – that pervade the
eclogue. Corydon had complained that his rustic gifts were
disgusting to his beloved (44), and the verb he used – *sordeo* ("to
be dirty, mean, despised") – had pointedly recalled his earlier
description of the country (*sordida rura*, 28) and contrasted
sharply with his description of Alexis in the following line: *huc
ades, o formose puer* (45, "Come hither, lovely boy"; cf. 1, 17).[25]
He now proceeds to envision the fruitful union of the *formosus*
and the *sordidus*. He imaginatively intertwines dark flowers with
light, and the blossoms of winter with those of summer; he
creates a rural landscape inhabited by bright and beautiful
Nymphs, and effectively unites concrete rusticity with sophisticated eroticism:[26]

> huc ades, o formose puer: tibi lilia plenis
> ecce ferunt Nymphae calathis; tibi candida Nais,
> pallentis violas et summa papavera carpens,
> narcissum et florem iungit bene olentis anethi;
> tum casia atque aliis intexens suavibus herbis

mollia luteola pingit vaccinia calta.
ipse ego cana legam tenera lanugine mala
castaneasque nuces, mea quas Amaryllis amabat;
addam cerea pruna (honos erit huic quoque pomo),
et vos, o lauri, carpam et te, proxima myrte,
sic positae quoniam suavis miscetis odores.   (45-55)

Come hither, lovely boy: the Nymphs bring baskets
Brimming with lilies; for you fair Naiads,
Plucking bright poppy heads and violets dim,
Will bind narcissus and flowers of fragrant dill;
Then twining cinnamon and pleasant herbs,
Brighten soft blueberries with marigolds.
Myself, I'll gather quinces, young and downy,
And chestnuts, which my [Amaryllis] used to love;
I'll toss in waxy plums and honor them too;
And oh you laurels and you myrtles, I'll
Pluck you together, to mingle sweetest smells.

The parallel between the unions Corydon creates and those
which he desires is emphasized in line 50. Here, he explicitly
recalls the *vaccinia nigra* ("dark blueberries") to which he had
earlier likened the rustic Menalcas (18); but whereas those dark
plants had been set against the *alba ligustra* ("white privets")
associated with *formosus* Alexis (17-18), the *mollia vaccinia* ("soft
blueberries") here complement the bright blossoms with which
they are joined; and the beauty of their union is mirrored in
the intertwining golden line. In the lines that follow, Corydon
continues to interweave old values with new, as he offers Alexis
the chestnuts "which my Amaryllis used to love" (52). And the
implied affirmation of his native countryside and its standards
leads him to become more involved in his imagined offering.
He first substitutes himself for the Nymphs as the bearer of the
gifts (51 ff.); he then effectively substitutes his offering for Alexis
as the object of his affections: he begins addressing the flowers
he has imagined, becoming erotically entangled in his own
creation (54-55).

As he does so, he necessarily realizes the limits of that
creation. The unions it contains are dependent upon – and can
only exist in – his own imagination. The qualities he has joined
are, in fact, particularly "hard to bring together in life," and in

the lines following the catalogue, they seem to be more unalterably opposed than ever; Corydon realizes that Alexis would despise his pathetic attempts at sophistication, and that his erotic imaginings are potentially destructive to the simple bucolic virtues he seeks to preserve:

> rusticus es, Corydon, nec munera curat Alexis,
> nec, si muneribus certes, concedat Iollas.
> heu heu, quid volui misero mihi? floribus Austrum
> perditus et liquidis immisi fontibus apros. (56–59)

> Corydon, you country boy! Alexis scorns
> Your gifts – nor could they match Iollas'.
> How could I, desperate wretch, want to unleash
> Tempests on flowers and boars on crystal springs?

While these lines severely question the power of the poetic image, however, they do not entirely discredit it. Alpers has commented that "[Corydon's] imaginative involvement in the catalogue of flowers lies behind both his turning on himself and the power and adequacy of his metaphors."[27] I would add that, by following the carefully balanced catalogue with Corydon's violent renunciation of it, Virgil enacts, on another level, the interweaving of the *formosus* and the *sordidus* that the catalogue had imaged. And the fact that Corydon has recognized the limitations of such images enables him to assert their power more convincingly, and to function as a more adequate image of the poet himself.

The paradox that is suggested here is most evident at the end of the eclogue. When Corydon resolves to abandon his dreams and concentrate on practical tasks, the occupation he proposes for himself – weaving something he really needs with twigs and soft rushes (*quin tu aliquid saltem potius, quorum indiget usus, / viminibus molliquae paras detexere iunco,* 71–72) – clearly reflects the imaginative interweaving he had been practicing earlier,[28] while it simultaneously implies a rejection of that activity (and of reflections in general). Similarly, when Virgil allows Corydon to end the poem he had begun – to stand, in effect, for "the poet" – he asserts the validity of substituting the fictive for the real;[29] this substitution seems plausible, however, only because Corydon himself has implicitly questioned its value.

A comparable moment occurs at the end of *Eclogue* 8, a poem
that once again allows us to observe Virgil's transformation of
Theocritean material. Virgil was clearly attracted to *Idyll* 2 –
upon which he based the second song of his eclogue – by the
implied analogy between the sorceress' sympathetic magic and
the artistic process: like the artist, the sorceress attempts to
control a painful reality by replacing it with a smaller, more
manageable image of itself. This parallel is, however, merely
suggested in *Idyll* 2, and it is only one aspect of that poem.
Virgil, typically, emphasizes it quite strongly and concentrates
on it to the exclusion of almost everything else: he eliminates the
history of the sorceress' love, downplays her pathetic attempts to
appear heroic, and insistently focuses on her *carmina* ("songs,"
"charms") as the essential component of her magic. As a result,
Theocritus' wide-ranging, paradoxical ironies are transformed
into an explicitly self-reflexive exploration of the efficacy of art.
Thus, a characteristically Theocritean passage, in which
Simaitha compares herself to several ill-fated, mythological
enchantresses – "Mak[e] these charms [*pharmaka*] prove no less
potent than the spells of Circe / Or of Medea, or the gold-haired
sorceress Perimede" (15–16)[30] – becomes, in Virgil's hands, a
paean to the powers of *carmina*:[31]

> *carmina* vel caelo possunt deducere lunam,
> *carminibus* Circe socios mutavit Ulixi,
> frigidus in pratis *cantando* rumpitur anguis.
>
> > (69–71; emphasis mine)

> Charms have the power to fetch the moon from heaven,
> Circe with charms transformed Ulysses' men,
> And incantations burst the clammy grass snake.[32]

And Virgil repeatedly calls our attention to this word in the
refrain:

> ducite ab urbe domum, mea carmina, ducite Daphnin.

> Fetch him, my charms, fetch Daphnis home from town.

The word *mea* is also significant here. In Theocritus' poem,
Simaitha's belief in her own skill was dependent upon her faith

that she was not entirely alone, that the universe was populated by more powerful beings who cared about her plight and were willing to come to her aid. Her song contains a series of addresses to these beings, and her two refrains – both of which invoke powers outside of herself ("O magic wheel," "O holy Moon")[33] – form part of that series. Virgil's sorceress is, by contrast, a more self-consciously isolated artist, and her refrain is appropriately addressed to her own creations.

A similar change is made in the model for the refrain of the first song of the eclogue. Here, Virgil recalls the refrain in *Idyll* 1 ("Lead now, I pray, dear Muses, lead you the pastoral song"); rather than invoking the Muses, however, his shepherd speaks to his own musical instrument:[34]

> incipe Maenalios mecum, mea tibia, versus.
>
> Begin these verses, [my] shepherd's pipe, with me.

The very fact that there are two complementary songs in the eclogue (both sung by fictional characters about fictional characters) is a further index of Virgil's self-conscious concern with the power of the poetic image. So, too, is the fact that both songs contain refrains: the refrain is perhaps the most precise artistic equivalent of the sorceress' magic; like her incantations, it distances and contains movement and pain through ritualistic repetition.

Finally, the context in which Virgil places both songs forces us to think about the limitations and strengths of his pastoral art. He begins by celebrating the power of the shepherds' songs to suspend movement and transform nature:

> Pastorum Musam Damonis et Alphesiboei,
> immemor herbarum quos est mirata iuvenca
> certantis, quorum stupefactae carmine lynces,
> et mutata suos requierunt flumina cursus,
> Damonis Musam dicemus et Alphesiboei. (1–5)
>
> Alphesibee's and Damon's rural muse –
> Whose contest drew the wondering heifer's mind
> From grazing, and whose song struck lynxes dumb,
> And made the rivers, transformed, stay their course –
> Alphesibee's we sing and Damon's muse.

He then turns away from the shepherds to address his patron, and in so doing, clearly designates the opening passage as a fiction – and a distressingly minor fiction at that:

> Tu mihi, seu magni superas iam saxa Timavi
> sive oram Illyrici legis aequoris, – en erit umquam
> ille dies, mihi cum liceat tua dicere facta?
> en erit ut liceat totum mihi ferre per orbem
> sola Sophocleo tua carmina digna coturno?   (6–10)

> Now, whether you skirt the Adriatic shore,
> Or get past great Timavus, with its rocks,
> Will the day come when I recite your deeds?
> Will I be allowed to carry through the world
> Your tragic songs, sole heirs of Sophocles?

He concludes, however, by expressing a characteristic wish that his pastoral poetry may be entwined with the heroic laurels he has been forced to renounce:

> a te principium, tibi desinam: accipe iussis
> carmina coepta tuis, atque hanc sine tempora circum
> intra victricis hederam tibi serpere lauros.   (11–13)

> You are my source, my end: accept the songs
> You bade me undertake, and let this ivy
> Entwine the conquering laurels on your brow.

And, on a smaller scale, his own poem appears to accomplish this end: the passions and ambitions expressed in both songs clearly reflect the heroic emotions he has left behind, and taken together, the two songs present us with a diminished image of the intertwining of limitation and power, tragedy and success.

The central question that the eclogue poses, on every level, is whether such imaginative substitutions – of the fictive for the real, of smaller fictions for greater ones – can be said to "work." The final line would seem to give us an affirmative answer, not merely because it is hopeful in tenor (*parcite, ab urbe venit, iam parcite carmina, Daphnis*, 109, "Leave off, my charms, Daphnis is coming from town"), but because, like the ending of *Eclogue* 2, it is itself such a substitution: it is simultaneously the sorceress' cry of triumph, Alphesiboeus' final refrain (the change in which answers the change in his partner's), and the last line of Virgil's poem. But, once again, this affirmation is possible only because the power of the artistic image has been radically questioned – not only by the poet and the first singer, but by the sorceress herself. Virgil's ending is actually both more and less hopeful than Theocritus'. It is perfectly clear, in *Idyll* 2, that Simaitha's magic is only a comforting fantasy; but Simaitha herself never entirely arrives at this conclusion. When she finally begins to doubt the efficacy of her love potions, she almost immediately reimagines herself as an even more powerful and deadly enchantress:

Now with these philtres will I strive to enchant him. But if still
He should grieve me, at Hell's gate soon, by the Fates, he shall
  knock:
Such evil drugs to work his bane here in a chest I store,
Whose use, dear Mistress, an Assyrian stranger taught me once.

(159–62)

And her renewed self-confidence enables her (typically two-edged) acceptance of her situation near the end: "And I will endure my misery still, even as I have borne it" (164). Virgil's sorceress, on the other hand, directly confronts the possibility that she may be deceiving herself; at the moment of her triumph she asks: *credimus? an, qui amant, ipsi sibi somnia fingunt?* (108, "Can it be true? or do those who love, themselves, fashion dreams for themselves?" [my trans.]). And her concluding words do not eradicate this question; rather, by claiming so much, they make it more pressing. The boundaries between "fiction" and "reality" are very hazy here:[35] we are uncertain, finally, whether the last line represents the triumph of art, or its ultimate deception.

This uncertainty recurs, in one form or another, in all the eclogues, from such a simple, positive poem as *Eclogue* 3 – in which the two shepherds briefly debate the relative value of their farm animals and two cups depicting human control of the world through art and science (35–48) – to the darker contemporary pastorals. Even the most extreme questionings of the power of art in these poems, however, simultaneously affirm its value. There is a moment towards the beginning of *Eclogue* 9, for example, when Moeris appears to despair utterly of the power of speech and song. Lycidas has just told him that "[he] had heard" (*audieram*) that their lands were preserved by Menalcas' songs (7–10); Moeris dismisses this as a worthless fable:

> Audieras, et fama fuit; sed carmina tantum
> nostra valent, Lycida, tela inter Martia quantum
> Chaonias dicunt aquila veniente columbas.   (11–13)

> You heard what people said; but all our songs,
> Lycidas, no more prevail with weapons of war
> Than the oracle's doves, they say, when eagles come.

But he can devalue the common word only by simultaneously invoking it (*dicunt*), and he can describe the worthlessness of poetry only by speaking metaphorically;[36] the metaphoric birds in his comparison, moreover, are effectively literalized in his next lines, as he himself appeals to another fable:

> quod nisi me quacumque novas incidere lites
> ante sinistra cava monuisset ab ilice cornix,
> nec tuus hic Moeris nec viveret ipse Menalcas.   (14–16)

> Had I not somehow cut fresh quarrels short,
> Warned by hearing a crow on a hollow tree,
> Your Moeris would not be alive – nor would Menalcas.

In his speech, Moeris is creating a myth about the death of myths, a song about the end of songs. This is a project that now seems characteristically "pastoral," largely because the *Eclogues* define it as such; and it is what these poems themselves accomplish: they create connections by explicitly confronting the experience of separation, and present us with fictions whose power depends upon their acknowledged fictionality.

CHAPTER 3

Pastime and passion: the impasse in the Old Arcadia

In the Renaissance, the suspensions that Virgil had effected begin to come apart. The proliferation of different pastoral forms during this period is, itself, a sign of the fragmentation that is taking place. While the eclogue continues to be centrally important, the form that best represents the problems and the possibilities of the mode for poets of the English Renaissance is the pastoral romance: even important eclogue collections of the time (e.g., *The Shepheardes Calender*) participate in the general movement towards narrative that is most fully realized in the romance.

In the following chapter, I will consider the attractions and the drawbacks of the Renaissance pastoral romance through an extended analysis of Sidney's *Old Arcadia*; I will then briefly examine the responses of Spenser and Shakespeare to the problems that Sidney locates in the form. Even more obviously than other English poets, Sidney sees the structure of pastoral romance as inherently problematic. In his later work, he expresses his dissatisfactions by moving away from a focus on pastoral *per se*. In his *Old Arcadia*, however, he makes the contradictions he perceives an integral part of his subject: he thus presents us with an especially clear picture of the difficulties that contemporary pastoralists were repeatedly confronting and attempting to resolve.[1]

In the romance, the balance of stasis and movement – of lyric and drama – that had characterized the *Eclogues* is necessarily disrupted: the introduction of narrative forces us to move beyond Virgil's suspended moments, to see what exists on the other side of their limits. The interconnection of the simple and

the complex – of naive shepherd and sophisticated poet – is
similarly made explicit, and, as a result, made less secure: the
heroes of romances are all, in effect, the children of Gallus –
sophisticated courtiers who journey to the countryside to
become shepherds. These developments all clearly reflect the
Renaissance humanist concern with the efficacy of art in the
external world; and they can all be seen as logical extensions of
Virgil's unpacking of Theocritus. The tensions that they
produce, however, eventually strain Virgil's suspensions to the
breaking point. The opposing perspectives that were already
held together only tenuously at the end of *Eclogue* 8 – *credimus?
an, qui amant, ipsi sibi somnia fingunt?* (108, "Can it be true? or do
those who love, themselves, fashion dreams for themselves?"
[my trans.]) – become disjoined, and the artist is faced with a
choice between seeing his creation as truly effective, issuing in
the "ending end of all earthly learning, ... virtuous action,"
and viewing it as a self-reflexive fantasy, trapping him forever in
"the zodiac of his own wit."[2] In the *Arcadia*, these opposing
beliefs are presented, paradoxically, both as interreflective and
as mutually exclusive – and they are ultimately seen as equally
untenable. The self-contradictory mechanisms of pastoral
poetry recoil upon themselves here, and they result in a poetics
of self-cancellation.

Sidney is not, of course, in a direct line from Virgil. His view of
pastoral was shaped, in large part, by his continental predecessors in the pastoral romance, Jacopo Sannazaro and Jorge de
Montemayor.[3] Sannazaro clearly saw himself as Virgil's legitimate heir, and later poets tended to agree. It was his *Arcadia* –
a series of twelve eclogues loosely joined by prose passages – that
initiated the movement toward narrative that characterizes
Renaissance pastoral. Some sense of his importance can be
conveyed by recalling Sidney's strictures, in the *Apology*, on
Spenser's linguistic experimentation in *The Shepheardes Calendar*:
"That same framing of his style to an old rustic language I dare
not allow, since neither Theocritus in Greek, Virgil in Latin, nor
Sannazaro in Italian did affect it."[4] Quite obviously, the
Italian *Arcadia* provided Sidney with more than a title and a

setting:[5] it functioned as a model that helped to define a genre for him – a model against which, ultimately, Sidney defined himself. To understand Sidney's perspective, it is therefore necessary to look briefly at Sannazaro's work.

The Italian writer apparently believed that suspension was the governing principle of pastoral: throughout his *Arcadia*, he delights in juxtaposing opposites. His alternation of prose with poetry is only one of many such juxtapositions; he similarly brings together strikingly different verse forms, themes, and moods. In his final eclogues, he explicitly contrasts the bucolic with the heroic, fiction with history.[6] And, in his descriptive passages, he repeatedly emphasizes the beauty of diverse qualities coexisting harmoniously. His comment in one such passage – a description of a number of nymphs intertwining different flowers in their hair – could serve as an epigraph for the work as a whole: "By the diversity of their bearing," he tells us, "they increased immeasurably their natural beauty" (50; *con la diversità de' portamenti oltra misura le naturali bellezze augmentavano*, 79).[7]

Sannazaro enhances the "natural beauty" of his own work by heightening the contrast between the oppositions he suspends, and by suppressing logical transitions. David Kalstone comments on the abrupt shift in tone in one poem: in *Eclogue* 10, one singer moves suddenly from sorrow to joy, and "no dramatic reason is given."[8] This omission would seem to be deliberate; it is certainly typical. In the opening paragraph of the romance, for example, Sannazaro begins by praising pastoral for its wild, uncultivated qualities:

Sogliono il più de le volte gli alti e spaziosi alberi negli orridi monti da la natura produtti, più che le coltivate piante, da dotte mani espurgate negli adorni giardini, a' riguardanti aggradare. (49)

More often than not the tall and spreading trees brought forth by nature on the shaggy mountains are wont to bring greater pleasure to those who view them than are the cultivated trees pruned and thinned by cunning hands in ornamented gardens. (29)

He ends by commending its carefully crafted tidiness:

Che certo egli è migliore il poco terreno ben coltivare, che 'l molto lasciare per mal governo miseramente imboschire. (50)

For surely it is a better thing to till a small field well, than to let a large piece wretchedly grow wild through ill government. (30)

These contrasting views are held together (insofar as they are held together at all) only by a brief reference to one of Virgil's many images of suspension – Corydon's pipe:

Onde io, se licito mi fusse, più mi terrei a gloria di porre la mia bocca a la umile fistula di Coridone, datagli per adietro da Dameta in caro duono, che a la sonora tibia di Pallade, per la quale il male insuperbito Satiro provocò Apollo a li suoi danni. (50)

Wherefore I, if it were permitted me, would think it more glorious to set my mouth to the lowly pipe of Corydon, given him long ago as a precious gift from Damoetas, than to the sounding flute of Pallas, with which the unhappy prideful Satyr provoked Apollo, to his own misfortune. (30)

Transitions between prose and poetry are handled in a similar fashion. As his most recent translator has noted, Sannazaro repeatedly calls our attention to discrepancies in time and setting between the eclogues and the narrative episodes that surround them.[9] And he pointedly contrasts the private emotional content of the songs to the fact of their public performance: "Tell me, for I will never breathe it to another" (*Dimel che con altrui mai nol commonico*, *Ecl.* 1.60), says one herdsman to his companion, as he persuades him to sing his love complaint before "almost all the neighboring shepherds" (31; *quasi tutti i convicini pastori*, 53).

The ease with which Sannazaro effects suspensions is inseparable from his confidence in the powers of art. As Kalstone points out, throughout his *Arcadia*, all emotion is insistently transformed into song.[10] Suspension becomes for Sannazaro a purely aesthetic principle, and while he often brilliantly imitates the formal techniques of his predecessors, he loses sight of the tensions and anxieties those techniques were created to express.[11]

These anxieties are further eased in Montemayor's *Diana*. Montemayor has been credited with the introduction of plot into the Renaissance pastoral romance;[12] while this may be somewhat of an overstatement, it is true that his romance translates the principle of unity in diversity into narrative terms. The *Diana* is structured around a series of analogous tales, all of which are concerned with problems of separation and connection in love. As Montemayor's characters journey, Wizard-of-Oz style, to Felicia's magic palace, their stories provide us with progressively darker examples of separation and disjunction; they move from absence and inconstancy to deception and death. In the second half of the romance, this pattern is reversed, as the more disturbing disruptions are repaired by resurrection and reunion. Throughout the *Diana*, as well as at its end, Montemayor creates a coherent (if somewhat static) narrative by rationalizing the logical discontinuities that had marked Sannazaro's work: suspension moves closer to union here, and contradictions are resolved.

While Sidney is clearly influenced by Montemayor's narrative, his own revision of the romance is strikingly different. He retains – and heightens – Sannazaro's logical discontinuities in his own *Arcadia*; the attitude he adopts toward these contradictions is, however, considerably less sanguine. He pointedly separates the eclogues in his romance from the surrounding narrative, and he repeatedly characterizes them as (or associates them with) "pastimes."[13] This term clearly denotes mere entertainment. During the Renaissance, however, "pastime" still retained its etymological sense: it also meant "a[n] ... elapsing of time."[14] And Sidney frequently calls our attention to the ways in which the two meanings are intertwined. In a contest with Lalus, a real shepherd, the disguised courtier Musidorus ("Dorus") responds to his partner's description of his pastoral pleasures by lamenting, "My pastimes none; time passes on my fall" (62.23). In another eclogue, the shepherd Mastix criticizes his fellow herdsmen:

> "Let us pass our time," each shepherd says.
> So small account of time the shepherd feels,
> And doth not feel that life is naught but time,
> And when that time is past, death holds his heels.
>
> (77.34–36, 78.1)

And Sidney himself opens the second book by declaring:

°

In these pastoral pastimes a great number of days were sent to follow their flying predecessors, while the cup of poison, which was deeply tasted of all this noble company, had left no sinew of theirs without mortally searching into it. (91)

The eclogues in the *Arcadia* are quite literally out of time: the first set is performed by the "artificial day of torches" (56), and the third, the celebration of Lalus' "marriage day," is re-counted to us "while the other greater persons are either sleeping or otherwise occupied" (244–45). Because they are removed from time and motion, these entertainments remain wholly fictional; the "real" shepherds who participate in them exist only in the "golden world" of pure art;[15] Sidney uses these shepherds to present the courtiers' problems in a simplified manner, but he does not allow them to intrude upon the rest of the romance.[16]

Unlike the shepherds, the courtiers must live and act in the fallen world; for them, art has value only in so far as it can affect that world. When he has adopted his disguise, Pyrocles responds to Musidorus' praise of his beauty by declaring:

If my beauty be anything, then will it help me to some part of my desires; otherwise I am no more to set by it than the orator by his eloquence that persuades nobody. (27)

The formal, external beauty that is the truth of the shepherds' existence, is, for the disguised courtiers, only a means to an end; the eclogues and the lyrics that they recite are therefore distinguished by the singers' desire to exit from the songs.

In his competition with Lalus, for example, Musidorus repeatedly transforms the simple externals of the shepherd's love lament into internalized metaphors. At the conclusion, Lalus offers his partner a conventional pastoral compliment: "Of singing thou hast got the reputation" (63.20). Musidorus returns the compliment – as the form of the contest requires. In so doing, however, he makes it clear that he doesn't care about winning the contest; he wishes instead to win the heart of his beloved:

> Of singing thou hast got the reputation
> Good Lalus mine; I yield to thy ability:

My heart doth seek another estimation.
But ah, my muse, I would thou hadst facility
    To work my goddess so by thy invention
    On me to cast those eyes where shine nobility:
Seen and unknown; heard, but without attention.

(63.21–23, 64.1–4)

Musidorus desires not an aesthetic victory, but a victory in the external world; and the inability of pastoral song to effect such a victory is the subject of his lament in another eclogue:

Silly shepherd's poor pipe, when his harsh sound testifies our woes,
Into the fair looker-on, pastime, not passion, enters.[17]   (84.5–6)

Sidney's treatment of the love complaint is paralleled by his treatment of the other main type of pastoral lament – the dirge. William Ringler notes that the dirge sung by Agelastus in the fourth eclogues differs from its model, Sannazaro's eleventh eclogue, in that it lacks an apotheosis; he attributes this omission to the fact that Sidney "is writing a lament by a pagan shepherd for a pagan ruler who did not have the comforts of Christian immortality."[18] But Ringler's reasoning is clearly specious here: Sidney's courtiers are, after all, quite capable of discussing the prospect of life after death; and Sannazaro's dirge is heavily indebted to "pagan" models.[19] The eternal life envisioned in Sannazaro's poem (and its classical prototypes) is, however, quite clearly connected to the immortalizing powers of song;[20] and it is this consolation that is missing from Sidney's poem:

The style of heavy heart can never fly
    So high as should make such a pain notorious.
    Cease muse, therefore; thy dart, O death, apply;
And farewell prince, whom goodness has made glorious.

(348.34–37)

As the courtiers' love complaints all seek an end in consummation, so their dirges all demand resolution in death; Agelastus closes an earlier lament:

No, no, our mischief grows in this vile fortune,
    That private pangs cannot breathe out in public

> The furious inward griefs with hellish wailing;
> But forced are to burden feeble nature
> With secret sense of our eternal damage,
> And sorrow feed, feeding our souls with sorrow.
>
> Since sorrow then concludeth all our fortune,
>   With all our deaths show we this damage public.
>   His nature fears to die who lives still wailing.
>
> (285.12–20)

Without an external outlet for emotion, each of Sidney's courtiers remains trapped in the "zodiac of his own wit," and normal pastoral consolations return upon themselves. Repetition becomes self-reflexive, intensifying grief rather than relieving it ("And sorrow feed, feeding our souls with sorrow"); stasis becomes imprisoning; and suspension becomes self-enclosed self-division. Sidney's double sestina (328–30) is the most famous example of this transformation of conventional pastoral form:[21] as his singers' reality becomes metaphoric, internal, and fallen, the repetitions of the form become the bars out of which their prison is made. A similar transformation occurs in the lyric lament, "Over these brooks." Here, the conventional responsiveness of nature becomes a sign of the speaker's frustration, an index of his inability to achieve an effective "discharge," a permanent "issue," an end to his "labour" (118.27, 22, 2). His plight is encapsulated in the second stanza:

> My thoughts, imprisoned in my secret woes,
> With flamy breath do issue oft in sound:
> The sound to this strange air no sooner goes
> But that it doth with echo's force rebound
>   And make me hear the plaints I would refrain:
>   Thus outward helps my inward grief maintain.
>
> (118.21–26)

The proximity of the words "rebound" and "echo" make it difficult not to read "refrain" as a pun;[22] and the pun seems particularly pointed because refrains are, of course, traditional pastoral means of assuaging and containing grief. Like the responsiveness of nature – of which they are the poetic equivalent – they express the paradoxical idea, central to classical pastoral, that the continuity of a problem is that problem's solution. Here, Sidney turns this paradox on its head: past solutions become part of his problem, as his speaker's desire to refrain (stop) becomes an endless refrain (repetition).

Everywhere Sidney's courtiers look they see their own reflections; and those reflections are endlessly divided against themselves.[23] Thus, Philisides "frame[s] a disputation betwixt himself and [the echo]" (160), taking both parts and countering his own arguments. And Pyrocles berates his muse for continually composing lyrics in which "the singer is the song's theme" (164.10); he then reports his muse's reply: "I am thine / So are thy pains my pains too" (164.15–16). The speakers of these poems seem trapped in an endless round of tautology and paradox; they are forever repeating "I am – and I am not – I."

When we consider these songs in the context of the surrounding action, Sidney's problems with pastoral become even more apparent. Like the eclogues, the static lyrics are "pastime": they are frequently interrupted and sometimes rendered nonexistent by the movement of the narrative. In the second book, for example, Gynecia remembers "an old song which ... did well figure her fortune" (122–23). This song describes an internal division that allows its singer no "rest" (123.5); and it remains unsung – because "[Gynecia's] leisure served her not as then to sing it" (123).

A similar moment occurs after Philoclea has begun to recognize her love for Pyrocles. She returns to a spot where she had engraved, upon a "fair white marble stone" (109), a vow of eternal virginity. This poem, which had expressed both her internal integrity and her unity with the external world ("Thou purest stone, whose pureness does present / My purest mind," 110.1–2) has now, appropriately, become illegible; and she composes a new lyric that is better suited to her present condition. Here, she laments the disjunction that exists between human inconstancy and an image of static perfection:

> [I] witness am, how ill agree in one,
> A woman's hand with constant marble stone.
>
> (110.33–34)

Once more, however, a lyric expressing disjunction remains unexpressed, and its nonexistence confirms its truth: Philoclea's poem was never written, Sidney tells us, because the princess "could not see so perfectly as to *join* this recantation to the former vow" (111; emphasis mine).

In both of these instances, the relation that exists between lyric and action is clearly not one of simple opposition: the circumstances that render both songs "pastime" simultaneously enact the divisions, disruptions, and frustrations that are contained within the songs in the external world. And a similar, self-contradictory relation obtains between most of the lyric laments and the action that surrounds them. Towards the end of the second book, for example, Philisides is singing a love complaint when he is interrupted by the Phagonian rebels; Sidney comments:

Before Philisides had finished the last accent of his song, the horrible cries of the mad multitude gave an untimely conclusion to his passionate music. (125)

The "horrible cries" that halt Philisides' lyric clearly translate his "passionate music" into action; and the limits of his song, while confining and frustrating in themselves, seem preferable to the unbridled passion of its enactment.[24]

Once again, Sidney seems to be disabling the solutions of earlier pastoralists: the relation that he constructs between lyric and drama – between pastime and passion – is a version of pastoral paradox of connection through separation: as we move from the static songs to the movement of the narrative, we are confronted with more disruptive and disturbing forms of self-enclosed self-division. In earlier pastorals, such a relationship was viewed as enabling; here, however, it is presented as self-defeating.

The paradoxical interconnection of lyric and drama in the *Arcadia* is matched by the similarly problematic relation that exists between the individual and the community. Sidney explores this relation most fully in a series of scenes involving overhearing, and his critical view of earlier pastoral is especially evident here. At the beginning of the second book, for example, Gynecia is complaining that her love for Cleophila (the disguised prince Pyrocles) makes her feel completely isolated and uniquely cursed; she then overhears a tune "suppressed with a kind of whispering note," and being "desirous to understand" the words, draws near "as softly as she c[an]" (92). The song to which she listens is a typically frustrated, self-enclosed, ineffective lyric; it is circular in structure, and it is built around the repetition of the word "vain" (93). Sidney comments at its close:

The ending of the song served but for a beginning of new plaints, as if the mind, oppressed with too heavy a burden of cares, was fain to discharge itself in all manners. (93)

There is a clear movement in this scene towards the creation of a fellowship based on mutual isolation. We are told that Gynecia drew near "in hope to finding some companion in misery" (92), and that after hearing the song, "she could not refrain to show herself, thinking such griefs could serve fitly for nothing but her own fortune" (94). This movement is, however, short-circuited when Gynecia confronts the hidden singer – who is, of course, none other than the disguised Pyrocles. The conflicting private desires of Sidney's characters make a harmonious union impossible. Indeed, the fact that Gynecia's emotions reflect those of Pyrocles intensifies his discomfort, rather than relieving it: as Philisides' "passionate music" is externalized, in a more frightening fashion, in the "horrible cries of the mad multitude," so Pyrocles' urge to "discharge" is given terrifying external expression in the "violent issue" that springs from Gynecia "great flood-gap of sorrow" (94). Simultaneously, the prince's frustration with self-enclosure is replaced by his fear of public exposure: "Cleophila," we are told, "fear[ed] lest she [Gynecia] had heard some part of the sorrows which she [Cleophila] had risen up that morning early of purpose to breathe out to herself" (94).[25]

Sidney is here recalling, revising, and implicitly criticizing a series of similar scenes in Montemayor's *Diana*.[26] In one such scene, Sylvanus, a shepherd whom Diana has always despised, encounters the nymph's rejected lover, Syrenus. Sylvanus repeats a song he overheard his more successful rival sing, when Syrenus had still enjoyed Diana's favors (19).[27] The song itself concerns reflection, and its repetition creates a perfect suspended moment: it brings together present and past, fulfillment and longing, rivalry and sharing; and these suspensions are intensified when Sylvanus goes on to repeat a song he heard Diana sing, in which she wishes the absent Syrenus were still "here" (21–23).[28] Later in the romance, in an even more striking encounter, Syrenus himself overhears two nymphs repeat songs that he and Diana had once sung to each other (59–75). In these scenes (and others), Montemayor rationalizes the unexplained conjunction of public performance and private emotion that had appeared in Sannazaro's *Arcadia* by appealing to the common idea that love, the most private and individuating of all emotions, is also the most widely shared: the song you overhear, he implies, may be (indeed, in some sense, *must* be) your own. He invokes this idea, in various forms, throughout the *Diana*: not only do the stories that his characters tell all reflect one another, they often focus explicitly on the similarities that exist among lovers; and his singers frequently take delight in repeating "the oldest songs they kn[o]w," altering the words slightly to suit their own situations (105 ff.).[29]

Sidney is no less aware of the potential interchangeability of all lovers. A good part of the comedy in the *Arcadia* depends upon this interchangeablity, and Sidney emphasizes the parallels between Pyrocles' and Gynecia's emotions, not only in the scene we have just examined, but also in a later episode that replays this one in reverse. Here, it is Pyrocles who overhears Gynecia and believes that he has encountered his own reflection; he exclaims:

O Venus , ... who is this so well acquainted with me, that can make so lively a portraiture of my miseries? ... I will seek thee out; for thy music well assures me we are at least hand fellow prentices to one ungracious master. (181)

Sidney further reminds us of the original scene by repeating many of its key phrases. "Cleophila" initially "hear[s] a whispering sound" (180; cf. 92) and draws near "as softly as she c[an]" (182; cf. 92). Sidney comments that "the general nature of man is desirous of knowledge, and sorrow especially glad to find fellows" (182; cf. 92); and Gynecia prays to achieve "some discharge to [her] overladen breast" (182; cf. 93). Once again there is a movement towards community, and once again this movement recoils upon itself when the identity of the singer is revealed.[30] The shared desires of the "general nature of man" are decisively overridden here by the particular motives and "motions" (i.e., passions) of specific men and women; and Montemayor's timeless suspensions are overwhelmed by the movement of Sidney's narrative – by the plot of his story.[31]

Pyrocles himself states the problematic behind these scenes in another overheard lyric. As Basilius listens behind a bush, the prince sings a song that begins, "Loved I am, and yet complain of love," and concludes:

> Yet thus much love, O love, I crave of thee:
> Let me be loved, or else not loved be.   (114.6, 18–19)

One might object that the paradoxes in these lines are more apparent than real: they are created only by omitting the particulars of Pyrocles' situation, and presenting it in abstract terms. But this is precisely Sidney's point: the abstract unities of love become self-contradictory when enacted in individual lives. And it is a point made repeatedly in the *Arcadia*. The particulars of Erona's situation (the "plot of her story"), for example, make her love inescapably self-defeating:

She had love against love. For if she loved him [Antiphilus] (as immeasurably she did), then could she condescend to no other; again, if she loved him, then must she save his life; which two things were impossible to be joined together. (68–69)

Neil Rudenstine has pointed to several important similarities between the *Arcadia* and the *Apology for Poetry*.[32] In the *Apology*, Sidney praises poetry because it gives us a sensuous image of virtue rather than a mere abstraction, and he defends it against its detractors by explaining that the abuses they ascribe to it are more properly referable to particular poets.[33] And in the *Arcadia*, Pyrocles defends love in strikingly similar terms:

For, if we should love virtue, in whom should we love it but in virtuous creatures? – Without your meaning be I should love this word of virtue when I see it written in a book. Those troublesome effects you say it breeds be not the fault of love, but of him that loves. (22)

Rudenstine seems to take Pyrocles' lines simply as a justification of love, and, when removed from the context of the narrative, they do indeed seem persuasive. But the whole of the *Arcadia* makes us uncomfortably aware that the "troublesome effects" the prince alludes to are the fault of *any* "him" that loves. Love and virtue remain mere "words" unless they are realized concretely, in an individual life; but this realization necessarily compromises and problematizes the abstract values it attempts to embody.

The similarities between the *Apology* and the *Arcadia* – and the parallels Sidney repeatedly draws between verbal and sexual intercourse – suggest that Sidney is questioning the viability of any abstract, communal truth. The scene that follows Pyrocles' paradoxical lyric reinforces this suggestion. After listening to the song, Basilius steps forward, and pleads for Pyrocles' love in language that the prince himself had used earlier in the romance (115; cf. 23). Pyrocles recoils, but declares that he would listen to "these same words in my lady Philoclea's mouth" (115). Clearly, it is the singer not the song that is important here. And indeed, throughout the *Arcadia*, the persuasive power of any given speech depends, not on the strength of the argument, but on the strength of the listener's feelings for the speaker.[34]

The scenes we have been examining do not, however, merely undermine the possibility of communal truth. They present us with two unsatisfactory, self-canceling alternatives: pastime and passion, self-enclosure and public exposure, a complete lack of "discharge" and an uncontrolled "flood." As the courtiers' lyric laments are realized in action, as their desires are reflected in another, they are simultaneously negated. This is not, of course, the external outlet that Sidney's characters seek. They do not wish to remain locked in lyric stasis, but neither do they wish to escape it entirely. What they desire – and it is this desire that makes the *Arcadia* pastoral – is, in effect, a union of the lyric and the dramatic, of self and other, of art and nature. They seek to create a pastime that is effective and to experience a passion that is past time – to bring together stasis and motion in a lyric moment that will last forever.

The desire to make the moment eternal is, of course, the motivating urge behind the entire romance. The events in the plot are set in motion when Basilius "undertake[s] a journey to Delphos, there by the oracle to inform himself whether the rest of his life should be continued in like tenor of happiness as thitherunto it had been" (5). He is "stirred," Sidney tells us,

with the vanity which possesseth many who, making a perpetual mansion of this poor baiting place of man's life, are desirous to know the certainty of things to come, wherein there is nothing so certain as our continual uncertainty. (5)

And his pastoral retreat is conceived in an effort to avoid the changes the oracle prophesies.

The other courtiers are similarly motivated. The two ends that they seek in their lyrics – sex and death – are sought precisely because they seem to translate the endlessness of the lyric moment into external fact. Early in the romance, Pyrocles praises the end of love – "enjoying" – "which end ends not no sooner than the life" (23), and although Musidorus takes issue with his perspective, both princes are soon content "to lose, nay to abuse, [their] time" (19) in pursuit of present pleasure. When they neglect their heroic obligations, Sidney makes it clear that they are disregarding the pressures of contingent time: "Considering that they had almost a year of time to succor [Erona], they resolved as soon as this present action (which had taken full possession of all their desires) were brought to any good point they would forthwith take in hand that journey" (71). And their courtship of the princesses is presented as a series of attempts to seize the moment. When Pyrocles first reveals himself to Philoclea, for example, he declares:

[Circumstances] compel me, not only *to embrace the smallest time I may obtain*, but to lay aside all respects due to yourself in respect of my own life, which is *now or never* to be preserved. (119; emphasis mine)

And, as he is about to consummate his love, Sidney comments:

For further ends of those ends, and what might ensue of this action, his love and courage well matched never looked after ... and the knowledge of any misery that might ensue this joyous adventure was recked of but as a small purchase of possessing the top of happiness. (228–29)

When he is confronted by the consequences of his actions, Pyrocles attempts to resolve all "in one instant" (293) by committing suicide; and Gynecia similarly looks toward death as a means of finally achieving the "rest" she has always longed for, the "end" she has always desired (383; cf. 368). The courtiers' pursuit of death is clearly an attempt to end self-enclosed self-division by effecting the ultimate separation: Gynecia thirsts "to be rid of herself whom she hated above all things" (281). And their more positive efforts are just as clearly attempts to achieve unity by bringing together all contraries "in one instant."

The unities that they desire are perhaps best imaged in the scene in which Pyrocles reveals himself to Philoclea. Here, the prince fulfills his promise to Basilius that he would listen to "these same words in my lady Philoclea's mouth." He is once more lamenting his inability to achieve an external outlet for his emotions, when he is overheard by his beloved. The princess' response recalls that of her mother: she feels that she is listening to "words which ... might with more cause have been spoken by her own mouth" (119). The confrontation that inevitably ensues, however, results not in withdrawal but in a temporary union. Philoclea "g[ives] herself to be seen unto [Cleophila/ Pyrocles], with such a meeting of both their eyes together, with such a mutual astonishment to them both as it well showed each party had enough to do to maintain their vital powers in their due working" (119). Pyrocles promises her that she will see "a living image and a present story of the best pattern love hath ever shown of his workmanship" (120); and he announces his true identity in a sentence that calls attention to itself as the climactic revelation in a romantic tale: "Behold here before your eyes Pyrocles, prince of Macedon" (120).[35] Sidney then describes Philoclea's reaction:

> The joy which wrought into Pygmalion's mind while he found his beloved image wax little and little both softer and warmer in his folded arms, till at length it accomplished his gladness with a perfect woman's shape, still beautified with the former perfections, was even such as, by each degree of Cleophila's words, stealingly entered into Philoclea's soul, till her pleasure was fully made up with the manifesting of his being, which was such as in hope did overcome hope. (120)

Here, the lovers seem to bring together successfully the opposites that Philoclea was unable to join before – "a woman's hand and constant marble stone." The Pygmalion image suggests that the "perfections" of art can be realized in human form. And the union of art and nature that is figured in the simile is inseparable from a union of self and other: both are suggested simultaneously by the phrase "his beloved image." This passage further insists on the union of desire and action ("it accomplished his gladness," "her pleasure was fully made up with the manifesting of his being"), and of male and female: the confusion of sexual roles in the romance is mirrored by a similar confusion in the passage itself.

The courtship of Pyrocles and Philoclea is clearly analogous to the story of Pygmalion: Pyrocles originally fell in love with a picture of the princess; he transformed himself into its image ("As for my name," he declared, "it shall be Cleophila, turning Philoclea to myself, as my mind is wholly turned and transformed into her," 18),[36] and it is this creature – an image of her own image – with whom Philoclea proceeds to fall in love. Sidney does not, however, associate this myth only with the young lovers, nor even with romantic love in general: the promise that it holds out represents, for him, the controlling fantasy of pastoral, and he thus invokes it at significant moments throughout the *Arcadia*. When Musidorus helps Pyrocles "put on his transforming apparel" in preparation for his entry into Arcadia, we are reminded both of Pygmalion and of his reverse image, Narcissus (26–27). And Basilius' attraction to pastoral is presented in similar terms; Sidney describes the growth of the duke's infatuation with Dametas' rusticity as follows:

The flattering courtier had no sooner taken the prince's mind but that there were straight reasons to confirm the duke's doing, and shadows of virtues found for Dametas. His silence grew wit, his bluntness integrity, his beastly ignorance virtuous simplicity; and the duke (according to the nature of great persons, in love with that he had done himself) fancied that the weakness was in him, with his presence, would grow wisdom. And so, like a creature of his own making, he liked him more and more. And thus gave he him first the office of principal herdsman. And lastly did he put his life in his hands. (31)

These passages clearly incorporate within themselves their own criticism. The confusion of pronouns in the above quotation ("the duke ... fancied that the weakness was in him, with his presence, would grow wisdom"), like the confusion of sexes in the description of Philoclea, underscores the self-projection that is occurring here. All the courtiers are, in effect, doing what Basilius eventually does in fact: they are attempting to make love to their own imaginations. Throughout the *Arcadia*, Sidney easily dismisses Basilius' desires and actions. He is, however, considerably more sympathetic to the young lovers, and he allows them a number of moments of apparent unity and repose, in which time appears to stop, and their dreams seem to be realized; like the lyric laments, however, these suspended moments invariably recoil upon themselves.[37]

Early in the romance, Pyrocles creates such a moment when he praises the beauty of Arcadia. He begins by dismissing both the pressures of time and the consequences of his actions: "And lord! dear cousin," he exclaims, "doth not the pleasantness of this place carry in itself sufficient reward for any time lost in it, or for any such danger that might ensue?" (15). He then proceeds to create a picture of harmony and perfection, in which all conflicts are resolved:

Do you not see how everything conspires together to make this place a heavenly dwelling? Do you not see the grass, how in colour they excel the emeralds, everyone striving to pass his fellow – and yet they are all kept in an equal height?... Doth not the air breathe health, which the birds, delightful both to the ear and eye, do daily solemnize with the sweet concent of their voices? Is not every echo here a perfect music? And these fresh and delightful brooks, how slowly they slide away, as loath to leave the company of so many things united in perfection! (15)

We are told, before Pyrocles speaks, that his words are merely an attempt "to breathe out some part of his inward evil" (15). Nevertheless, we are drawn into the balanced beauty of his description. Rudenstine has – quite correctly, I believe – characterized this passage as "lyric";[38] it is a moment in which Sidney deliberately halts the flow of the narrative, and forces us to "stop here." We are therefore inevitably brought up short by the description of Pyrocles that follows:

Musidorus had all this while held his look fixed upon Pyrocles' countenance, and with no less loving attention marked how his words proceeded from him. But in both these he perceived such strange diversities that they rather increased new doubts than gave him ground to settle any judgement; for, besides his eyes sometimes even great with tears, the oft changing of his colour, with a kind of shaking unstaidness over all his body, he might see in his countenance some great determination mixed with fear, and might perceive in him store of thoughts rather stirred than digested, his words interrupted continually with sighs which served as a burden to each sentence, and the tenor of his speech (though of his wonted phrase) not knit together to one constant end but rather dissolved in itself, as the vehemency of inward passion prevailed. (15–16)

The static harmony that we have admired does not, in fact, exist at all. Pyrocles' speech is marked by "strange diversities" that "[un]settle" his audience: it is distorted by the speaker's frequent "change[s]," "shaking unstaidness," "mixed" emotions, and "stirred" thoughts; it contains its own "interrupt[ions]"; and the only "end" it reaches is self-dissolution.

The movement that occurs in this scene recurs throughout the *Arcadia*. Pyrocles' "affected praising of the place" (16) is, for example, matched later in the romance by Sidney's description of the "fair meadow appointed for [the] shepherdish pastimes" (46). Sidney first informs us that these pastimes have been violently interrupted; he then proceeds to praise their setting, and we are once more drawn into a vision of unity and peace:

It was, indeed, a place of great delight, for through the midst of it there ran a sweet brook which did both hold the eye open with her beautiful streams and close the eye with the sweet purling noise it made upon the pebble-stones it ran over; the meadow itself yielding so liberally all sorts of flowers that it seemed to nourish a contention betwixt the colour and the smell whether in his kind were the most delightful. Round about the meadow, as if it had been to enclose a theatre, grew all sorts of trees as either excellency of fruit, stateliness of growth, continual greenness, or poetical fancies have made at any time famous. In most part of which trees there had been by art such pleasant arbours that it became a gallery aloft, from one tree to the other, almost round about, which below yielded a perfect shadow, in those hot countries counted a great pleasure. (46)

This harmonious description seems particularly compelling because it appears to heal a breach that has just occurred. At the beginning of this paragraph, Sidney had described Musidorus' entry into pastoral life in positive terms; he had spoken approvingly of the "contentment" that the prince experienced:

And thus went they to the lodge, with greater joy to Musidorus (now only poor shepherd Dorus) than all his life before had ever brought forth unto him – so manifest it is that the greatest point outward things can bring a man unto is the contentment of the mind, which once obtained, no state is miserable; and without that, no prince's seat restful. (44–45)

He had then implicitly criticized the assumptions in this passage by juxtaposing it with a description of Basilius:

Poor old Basilius, now alone..., had a sufficient eclogue in his own head betwixt honour, with the long experience he had of the world, on the one side, and this new assault of Cleophila's beauty on the other side. There hard by the lodge walked he, carrying this unquiet *contention* about him. (45; emphasis mine)

The word play in these lines reminds us that bucolic "contentment" springs from – and issues in – "unquiet contention";[39] here again, normal pastoral consolations seem to return on themselves.

In his description of the "fair meadow," Sidney appears to resolve this dilemma by providing us with a vision of a contention that yields content. The pleasure and delight that can be derived from "contending" contraries is the governing idea of the description; and this idea is made explicit when Sidney praises the meadow for "yielding so liberally all sorts of flowers that it seemed to nourish a contention betwixt the colour and the smell whether in his kind were the most delightful."[40] But this apparent resolution recoils upon itself once more, as the meadow is invaded by a lion and a bear, and the courtiers are forced into contention with the wild beasts who are clearly associated with their own appetites.[41]

Both the preceding scene and Pyrocles' encomium of Arcadia imply that pastoral harmony is undermined by the very desires that create it. As the narrative proceeds, and Sidney follows those desires through to their necessary ends, this implication becomes more insistent; it is made brutally explicit in the third book, when Musidorus and Pamela elope.

The young lovers' woodland idyll is clearly presented as an attempt to enact a pastoral fantasy. In preparation for their departure, Musidorus deceives Miso, one of the princess' rustic guardians, by telling her a tale designed to appeal to her jealousy; he describes an encounter he claims to have witnessed between a shepherdess and her beloved shepherd. At the center of his tale is one of the most lovely – and most frequently anthologized – lyrics in the *Arcadia*; the shepherdess, in an "angelic voice" (190), sings the following song:

> My true love hath my heart, and I have his,
> By just exchange, one for the other given.
> I hold his dear, and mine he cannot miss:
> There never was a better bargain driven.
>
> His heart in me, keeps me and him in one,
> My heart in him, his thoughts and sense guides.
> He loves my heart, for once it was his own,
> I cherish his, because in me it bides.
>
> His heart his wound received from my sight:
> My heart was wounded, with his wounded heart,
> For as from me on him his hurt did light,
> So still methought in me his hurt did smart:
>   Both equal hurt, in this change sought our bliss:
>   My true love hath my heart, and I have his.
>
>   (190.25–32; 191.1–6)

The beautifully balanced verse of this lyric repeatedly emphasizes the perfect unity of love. Its abstract courtliness is, in turn,
balanced by the comic and sensual rusticity of the shepherd's
reply; and Sidney underscores the responsiveness of the lyrics in
the bridge between them:

But, as if the shepherd that lay before her had been organs which were
only to be blown by her breath, she had no sooner ended with the
joining her sweet lips together but that he recorded to her music this
rural poesy:

> O words which fall like summer dew on me,
> O breath more sweet than is the growing bean,
> O tongue in which all honeyed liquors be,
> O voice that doth the thrush in shrillness stain,
>   Do you say still, this is her promise due,
>   That she is mine, as I to her am true.
>
> Gay hair, more gay than straw when harvest lies,
> Lips red and plum, as cherry's ruddy side,
> Eyes fair and great, like fair great ox's eyes;
> O breast in which two white sheep swell in pride
>   Join you with me, to seal this promise due,
>   That she be mine, as I to her am true.
>
> But thou white skin, as white as cruds well pressed,
> So smooth as sleekstone-like it smooths each part,
> And thou dear flesh, as soft as wool new dressed,
> And yet as hard as brawn made hard by art;
>   First four but say, next four their saying seal,
>   But you must pay the gage of promised weal. (191.11–28)

Tension clearly exists between the terms of the second song and
those of the first; but that tension is held in suspension by the
lyric form. Taken together, the two songs present us with an
image of the harmonious union of the spiritual and the physical,
the abstract and the concrete, high idealism and low comedy,
the sentimental and the naive. In the succeeding lines, however,
this image is destroyed. The shepherd asks that the desires
contained in his blazon be realized in fact; he demands of his
beloved: "When shall I enjoy the rest of my toiling thoughts,
and when shall your blissful promise (now due) be verified with

just performance?" (191). And it is at this point, significantly, that we are reminded that the lyrics are a trick: Musidorus assigns the second song to a "real" shepherd – the rude and crude Dametas; and the disruption that we inevitably experience here is paralleled by Miso's interruption of Musidorus' sentence:

"With that I drew nearer to them, and saw (for now he had lifted up his face to glass himself in her fair eyes) that it was my master Dametas" – but here Miso interrupted his tale with railing at Dametas with all those exquisite terms which I never was good scold enough to imagine.[42] (191–92)

Sidney is clearly suggesting that Musidorus' fiction represents a deception greater than the one that is practiced upon Miso.

This suggestion is borne out when Pamela and Musidorus flee Arcadia. After journeying for a while, "maintaining their hearts in that right harmony of affection which doth interchangeably deliver each to the other the secret workings of their souls" (197), the lovers arrive at a perfect pastoral *locus amoenus*, "a fair thick wood, which did entice them with the pleasantness of it to take their rest" (197). Here, they effectively reprise – in extended form – the lyrics with which Musidorus had deceived Miso. Pamela carves in the barks of the trees "pretty knots which tied together the names of Musidorus and Pamela, sometimes intermixedly changing them to Pamedorus and Musimela" (198). And they sing a series of suspended, responsive lyrics, which repeatedly emphasize their own perfect harmony, and hold out the possibility of reconciling pleasure to virtue: "In this virtuous wantonness," Sidney tells us, they "suffer[ed] their minds to descend to each tender enjoying their united thoughts" (200). Finally, Pamela falls asleep, and Musidorus mentally catalogues her beauties in a prose blazon (201) that recalls the second song in his pastoral fiction. But the young lovers do not, of course, merely live out Musidorus' lyrics; they end by replaying the entire earlier scene. As the rustic sensuality of the second song had – shockingly but appropriately – found its realistic counterpart in Dametas' crudity, so the desires contained in Musidorus' praise of Pamela are, inevitably, realized in his attempt to rape his beloved; and this attempt is itself almost immediately interrupted by the arrival of a rude, ungovernable rabble:

And now he began to make his approaches when (to the just punishment of his broken promise and most infortunate bar of his long-pursued and almost-achieved desires) there came by a dozen clownish villains, ... [who] seemed to bear a great conformity with the savages. (202)

In his exquisitely intrusive parenthetical phrase, Sidney makes it clear that the circumstance that hinders the fulfillment of his character's longings simultaneously embodies them: it is both a "just punishment" and a "most infortunate bar." And this double vision is possible because those longings themselves represent both an interruption and an end: the logical, parallel structure of the phrase is at odds with its paradoxical content; Musidorus' "broken promise" and his "long-pursued and almost-achieved desires" are not, after all, two separate things, but the same thing. His desires are, in effect, self-interrupting; they necessarily destroy the perfect unity they seek to enact.[43]

Nancy Lindheim has argued that the controlling idea of the *Arcadia* is the "vanishing distinction":[44] Sidney repeatedly presents us with two antithetical qualities or ideas, only to prove that "at their extremes ... opposing values are actually identical"; the ultimate effect of the romance is thus one of "reciprocity" and "harmonious interchange."[45] As we have seen, Lindheim is accurately describing only the controlling fantasy of the *Arcadia*; the reality with which Sidney confronts us is the reverse image of her model: while his characters strive to assert the identity of opposites, they repeatedly find that each one of their desires and impulses is inescapably divided against itself; like Erona, they all, in effect, "ha[ve] love against love ... which two things [are] impossible to be joined together." As Richard McCoy has noted, the "protagonists' principal characteristic is a kind of heroic pathos in which they are defeated by their own impulses and exertions."[46] A pattern of self-frustration dominates the work as a whole – from Basilius' original abdication of responsibility (on which Philanax comments, "Why should you deprive yourself of governing your dukedom for fear of losing your dukedom, like one that should kill himself for fear of death," 7), to Dametas' parody of his actions ("sometimes for dread of hanging he meant to hang himself," 272), to the final irony that the princes' efforts to outwit the authorities and win the princesses almost undermine the marriages that Pyrocles' father had originally planned. In this context, of course, the traditional plot device of fulfilling an oracle by attempting to avoid it takes on particular significance. Like Theocritus, Sidney seems acutely aware that "you can't get rid of the damn thing"; but this awareness is no longer liberating: whether the longings his characters express in their lyrics are immediately thwarted or (as we shall see) apparently fulfilled, they remain trapped in an endless cycle of self-enclosed self-division.

The problems and desires that are explored in *Arcadia* are clearly not those of the characters alone. In Virgil's *Eclogues*, we will recall, the suspensions that the characters created – between the lyric and the dramatic, the fictional and the real – mirrored the suspension that existed between the poet and his own creations; so, too, are the disjunctions at the heart of *Arcadia* reflected in and expressive of Sidney's relation to his fictional self-representations. We are presented here with a proliferation of personae – with a number of disjoined representations of the author, existing on different levels of the text.

Critics usually simply identify Philisides as "Sidney's fiction-alized self-portrait,"[47] pointing out, as they do so, that he is a descendant of Sincero, the melancholy lover in Sannazaro's *Arcadia*.[48] But the similarities that exist between these characters make their differences more striking. Sincero is not, after all, merely a figure for the suffering poet-lover; he is also the narrator of the romance, and, insofar as there is action in Sannazaro's work, he is its principal actor.[49] Philisides, by contrast, is the world's most peripheral authorial persona: except for the brief episode we have already examined (in which his lyric expression of frustration is interrupted by action that embodies it in a more frightening fashion), he exists only in the

eclogues. Richard McCoy feels that Sidney's identification with
Philisides leads him to present the "stranger shepherd" in a
particularly sympathetic light; he comments:

Philisides...has the singular advantage of representing his author
in debate, and a certain favoritism is shown him from his first
appearance...Unlike Basilius, he incurs no reproach for pastoral
retirement.[50]

But McCoy is clearly comparing the incommensurable here,
and confusing cause with effect. Unlike Basilius, Philisides is
purely a creature of lyric "pastime"; his desires have no
consequence in the world of action. And it is precisely because
his emotions are so clearly distanced, fictionalized, and contained that he can be so clearly identified with Sidney himself.
    The narrator of the *Arcadia* – who is straightforwardly pre-
sented as "Sidney" – is, of course, past time in another way: he
is able to enter the realms of lyric and drama but he is bound by
neither; he presents us with an image of the poet as truly free. If
Philisides' desires remain completely internal and fictional, his
perspective is wholly communal and "real"; and Philisides'
static, self-enclosed lyrics are matched by his public *sententiae*,
which provide us – temporarily – with moments of closure in
the narrative.[51]
    As McCoy's comments suggest, the truly problematic charac-
ters in the *Arcadia* are those who inhabit the realm of passion;
and of these characters, the ones who most fully enact what one
critic (oxymoronically) terms "the drama of Philisides"[52] are,
of course, Pyrocles and Musidorus. Most readers have felt that
clear connections exist between the princes (particularly Pyrocles) and Sidney's other self-representations;[53] but these connections are never fully acknowledged, and for most of the
Arcadia, Sidney's principal personae[54] remain discrete. For one
brief moment, however, they seem to come together; and this
moment is, significantly, the greatest moment of unity that the
characters experience. When Pyrocles is about to consummate
his love for Philoclea, the narrator tells us:

There came into his mind a song the shepherd Philisides had in his
hearing sung of the beauties of his unkind mistress, which in Pyrocles'

judgement was fully accomplished in Philoclea. The song was this:...
(238)

He then proceeds to repeat the lyric, "What tongue can her
perfections tell."

The suspension of pastime and passion – of stasis and
motion – that is figured in one way by the sexual union of
Pyrocles and Philoclea, is figured in another by the verbal union
of Philisides and Pyrocles. By bringing together his lyric and his
dramatic personae, Sidney (in effect) unites fiction and reality,
eternity and contingent time. Pyrocles and Philoclea's requited
love also represents the perfect union of self and other; it
provides us with an image of a discharge that is not a flood. And
Sidney presents us with the verbal equivalent of this image by
describing an overheard, lyric expression of love that is successfully transferred from one individual to another. By identifying Philisides simply as a shepherd here,[55] Sidney further seems
to effect a suspension between shepherd and courtier, the simple
and the complex. And he explicitly brings together frustration
and fulfillment, desire and action: the beauties of Philisides' unkind mistress are "fully accomplished" in the kind and willing
Philoclea.

This is, of course, not simply the greatest moment of unity in
the text; it is also the most memorable of the moments that are
not there at all: it is, inevitably, interrupted by its own
fulfillment in action. After presenting us with a static blazon
(the third in a series of blazons)[56] that continues for 146 lines,
the narrator picks up the thread of the story where he has left it,
and remarks: "But do not think, fair ladies, his thoughts had
such *leisure* as to run over so long a ditty" (242; emphasis mine).
While the narrator has been repeating Philisides' praises of the
lady "in whose each part all pens may dwell" (238.7; 242.10),[57]
Pyrocles has been "using the benefit of the time" (242) to fully
accomplish these praises in Philoclea.

It is instructive to compare this fleeting moment of unity to the
similar moment that occurs upon Mount Acidale in Book 6 of
The Faerie Queene. Throughout Book 6, Spenser has faced

problems similar to those in the *Arcadia*, and he has expressed them in a similar manner: like Sidney, he creates a number of discrete self-representations, and like Sidney, he presents us with a series of broken moments of repose – static idyllic moments that are destroyed by the intrusion of the active world. The characteristic movement of the book is emblematized in canto 9, when Spenser compares Calidore to Paris; the courtier turned shepherd is depicted as enjoying a brief moment of peaceful love before an impending disruption:

> ... who had seene him then, would have bethought
> On *Phyrigian Paris* by *Plexippus* brooke,
> When he the loue of fayre *Oenone* sought,
> What time the golden apple was vnto him brought.   (9.36)[58]

In canto 10, however, this movement is reversed. When Spenser is describing the Graces, he compares "the beauty of this goodly band" (14) to that of Ariadne's crown:

> Looke how the Crowne, which *Ariadne* wore
> Vpon her yuory forehead that same day,
> That *Theseus* her vnto his bridale bore,
> When the bold *Centaures* made that bloudy fray,
> With the fierce *Lapithes*, which did them dismay;
> Being now placed in the firmament,
> Through the bright heauen doth her beams display,
> And is vnto the starres an ornament,
> Which round about her moue in order excellent.   (10.13)

In these lines, a chaotic disruption is itself seen as a momentary experience: it is preceded by the joys of earthly love, and it is resolved into a cosmic harmony. It seems significant that the ultimate "order" that Spenser envisions here is explicitly aesthetic in nature. Throughout Book 6, he had investigated self-conscious artifice as one possible response to a world beyond one's control;[59] in the Ariadne simile, he imagines the final triumph of art – and that triumph prefigures the one that occurs on Acidale.[60]

Here, for the only time in Book 6, we are presented with a broken moment that is healed – and it is healed through the power of an art acutely conscious of its own limitations. Calidore, seeking to know, significantly, whether the Graces are

real or "enchaunted show" (10.17), intrudes upon Colin's lyric
vision, and causes it to disappear. In the act of mourning its
passing, however, the shepherd-singer effectively recreates what
has been lost. As he extolls the beauty of his beloved, he becomes
progressively more involved in his description, and the tenses of
his speech shift subtly into the present (10.25–27). Simultaneously, he begins to echo words spoken earlier by the
narrator. When Spenser was describing Colin's love, he had
been so moved that he had turned to address his own character:

> Pype iolly shepheard, pype thou now apace
> Vnto thy loue, that made thee low to lout:
> Thy loue is present there with thee in place,
> Thy loue is there aduaunst to be another Grace. (10.16)

Now, in a very Virgilian passage, Colin "repeats" this address:

> ... the Graces that here wont to dwell,
> Haue for more honor brought her to this place,
> And graced her so much to be another Grace.

> Another grace she well deserues to be,
> ... all her peres cannot with her compare,
> But quite are dimmed, when she is in place.
> She made me often pipe and now to pipe apace. (10.26–27)

Clearly, the distinctions between loss and consolation, reality
and fiction, "heroic" author and "bucolic" character are here
beginning to be erased. This movement culminates in stanza 28,
in which Colin turns to address Gloriana, and the fictional
shepherd stands revealed as the author of *The Faerie Queene*:

> Sunne of the world, great glory of the sky,
> That all the earth doest lighten with thy rayes,
> Great *Gloriana*, greatest Maiesty,
> Pardon thy shepheard, mongst so many layes,
> As he hath sung of thee in all his dayes,
> To make one minime of thy poore handmayd,
> And vnderneath thy feete to place her prayse,
> That when thy glory shall be farre displayd
> To future age of her this mention may be made. (10.28)

In these lines, moreover, Spenser expresses confidence that the
ravages of time and fortune can be healed through the power of
song, which can make what has been lost seem present.

The suspension that is achieved here is much more complete than the comparable suspension that occurs in the *Arcadia*. Sidney's brief moment of unity is explicitly created and controlled by his godlike narrator, but Spenser's narrator cedes control to his own fictional, lyric creation: Colin (like his forerunner, Virgil's Corydon) effectively becomes "the poet." And while the perfection of Sidney's moment is destroyed by the exertions of his active hero, Spenser incorporates a similar disruption into the harmony he finally envisions – indeed, he makes that harmony depend upon Calidore's disruption.

Like the union in the *Arcadia*, the harmony in *The Faerie Queene* is, from one perspective, necessarily ephemeral. The permanence that Colin imagines in his lyric speech cannot be realized in an individual life or represented in a continuous narrative. Calidore must return to his love-idyll with Pastorella (which, in this canto, is seen both as a more earthbound, individuated version of Colin's relationship with his beloved and as the diminished reflection of Calidore's heroic quest); and that idyll itself is inevitably disrupted by an intrusion from the outside. Moreover, the confidence in art that is expressed here will be radically questioned by the end of the book. Nevertheless, the experience upon Acidale permits Spenser to assert, for the first time in Book 6, that the very briefness of moments of earthly happiness increases their value. He begins the next canto with a stanza in which he suspends notions of limitation and power, of value and loss:

> The ioyes of loue, if they should euer last,
>   Without affliction or disquietnesse,
>   That worldly chaunces doe amongst them cast,
>   Would be on earth too great a blessednesse,
>   Liker to heauen, then mortall wretchednesse.
>   Therefore the winged God, to let men weet,
>   That here on earth is no sure happinesse,
>   A thousand sowres hath tempred with one sweet,
> To make it seeme more deare and dainty, as is meet.   (11.1)

The parallel infinitives here (lines 6–7, 9) present us with conflicting explanations for, and attitudes toward, the loss of perfection that marks quotidian life.

Sidney's narrator also expresses sympathy for his lovers, "who had but small respite of their fiery agonies" (243). But this sympathy is itself short-lived. As the narrative continues, Pyrocles' and Philoclea's actions inevitably recoil upon themselves, and the narrator's perspective shifts to one of condemnation. After the "small respite" of the eclogues, he opens Book 4 with a scathing denunciation of our self-defeating desires:

The everlasting justice (using ourselves to be the punishers of our faults, and making our own actions the beginning of our chastisement, that our shame may be the more manifest, and our repentance follow the sooner) took Dametas at this present (by whose folly the others' wisdom might receive the greater overthrow) to be the instrument of revealing the secretest cunning – so evil a ground does evil stand upon, and so manifest is it that nothing remains strongly but that which hath the good foundation of goodness. (265)

Unlike the conflicting perspectives in *The Faerie Queene*, the contradictory attitudes that Sidney's narrator adopts are presented as ultimately irreconcilable; and the disjunction between them mirrors the other disjunctions in the *Arcadia*. Our awareness of these disjunctions, of course, depends upon the exemption of the narrator from the strictures he places upon his characters: our understanding of the nonexistence of the moments of perfect unity in the *Arcadia* rests upon the narrator's ability to make them present. So, too, does the repeated undermining of communal truth rely on the narrator's communal speech, and the repeated demonstration of the illusoriness of fiction, on his skills at fiction-making. For most of the *Arcadia*, Sidney avoids the implications of this paradox: as he follows his characters' desires through to their necessary ends, however, he inevitably pursues the consequences of his own.

At the conclusion of the romance, Sidney attempts to satisfy all of his conflicting impulses – and, simultaneously, to show us the gap between them. He finally presents us with a character – Euarchus – who is capable of separating the singer from the song, of subordinating individual desires to the dictates of reason. As he had earlier investigated the consequences of the princes' passions, he now takes Euarchus' reason to its logical conclusion; and the result has made most readers distinctly uncomfortable.[61]

The discomfort that we experience during the trial does not, however, arise merely from our sympathy for the princes' desires, but from our own analogous desire for a conclusion that resolves all conflicts "in one instant" – for an appropriate conclusion, that is, to a pastoral romance. The point at which we completely lose sympathy with Euarchus is the point at which most of the characters do – not, that is, when he makes his original judgment against the princes (this verdict is expected as well as deserved), but when he holds fast to that judgment after their relation to him has been revealed. Sidney leads up to the revelation that we have been awaiting with a sentence that holds forth the promise of instantaneous reversal and resolution:

> But as with great number of armed men Philanax was descending unto them, and that Musidorus was beginning to say something in Pyrocles' behalf, behold Kerxenus that with arms cast abroad and open mouth came crying to Euarchus, holding a stranger in his hand that cried much more than he, desiring they might be heard speak before the prisoners were removed. (408)

When he exclaims "behold," Sidney halts the movement of his sentence, and fuses past and present, the world of the story and the world of the reader. Philanax, we are told in the following lines, is at this instant "stopped ... betwixt entreaty and force from carrying away the princes" (408); and our reading experience is similarly held in suspension. Sidney's exclamation itself, moreover, clearly leads us to expect a magic moment of revelation and resolution; we are reminded of the words Pyrocles had used when he announced his identity to Philoclea: "Behold here before your eyes Pyrocles, prince of Macedon" (120).

The recognition scene that follows would, in another work, satisfy our expectations. Recognition scenes traditionally occur at the ends of romantic narratives – and for good reason: they enact the idea of unity achieved in an instant. They present us with an image of separation become connection, of absence become presence, of chaotic chance become providential order. It is precisely this image of miraculous harmony that so moves Sidney's characters:

Even Philanax's own revengeful heart was mollified when he saw how from diverse parts in the world so near kinsmen should meet in such a necessity.(410)

The contentment that Philanax finds in the thought of familial unity is matched by the pleasure that we ourselves experience in the anticipation of narrative unity. When Euarchus fails to respond to the revelation in a conventional manner, the other characters are troubled by his coldness as a father. We are equally troubled by his recalcitrance as a character: Euarchus, in effect, misses his cue.

It might be objected that Sidney is imitating Heliodorus here;[62] and so he is – up to a point. Like Euarchus, Hydaspes, the king in *An Aethiopian History*, refuses to reverse his decision when he discovers that he has sentenced his own child to death. He thus demonstrates that he will not "yeelde to affection"; he tells the assembled multitude: "So wil I make more account of your weale publike, then mine owne private commoditie" (272).[63] Unlike Euarchus, however, he places the final decision in the hands of the people; and they, of course, vote to let his daughter live. Heliodorus' king, in other words, gets to have it both ways; and having it both ways is precisely what Sidney will not, finally, allow his characters or his readers – or himself.

Euarchus' decision leaves us with a gap between an image of resolution and the reality it purports to resolve. Sidney then presents us with another image – really a variant of the same image – and this time he lets it work. The resurrection of a character presumed dead – like the recognition scene – enacts the idea of recovery achieved through loss. The two devices are frequently used together at the end of romances to signal emotional recovery and narrative resolution. Montemayor's *Diana* ends in this manner; so, too, do *The Winter's Tale* and the sixth book of *The Faerie Queene*. In these works, however, the images of resurrection and recovery operate in conjunction with the emotional development of the characters and the progress of the action. In the *Arcadia*, they do not. For Sidney's "solution" – the revival of Basilius – notoriously solves nothing at all: the princes have not been convicted of murdering the duke, but of kidnaping and seduction – charges of which they remain guilty. Once more, we are faced with a disjunction between idea and action; and the discomfort we experience here is equivalent to that which we experienced during the recognition scene.

I have no doubt that Sidney intended his conclusion to be unsatisfactory. Here, as throughout the *Arcadia*, he is confronting us with two contradictory, reflecting options, "which two things [are] impossible to be joined together." What we desire for the princes is a simultaneous acknowledgment of their faults and their virtues, a simultaneous punishment – or pardon – and reward. In his encounter with the brigands, Musidorus had patiently explained that "reward" and "pardon" cannot easily "go together, being of so contrary a making" (315);[64] and during the trial, Euarchus argues – to the princes' dismay and our own – for an even more stringent version of this distinction: "Reward is proper to well doing, punishment to evil doing, which must not be confounded no more than good and evil are to be mingled" (405). Similarly, what we desire for the narrative is a simultaneous expression of recovery and loss, of resolution and impermanence; and Sidney presents us with the negative image of the suspension we expect. Basilius' miraculous revival is, moreover, the culmination of a pattern of death-and-resurrection imagery that has appeared throughout the narrative: whenever Pyrocles is in danger of losing an argument to a more reasonable opponent, he falls into a deadly swoon – and his antagonist immediately relents.[65]

Sidney also signals the unsatisfactoriness of his conclusion as it occurs. He incorporates into it a mini-romance, the story of Gynecia's grandmother, in which a number of unacceptable actions – strikingly similar to those in the *Arcadia* – are suddenly brought to a happy ending. The heroine of this tale disobeys her father, rapes her beloved while he sleeps, and flees the kingdom with him; her story is then abruptly resolved in the middle of a sentence: "...and after many strange adventures [they] were reconciled to the king, her father, after whose death they

reigned" (415–16). Sidney calls our attention to the abruptness
of his own, similar resolution when, shortly afterwards, he
suddenly shifts his focus from Gynecia to the princes:[66]

Then with princely entertainment to Euarchus, and many kind words
to Pyrocles (whom still he [Basilius] dearly loved, though in a more
virtuous kind) the marriage was concluded, to the inestimable joy of
Euarchus (towards whom now Musidorus acknowledged his fault),
betwixt these peerless princes and princesses. (416–17)

The phrases that separate "concluded" from "betwixt" allow
the verb to assume its full force – and one is compelled to
wonder when this "conclusion" began. Here, as in the story of
Gynecia's grandmother, some transitional explanation seems to
be missing.

   Having said all this, I must also say that I do not find the
conclusion of the Old Arcadia satisfactorily unsatisfactory. I do
not believe that we really feel, as several critics have main-
tained,[67] that our own desires have been effectively challenged
or questioned; on the contrary, most readers' initial reaction –
and many readers' final one – is that Sidney has made some sort
of mistake.[68] And the reason we do not acknowledge our
complicity in the ending is clearly that Sidney never fully
acknowledges his own. To a certain extent, the conclusion has
affinities with the last line of one of Sidney's sonnets. In Astrophil
and Stella 71 – to cite the most well-known example – a carefully
built structure is overturned by a last-minute assertion of the
claims of desire: "'But ah,' Desire still cries, 'give me some
food.'" (14). But the desire in the sonnet is simultaneously
acknowledged, located, and contained: the line is spoken by
Sidney's fictional, lyric persona (who, in turn, attributes the
"cry" to a personification of his own emotion),[69] and it provides
us with a provisional, lyric resolution. The Old Arcadia similarly
leaves us in the realm of desire, but the desire here is completely
unlocatable; it leaves us in the realm of fiction, but it does so in
a voice that has been designated as "real." McCoy has
accounted for Sidney's failure here in psychological and
historical terms;[70] I am thoroughly persuaded by most of his
analysis, but I would argue that the difficulties Sidney is

experiencing are formal as well. There is really no way, within the terms of the narrative, that he *can* arrive at a satisfactory conclusion. He cannot, in the voice of his communal narrator, conclusively assert the supremacy of desire; but neither can he wholly distance himself from its claims. And he cannot – given the disjunctions he has effected – finally do both at the same time: to do so would require merging his "real" and his fictional personae, as Virgil does at the end of *Eclogue* 2; it would require suspending pastime and passion, "which two things [are] impossible to be joined together."

Sidney is ultimately caught in the same self-contradiction as his characters – and he seems to be aware of this fact. Philoclea's inability to unite human inconstancy and an image of artistic perfection was, we will recall, demonstrated by the nonexistence of the lyric she had composed to lament her condition; Sidney had repeated her poem, and then declared: "But seeing as she could not see so perfectly as to join this recantation to [her] former vow, ... for a while the poor soul did nothing but turn up and down and hide her face" (111). His comment had implicitly acknowledged that our awareness of Philoclea's predicament depended on the presence of a narrator who *could* see perfectly enough to join conflicting perspectives – if only to declare that they were irreconcilable. But this narrator cannot possibly get his mind around his own conflicting impulses. As the truth of Philoclea's "recantation" was proven by its nonexistence, so the integrity of Sidney's vision in the *Old Arcadia* is, in a sense, demonstrated by its ultimate failure. And there is no meta-narrator available to explain, "But seeing as he could not see ... "

Sidney's prefatory letter to the Countess of Pembroke is, perhaps, an attempt to provide himself with such an overview. Here, and only here, he presents his own efforts to communicate in the same terms as he has presented those of his characters. Like Pyrocles, he is "desirous to speak to breathe out some part of his inward evil" (15):

In sum, a young head not so well stayed as I would it were (and shall be when God will) having many fancies begotten in it, if it had not been in some way delivered, would have grown a monster, and more sorry might I be that they came in than that they gat out. (3)

But he does not wish his discourse to become completely public; he continues: "But his chief safety shall be the not walking abroad" (3). He desires, in sum, a discharge that is not a flood, an issue that does not issue. He therefore directs his words to their only proper receptacle – his other self, his sister: "Now it is done only for you, only to you" (3). He asks her to share it only with those who can hold justice and mercy in suspension, whose judgment of his song will be tempered by their affection for the singer:

If you keep it to yourself, or to such friends who will weigh errors in the balance of goodwill, I hope, for the father's sake, it will be pardoned, perchance made much of, though in itself it have deformities. (3)

And throughout the letter, of course, he repeatedly characterizes the entire romance as "pastime":

Here now have you (most dear, and most worthy to be most dear, lady) this idle work of mine ... For severer eyes it is not, being but a trifle and that triflingly handled ... Read it then in your idle times, and the follies your good judgement will find in it, blame not, but laugh at. (3)

It seems only fitting that for hundreds of years the *Old Arcadia* was, in fact, a wholly private utterance, a fictional moment of repose that was not really there at all.

Sidney's own dissatisfaction with the *Old Arcadia* is evident in the revisions he later made. In the *New Arcadia*, the princes are guiltless of the crimes they had committed in the earlier version.[71] More important, Sidney seems less interested in focusing on the problems and attractions of pastoral poetry. He moves away from the bower both literally (a good part of the story takes place outside Arcadia) and structurally (the *New Arcadia* is considerably more dramatic than the original version). He devalues "pastime" throughout the work, and places us more completely in the world of action.

An essential element in this movement towards movement is the effacing of both of the author's static self-representations.

Philisides and the narrator still exist, of course, but their roles
are significantly reduced. Philisides' songs are systematically
reassigned, so that he no longer functions as a lyric reflector of
the action; his part is limited to a brief appearance in the
Iberian tournament,[72] and it has the force of a Hitchcockian
cameo. The narrator's *sententiae* are also reassigned. In the *Old
Arcadia*, for example, when the Phagonian rebels relented after
listening to Cleophila's speech, the narrator had exclaimed:

O weak trust of the many-headed multitude, whom inconstancy only
doth guide at any time to well doing! Let no man lay confidence there
where company takes away shame, and each may lay the fault in his
fellow. (131)

The sentiment expressed in these lines is one to which Sidney
clearly subscribed, and it remains intact in the revised version;[73]
it is immediately followed, however, by this explanation:

So said a craftie felow among them, named *Clinias*, to himselfe, ...
when he saw the worde no sooner out of *Zelmanes* mouth, but that there
were some shouts of joy. (319)

Sidney's public statement has now become completely private
and untrustworthy: it is uttered by a particular individual –
and a "craftie" one at that – to no one but himself. The
discussion of Clinias' past motives and future plans that proceeds
naturally from this attribution further undermines the closure of
the *sententia*; and we learn in this discussion that Clinias'
particular form of "craftiness" – which enabled him to start the
rebellion in the first place – consists in his skill at manipulating
language and assuming feigned roles:

This *Clinias* in his youth had bene a scoller so farre, as to learne rather
wordes then manners, and of words rather plentie then order; and oft
had used to be an actor in Tragedies, where he had learned, besides a
slidingnesse of language, acquaintance with many passions, and to
frame his face to beare the figure of them. (319)

Sidney's *sententia* has here been effectively transformed into a
nonexistent moment of repose.

While this is one of the most striking transformations of the
narrator's speech in the *New Arcadia*, it is far from the only one.
In the original version, we will recall, Sidney had forced us to

reevaluate his positive assessment of Musidorus' pastoral retirement by contradicting it in succeeding lines, and by undermining it in the events that followed (31 ff.); now, however, he immediately calls this praise of bucolic "contentment" into question by attributing it to Musidorus himself (116). We are no longer presented with abstract, communal truths – not even with contradictory ones. All statements of belief have become private opinions, uttered for personal reasons that are clear only to those familiar with the speaker's past history. Personal history assumes an importance here that is foreign to the *Old Arcadia*: we cannot, for example, understand Pyrocles' disguise (as "Zelmane") until we know his history (which also helps to explain why he falls in love with Philoclea). Even Basilius' actions are made more comprehensible by the addition of a comment on his past. His infatuation with the young Zelmane is not, it would seem, an isolated incident; Kalender tells the princes: "He being already well striken in yeares, married a young princes, named *Gynecia* ... " (19). The characters in the *New Arcadia* are thus made more "individual," their psychology seems more modern, and the narrative as a whole is considerably less static and less securely grounded in the present. And while the narrator still occasionally functions to make private thoughts public (e.g., Clinias' evaluation of the rebels), we usually receive important information only when the other characters do (e.g., the true identities of Pyrocles and Musidorus, the reason for Pyrocles' assumed name, the news of Basilius' retirement, the secret of the oracle). As a result, we are more often confused and more frequently surprised than we were in the original version.[74] Sidney not only avoids an ultimate conclusion here, he avoids intermediary ones as well; and he produces a work that is considerably more disturbing than its predecessor – and considerably less problematic.

* * *

The difficulties that Sidney locates and experiences in his pastoral romance reappear in the romances of his contemporaries and successors; so, too, does Sidney's undeniable attraction to pastoral. Insofar as Spenser and Shakespeare find the mode a more adequate one – and to varying degrees they do – it is because they are more willing to see the oppositions we have been examining as intertwined. The problems Sidney poses thus become an integral part of the "solution" each of them proposes.

As we have noted, the sixth book of *The Faerie Queene*, like the *Arcadia*, makes the problematic structure of the pastoral romance an explicit part of its subject: whenever Spenser's characters are experiencing an interlude of peace and contentment, they are likely to be surprised by an unwelcome intrusion, and forcibly reminded of the existence of the active world. But Spenser's attitude toward these intrusions is significantly different from Sidney's: while they serve to demonstrate the limits of the moments of harmony they disrupt, they do not necessarily invalidate them. Like Calidore's retreat into pastoral, each of those moments provides Spenser, his characters, and his readers not (as Calidore first wishes) with a "safe retyre" (9.27), but with "some small repose" (9.31) – with a momentary stay against the confusions of the surrounding world. This difference is clearly connected to another: while the disruptions in the *Arcadia* were all traceable to the heroes' flawed desires, those in the sixth book of *The Faerie Queene* are just as likely to be the result of blind chance, to be the hero's "fortune, not his fault" (3.21). They are among the many signs in Book 6 that the universe is imperfectly proportioned to human beings, that all men and women are foundlings, lost without a guide in a world where virtue and sin are not properly rewarded.

The diminished confidence in heroic activity that Spenser evidences throughout this book leads him to return to pastoral here, and to reconsider the value of admittedly limited experiences. And, in the pastoral cantos, he does manage successfully to suspend notions of loss and recovery, limitation and value. This suspension is most complete, as we have seen, in the lyric moment upon Acidale, when Colin recreates his disrupted vision in the act of mourning its loss; but Spenser is able to maintain an image of that balance throughout Calidore's momentary stay among the shepherds. As he moves outward in the narrative, however, he experiences more difficulty, and he frequently either offers us a recovery that seems too easy (e.g., the episode of Calepine, the baby, and the bear), or descends into unrelieved bitterness and despair (e.g., the end of the book). He is unable consistently to hold these opposite perspectives together, and he thus makes us aware of a gap between them.

Shakespeare is more successful in *The Winter's Tale*, partially because he revives the classical idea of an imperfectly innocent innocence. The play as a whole rejects the pure, static, prelapsarian pastoral that Polixenes evokes at its beginning, in his wistful recollection of the boyhood that he and Leontes shared ("We were as twinn'd lambs that did frisk i' th' sun / And bleat the one at th' other. What we chang'd / Was innocence for innocence," 1.2.67–69; see also 62–65, 69–75).[75] The desire for absolute innocence that Polixenes now shares with his fellow king is clearly connected here with the fear of time, death, sex ("blood"), and artifice ("play"). All of these fears are summoned up simultaneously in Leontes' meditation on Mamillius:

> Looking on the lines
> Of my boy's face, methoughts I did recoil
> Twenty-three years, and saw myself unbreech'd
> In my green velvet coat, my dagger muzzled,
> Lest it should bite its master, and so prove
> (As ornament oft does) too dangerous.   (1.2.153–58)

In the first half of the play, the desire for purity "recoils" upon itself (154; cf. 2.3.20) in a frightening manner; here, as in the *Arcadia*, the qualities that are desired metamorphose into the negative mirror images of themselves: the longing for absolute truth and permanent rest produces absolute falsity and permanent sleeplessness, self-protection turns into self-destruction, and the eternal static spring of Polixenes' nostalgic vision becomes the deathlike "still winter" of Leontes' repentance (3.2.212).

In its fourth act, however, *The Winter's Tale* presents us with an alternative version of pastoral; it moves toward an image of its own creation similar to the one Perdita constructs at the sheepshearing festival when she begins to "play" (4.4.130, 133). In a speech that recalls and builds upon Corydon's flower passage in Virgil's second eclogue, Perdita imagines a vanished spring that is itself suffused with impurity – with sexual longing, violation, movement, pain, and death:

> Now, my fair'st friend,
> I would I had some flow'rs o' the spring that might
> Become your time of day – and yours, and yours,
> That wear upon your virgin branches yet
> Your maidenheads growing. O Proserpina,
> For the flow'rs now, that, frighted, thou let'st fall
> From Dis's waggon! daffidils,
> That come before the swallow dares, and take
> The winds of March with beauty; violets, dim,
> But sweeter than the lids of Juno's eyes,
> Or Cytherea's breath; pale primeroses,
> That die unmarried, ere they can behold
> Bright Phoebus in his strength (a malady
> Most incident to maids); bold oxlips, and
> The crown imperial; lilies of all kinds
> (The flow'r-de-luce being one). O, these I lack,
> To make you garlands of, and my sweet friend,
> To strew him o'er and o'er!   (4.4.112–29)

The losses that Perdita builds into her creation clearly mirror the absence and insufficiency that forces her to create it ("O, these I lack"). By acknowledging that insufficiency, she is able temporarily to overcome it; more precisely, she is able to make that absence itself seem present. Unlike Polixenes' speech, and unlike the idyllic experiences in the *Arcadia*, Perdita's "moment of repose" self-consciously contains its own interruption; it can therefore sustain interruption from the outside. This is true of the entire pastoral sequence, and, ultimately, of *The Winter's Tale* as a whole: the play, in which Time is not only the creator and the destroyer of fictions, but also a fiction himself, finally suspends stasis and motion, pastime and passion.

The suspensions that characterize the central, lyric speeches of both *The Winter's Tale* and the sixth book of *The Faerie Queene* are worked out, in more linear terms, in the death-and-resurrection sequences of the two romances; in *The Winter's Tale*, the presence of (absent) Proserpina in Perdita's speech makes this connection explicit. As Sidney's problematic conclusion suggests, the resurrection motif is central to the pastoral romance: its history encapsulates the history of the mode that I have been tracing to this point. The revival of a character presumed dead is clearly the linear (narrative or dramatic) expression of the mechanics of the pastoral dirge; in innumerable dirges, a dead singer "lives again" as another mourns his loss. This paradox appears in its most radical form in Theocritus' first idyll; here, we will recall, Thyrsis affirms the continuing life of pastoral song by repeating Daphnis' prayer that it might die with his death. When Virgil imitated this idyll in *Eclogue* 5, he characteristically made explicit and rationalized the elements of Theocritus' paradox: his eclogue consists of two songs, one of which mourns Daphnis' death, and one of which celebrates his apotheosis. This balanced opposition is exaggerated in Sannazaro's *Arcadia*, and it falls apart in the works of his followers; as Sidney is well aware, the perfect suspension of loss and recovery is more difficult to achieve in a narrative or a drama: someone is, after all, "really" alive – or s/he is not. Montemayor attempts to retain some suspension in his conclusion by leaving his least disturbing story unresolved; but the overwhelming effect of the end of the *Diana* (which is filled with surprising resurrections and countless swoons and revivals) is one of unity and recovery. And when Shakespeare, early in his career, attempts to imitate (and to criticize) the *Diana* in *The Two Gentlemen of Verona*, he achieves a result similar to Sidney's: Julia's swoon and recovery precipitate another notoriously problematic conclusion.

When Spenser and Shakespeare do, finally, make the resurrection image function adequately, they do so in a somewhat similar fashion: by engineering the death of other major characters. Spenser calls our attention to the implications of this event in a particularly striking fashion. Towards the end of canto 11, Calidore rescues Pastorella from the brigands, revives her emotionally and physically, and carries her up from her underground prison into the light of day; as he does so, the

numerous images of death and rebirth that have been running
throughout this episode reach a climax:

> So he vneath at last he did reuiue,
> That long had lyen dead, and made againe aliue.   (11.50)

The canto then ends with this notation:

> And also all those flockes, which they before
> Had reft from *Meliboe* and from his make,
> He did them all to *Coridon* restore.
> So droue them all away, and his loue with him bore.   (11.51)

These lines are worth considering in some detail. By emphasizing the verb "restore" at the end of line 8, Spenser clearly
suggests that the sheep have not simply been "given" to
someone; they have been "given back." And this suggestion is
consonant with the images of recovery that pervade the canto.
At the same time, however, he pointedly reminds us of
something we may have temporarily forgotten – that the
original owners of the sheep (the archetypal shepherd and his
wife) are irretrievably dead. Spenser thus manages to imply
simultaneously that an earlier, happier state of being has been
recovered, and that such a recovery is impossible to achieve,
and he effectively balances his pastoral resurrection with an
image of the death of pastoral.[76]

In *The Winter's Tale*, Shakespeare uses a similar technique to
make explicit the criticism of idealizing pastoral that was
implied by the problematic endings of *The Two Gentlemen of
Verona* and the *Old Arcadia*, and he attempts to satisfy the
conflicting impulses underlying both these works. Early in the
play, he presents us with a death-and-resurrection image that is
clearly inadequate to problems it pretends to resolve. When
Hermione falls into a swoon upon hearing of Mamillius' death,
Leontes repents and confidently expects that all will be well. His
confidence is then shattered by Paulina, who breaks into his self-
enclosed reverie – with a speech replete with images of breaking
("O, cut my lace, lest my heart, cracking it, / Break too,"
3.2.173–74) – and declares that the queen is dead. The death-
and-resurrection pattern is, of course, finally fulfilled; but it is
accompanied by an acknowledgment of the irremediable losses

that have been sustained "in this wide gap of time" (5.3.154):
Hermione's wrinkles, Antigonus' death, and (at a distance)
Mamillius' untimely end.

It seems doubtful, however, that the self-consciously limited
and artificial – and ultimately quite affirmative – conclusion of
The Winter's Tale would have satisfied Sidney. While the
suspensions that Shakespeare creates here can sustain some
interruption, they are always open to being more decisively
broken, and they can always be made to recoil on themselves –
as Shakespeare himself had already demonstrated at the end of
King Lear: there, pastoral recognition and resurrection become
separation and death once more, and the now-alive, now-dead
motif is transformed into Lear's final, painful oscillation
between a comforting fantasy and an unbearable reality. The
disjunctions that Shakespeare deploys so effectively at the end of
King Lear, of course, push us out of the realm of pastoral
altogether – even more certainly than the revisions in the *New
Arcadia* do. In the *Old Arcadia*, Sidney would seem to take the
pastoral criticism of pastoral as far as – and indeed further than
– it can comfortably go. If we are to continue to pursue his self-
contradictory impulses, we must leave the romance, and turn to
the seventeenth-century lyric – and to Andrew Marvell.

CHAPTER 4

Complaints themselves remedy: Marvell's lyrics as problem and solution

I

By the seventeenth century, the severing of pastoral connections that began in the early Renaissance appears to be complete. The interest in the lyric form during this period coincides with the development of a version of pastoral that is more self-reflexive, internalized, and metaphoric – a thoroughly self-conscious, "sentimental"[1] pastoral that is epitomized by the poetry of Andrew Marvell. The problems that are posed by all of Marvell's pastorals appear in their most concentrated form in his Mower poems; Rosalie Colie comments: "Pastoral is cruelly intellectualized in these poems – and to intellectualize is radically to invert pastoral values in any case, which frankly relinquish intellectual burdens for the embrace of a comfortable natural passivity."[2] Colie's assessment clearly involves a radical oversimplification: she is ignoring the extent to which pastoral poetry has always been intellectualized, has always contained elements that seem antithetical to it. Nevertheless, we can appreciate the force of her insight: Marvell so insistently magnifies these elements in the Mower poems, and so consistently suppresses their opposites, that the ideals we traditionally associate with pastoral seem irretrievably lost. The condition of the inhabitants of these lyrics – and of their creator – approximates that of Sidney's courtiers; the self-enclosed self-division[3] that Sidney feared seems fully realized here. But Marvell sees disjunction itself as the means of establishing continuity, and his apparent movement away from traditional bucolic values is, in fact, a movement back: he is self-consciously reinventing the paradoxical relationship of separation and connection upon which the classical pastoralists relied.

We can begin to understand Marvell's version of this relationship by examining a poem that explicitly concerns itself with distance and separation – "The Mower to the Glo-worms." In the first three stanzas of this poem, the Mower lovingly describes the innocent existence that he has lost:

> Ye living Lamps, by whose dear light
> The Nightingale does sit so late,
> And studying all the Summer-night,
> Her matchless Songs does meditate;
>
> Ye Country Comets, that portend
> No War, nor Princes funeral,
> Shining unto no higher end
> Than to presage the Grasses fall;
>
> Ye Glo-worms, whose officious Flame
> To wandring Mowers shows the way,
> That in the Night have lost their aim,
> And after foolish Fires do stray...   (1–12)

The picture he paints is not, however, completely idyllic. The poem becomes progressively darker as it continues:[4] the second stanza suggests that even innocent nature suffers death, and the third confronts us with an image of human loss and confusion. The mere fact that these stanzas are progressive is a further indication of their distance from perfect innocence: movement is associated with "displac[ement]" (15) here; it is a sign of the Fall. Accordingly, as suggestions of loss become more insistent, so, too, do suggestions of movement: the stationary nightingale of the beginning gives way to the grass that is about to fall, and then to the mowers who wander and stray; and, while the creatures in the first stanza remain perfectly centered in the present moment, those in the next two direct their energies toward future "ends" and "aims." Nevertheless, the indications of pain and movement here are carefully contained: the losses are presented as harmless and remediable; and the progress of the stanzas is effectively countered by their suspended syntax and parallel structure.

Like the earliest pastoral poems, then, the first three stanzas of the "The Mower to the Glo-worms" present us with a world that contains disturbances, but remains essentially secure. The relative innocence of this world is conclusively established by the final stanza:

> Your courteous Lights in vain you wast,
> Since *Juliana* here is come,
> For She my Mind hath so displac'd
> That I shall never find my home.   (13–16)

Unlike the creatures he had described, the Mower is permanently "displac'd." His loss is different in degree because it is different in kind: while the earlier misfortunes were external events, the Mower's dislocation occurs internally; a gap has been opened between physical nature and the realm of the mind that seems impossible to bridge. Thus, for the first time, the Mower uses the word "I," distinguishing and isolating himself from the anonymous mowers in the third stanza. And, for the first time, he makes uses of logical connectives ("Since," "For," "so ... That"), transforming his world into a series of hierarchical cause and effect relationships. Inevitably, the repeated apostrophes and suspended syntax of the previous stanzas now vanish from his speech; and their disappearance seems to mark the disappearance of innocent stability from the poem.

As a result of this loss, however, "The Mower to the Glo-worms" achieves a stability of a different kind; quite simply, it comes to an end: the displaced syntax of lines 13–15 unwinds in the direct, plain statement of the close, coming to rest, significantly, on the word "home." This conclusion provides the earlier stanzas with both meaning and syntactic completion, and, in so doing, it supplies them with the "end," the "aim" – and the future ("shall," 16) – that their imagery had "presaged." The poem, then, acquires direction through an acknowledgment of the loss of direction, and rest through a lament for the inability to rest. And the Mower is similarly "placed" by confronting his displacement: it is only in the final stanza that words specifying location appear ("here" as well as "home"); and the Mower's self-reference in the last line seems therefore not merely an acknowledgment of isolation, but a gesture of self-recognition – an attempt to situate himself.

The end of "The Mower to the Glo-worms" clearly mirrors its beginning; the fallen but stable state the Mower attains in the final stanza reflects the innocent but fallen condition that he feels he has lost. The two sections of the poem are just as clearly opposed. The decisive closure of the despairing conclusion is alien to the first three stanzas, as it is alien to more naive pastoral. The final stanza suggests, however, that "naive" pastoral is necessarily the creation of sophisticated poets: as "home" is a concept that is fully available only to the displaced mind, so "suspension" (the absence of conclusive meaning or ending) is comprehensible to us (acquires meaning, that is) only because we are familiar with its opposite. Our conceptions of – and connections to – innocence depend entirely upon our separation from it.

The poem makes this point in other ways as well. Each of the initial stanzas is itself both the image and the antithesis of the Mower's present state. They are all different versions of one of Marvell's central concepts – the harmless fall. The difficulties involved in this idea are most apparent in the second stanza:

> Ye Country Comets, that portend
> No War, nor Princes funeral,
> Shining unto no higher end
> Than to presage the Grasses fall.

Donald Friedman comments on these lines:

Death in the country is limited to the death of green things; but they symbolize the greater deaths of mind and body in so far as the concept of communion between man and nature is accepted seriously. If it is, "the Grasses fall" is the highest, the most significant, "end" that any comet could prophesy.[5]

Friedman's remarks point to some of the paradoxes here. Our connection to innocent Nature – our "communion" with her – depends upon our conceiving of her condition as reflecting our own. But in a poem that – like all of Marvell's poems – identifies

distance from external reality with displacement, the mere fact
that "innocence" is symbolic is evidence of separation from it;
and what it symbolizes, of course, is that separation itself – the
Fall. Separation thus becomes both the means of connection,
and the point at which connection is made.

But the stanza does not, of course, literally say that. While
making it impossible to avoid "compar[ing] great things and
small," it expressly forbids us to do so.[6] The relative innocence
of Nature, we are told, consists precisely in the fact that her falls
are truly harmless, that they do not reflect our own. But this
approach is even more paradoxical. Nature's independent
existence can be imagined only by creating a diminished image
of our fallen state – and declaring that this image represents
nothing but itself.[7] The condition of not being symbolic is made
to rely on that of being symbolic, and "innocence" is presented
as a creation of the Fall.

The interdependent ideas of reflection and exclusion, which
are perfectly balanced in the second stanza, are present, with
different emphases, in the other two as well. They are suggested,
of course, by the Mower's various epithets for the glowworms,
each of which seems to imply simultaneously that "great things
and small" are fundamentally different, and that they are
essentially similar.[8] And these suggestions are fulfilled in the
body of each of the stanzas.

In the third, more fallen stanza, the reflection of opposites is
made explicit. The "officious Flame" that aids the mowers is,
both ideationally and aurally, the mirror-image of the "foolish
Fires" that mislead them. If, with Elizabeth Story Donno, we
assume that these "Fires" are meant specifically to evoke the
illusory desires of love,[9] the "Flame" of the glowworms
naturally suggests a more harmless form of that passion. Not
only is "flame" (like "fire") a word traditionally associated
with sexual desires, the very name of the "Glo-worms" implies
a phallic symbolism that it simultaneously negates: the sexual
connotations of the second syllable – with its unavoidable
reminder of the Fall – are countered by the spiritual connotations of the first. The light that the glowworms provide is the
light of the harmless fall: it emanates from an "innocent"

desire, which, inevitably, reflects the desire against which it protects.

In the innocent initial stanza, the idea of exclusion is dominant. Marvell is appealing here to an ideal of painless, natural, stable song – but he is doing so in a most peculiar fashion. In a song that is the result of pain and displacement, that owes its existence to the intrusion of sexuality and the loss of home, he is presenting us with a nightingale – the traditional type of song achieved through these means – and he is leaving out her pain. He is doing indirectly what he does more explicitly in stanza 65 of *Upon Appleton House*. There, he begins by evoking the wound of the nightingale's violation:

> The *Nightingale* does here make choice
> To sing the Tryals of her Voice.
> Low Shrubs she sits in, and adorns
> With Musick high the squatted Thorns.   (513–16)

And he ends by banishing it:

> The Thorn, lest it should hurt her, draws
> Within the Skin its shrunken claws.   (519–20)

First, however, he transforms it into a metaphor – a metaphor, moreover, that itself transforms the experience of pain (and of sexual pain in particular) into the experience of song:

> But highest Oakes stoop down to hear,
> And listening Elders prick the Ear.   (517–18).

In the initial stanza of "The Mower to the Glo-worms," Marvell is similarly making the innocence that is present depend on the experience that is left out: more obliquely than in the second stanza, but just as surely, he is creating an untroubled reality by treating an image of suffering as if it referred to nothing but itself. And the transformation into metaphor that occurs in *Upon Appleton House* occurs here as well. The reflection of the Mower that is suppressed in the peaceful description of the nightingale is expressed in another way: the bird is thoroughly personified; it is presented as a human artisan.[10] As the poem becomes progressively more "fallen," and the condition of the innocent creatures the Mower describes begins more nearly to approximate his own, his need to understand those creatures by seeing them as something other than themselves decreases. And when, in the concluding stanza, he presents us with a completely displaced and internalized vision, he does so in comparatively literal terms: in the world of the poem, the final quatrain suggests nothing but itself; it is the point of reference upon which the earlier images depend. All of the stanzas therefore ultimately seem, in different ways, equally expressive of both unity and disjunction, equally "displac'd," and equally connected to "home"; and the movement away from external nature that the poem appears to trace is effectively countered by a movement towards a new "literal" reality – the reality of the life of the mind.

The relation that exists between the Mower and the harmless falls he creates is duplicated, at one more remove, in the relation between the Mower and his own creator. Marvell is able – as poets of the earlier Renaissance were not[11] – to imagine the speaker of his pastorals as a naif because he imagines him as not completely naive: here, and in all the Mower poems, the speaker is a fallen innocent, a "Country Comet," whose condition is the diminished image of our own.

And, as I have been suggesting, a similar relation obtains between "The Mower to the Glo-worms" and earlier pastoral poetry. The conception of an imperfectly innocent innocence here seems specifically Virgilian in origin, and Marvell makes this relation explicit by recalling one of Virgil's most important pastorals – the first eclogue. *Eclogue* 1 is a conversation between two shepherds: Meliboeus, who has been forced into exile by the Roman land expropriations, and the more naive Tityrus, who continues to lead a comparatively stable, but not completely idyllic, life. During the course of the poem, Meliboeus imaginatively recreates the home he has lost, and the two shepherds establish connections with each other, despite their different points of view. The situation of Marvell's poem clearly resembles that of Virgil's, and Marvell underscores this basic resemblance by repeating some of his predecessor's most well-known locutions. In the opening lines of *Eclogue* 1, Meliboeus addresses his friend:

Tityre, tu patulae recubans sub tegmine fagi
silvestrem tenui musam meditaris avena;
nos patriae finis et dulcia linquimus arva.
nos patriam fugimus; tu, Tityre, lentus in umbra
formosam resonare doces Amaryllida silvas.   (1–5)

You, Tityrus, under the spreading, sheltering beech,
Tune woodland musings on a delicate reed;
We flee our country's borders, our sweet fields,
Abandon home; you, lazing in the shade,
Make woods resound with lovely Amaryllis.

"The Mower to the Glo-worms" also opens with a displaced rustic describing a stationary singer who "meditates" his song;[12] and the repeated vocatives in Marvell's poem seem to derive from this passage as well. While these echoes call our attention to the relationship between the two poems, however, they also point to their differences. The most striking of these is the absence of dialogue in "The Mower to the Glo-worms": in Marvell's poetry, innocence never has a speaking part (it is necessarily *infans*).[13] As a result, the Mower seems more distant than Meliboeus from the tranquility he envies; and, while the connections between Virgil's shepherds are reciprocal, the bonds the Mower forges are necessarily the products of his own mind. A similar difference exists in the subject of the two poems: while Meliboeus has literally lost his home, the Mower's displacement is purely metaphoric. The shared, external reality of Virgil's poem has now become completely solitary and internal. But, once more, Marvell makes separation a point of connection. The two poems are related, first of all, because they both deal with our responses to displacement. Marvell's separation from Virgil – like Virgil's from Theocritus – thus ensures that the problematic with which both poets are concerned will be reproduced in the distance between them. One could say that Marvell is playing Meliboeus to Virgil's Tityrus here:[14] he is using his "exile" to reinvent the community he has left behind.

But Marvell is doing more than that. He is not merely intensifying the problematic in Virgil's poem; he is inverting it.

Here, and in all his works, he is making the metaphoric content of earlier poems the literal content of his own; he is reversing the accepted priorities of fact and fiction, connection and separation, innocence and loss. And, in so doing, he is reaching beyond Virgil's suspensions to create a latter-day version of Theocritus' original paradox – the coincidence of distance and identity. Criticism of Marvell's poetry has repeatedly presented us with contradictory accounts of his relation to pastoral conventions: he is seen simultaneously as deeply attached to pastoral and as decisively separated from it, as coolly ironic and as fundamentally nostalgic.[15] It is no accident, I believe, that these contradictions are reminiscent of those in critical analyses of Theocritus' relation to heroism. Standing at a similar point at the end of a poetic tradition, Marvell is reinventing the fundamental ironies with which Theocritus began. And the fact that his self-consciously belated version of these ironies necessarily results in a "radical inversion"[16] of Theocritus' original values cements the connection between the two poets at the same time that that it confirms their distance.

The relation between a limited life and a heroic one, which was central to Theocritus' *Idylls*, is still important in Marvell's poetry, as we shall see. But it is supplemented, and to a certain extent supplanted, by the parallel relation – whose centrality is Virgil's legacy – between the artistic image and the reality it represents. "The Mower to the Glo-worms" suggests that the separated mind establishes connections with innocence by creating diminished images of itself. These "harmless falls" are both reflective of and opposed to the separation upon which they depend; they both are – and are not – innocent. And these conflicting perspectives themselves are necessarily related to and reflective of each other. Any attempt to insist on one alone necessarily recreates the other, and, at either extreme, separation is equated with connection, art replaces reality, displacement is conflated with purpose, and the image "becomes" the thing itself.

The other Mower poems bear this out. "The Mower against Gardens" represents one extreme. Here, the "innocent," bucolic perspective of the nightingale stanza is taken to its logical conclusion. Alone among the Mowers, the speaker of this poem does not perceive himself as fallen; indeed, he does not perceive himself as fully human. He attempts to dissociate himself entirely from "Luxurious Man" (1), refusing even to acknowledge that he possesses a separate, individual consciousness: he is the only Mower who never uses the first person singular. And critics have frequently taken him at his word. Thus, we are told that unlike the other "double-minded" Mowers, this speaker takes a "single, natural point of view,"[17] and that he rightly attacks fallen man who, "instead of gazing into the mirror of natural innocence ... narcissistically forces Nature to give him back his own image."[18] But the Mower's single-mindedness necessarily reproduces the double-mindedness it eschews. Friedman describes the antitheses upon which the poem is structured as follows:

The values opposed to those of "Luxurious Man" are characterized succinctly in the next distich: "And from the fields the Flow'rs and Plants allure, / Where Nature was most plain and pure" (lines 3–4) ... "Plain" and "pure" are self-defined values; their monosyllabic simplicity is the best assertion of what Nature stands for to Damon.[19]

As the poem progresses, however, the meaning of these "self-defined" words becomes anything but pure and simple: they take on human, sexual connotations, as Nature is transformed into a fully sentient, sensual being, who is capable of whorish behavior when "seduce[d]" (2; cf. 11–14), but who will freely "dispence" her "wild and fragrant Innocence" to those who do not "enforc[e]" her (31–34). The only way the Mower can lament the human violation of Nature is by involving himself in it; and his attempt to efface his own humanity results, perforce, in a more radical humanization than that which he decries: because he does not recognize his individual separation, when he "gazes into the mirror of natural innocence" he can see nothing but his own reflection.[20] One cannot say simply that the extravagant personification in the poem intensifies "the correspondence between Damon and the denizens of pure nature"[21] without first noting that it destroys the very purity it seeks to preserve.

The Mower is, in fact, naively acting out the ironic vision of stanza 3 of "The Garden":

> No white or red was ever seen
> So am'rous as this lovely green.
> Fond Lovers, cruel as their Flame,
> Cut in these Trees their Mistress name.
> Little, Alas, they know, or heed,
> How far these Beauties Hers exceed!
> Fair Trees! where s'eer your barkes I wound,
> No Name shall but your own be found.   (17–24)

Rather than defacing innocent Nature by making it reflect the images of women,[22] he is "wounding" it with an image of Nature itself. And he is countering erotic desire, not with innocence, but with the desire for innocence – the desire, that is, for the lack of desire.

Nevertheless, "The Mower against Gardens" is hardly a single-minded irony against its speaker. By unthinkingly re-creating Nature in his own likeness, the Mower does, in fact, achieve unity with it. And, while he never becomes aware of the contradictions inherent in his position, he alters his stance somewhat in the final lines of the poem:

> And *Fauns* and *Faryes* do the Meadows till,
>   More by their presence then their skill.
> Their Statues polish'd by some ancient hand,
>   May to adorn the Gardens stand:
> But howso'ere the Figures do excel,
>   The *Gods* themselves with us do dwell.   (35–40)

Here, self-conscious art is seen not only as the opposite of the Mower's vision, but also as its reflection.[23] And this change is matched by a change in the Mower's self-image. His union with humanized Nature allows him to acknowledge, to some degree, his own humanity: he never recognizes his separate existence, but he does acknowledge the existence of an "us" – an "us" that seems to refer interchangeably (for the two meanings have become identical) to the Mower and the meadows and to the Mower and other human beings.

The ironies in the poem are further complicated by the fact that Marvell is involved here in a self-conscious version of the

Mower's enterprise. More insistently than any other Mower poem, "The Mower against Gardens" evokes an image of the greater world that it simultaneously excludes. Rosalie Colie points to some of the issues that the Mower's diatribe inevitably raises:

The Mower's morality speaks out, as in the great Homilies, against popular disturbance, against adultery, against insurrections; in such a context, the moral notion of social hierarchy is made ridiculous by its application to the vegetable world.[24]

Colie's somewhat dismissive conclusion hides a genuine perception. For the peculiarity of the poem lies precisely in the fact that the Mower is *not* using the example of Nature to make a broader statement about politics or human sexual behavior, as some critics have claimed:[25] he is not delivering a sermon against adultery; he is saying, in effect, "Don't screw around with plants."[26] The extravagance of his vision clearly depends on the extremity of its limits. But the existence of those limits just as clearly depends on the poet's lack of them. Not only is the Mower creating trees with the word "Tree" inscribed upon them, he is himself such a creature. Like the Mower, Marvell is "graft[ing] upon the Wild the Tame" (24); and, in so doing, he is bringing together the two versions of pastoral that Sidney forced apart. He is presenting pastoral both as the diminished reflection of a greater, uncontrollable reality, and as the metaphoric recreation of a simpler, more innocent existence. And he is making it clear that the second version – which is as close to innocence as we can get – is necessarily dependent upon the first.

The double displacement by which he is approaching innocence here is perhaps best glossed by another passage from "The Garden":

> *Apollo* hunted *Daphne* so,
> Only that She might Laurel grow.
> And *Pan* did after *Syrinx* speed,
> Not as a Nymph, but for a Reed. (29–32)

In these lines, Marvell first insists that the object of desire is its own containment in art. He then repeats this displacement, on another level, by literalizing metaphors for art (metaphors, that is, for the process of creating metaphors) to produce two examples of "pure" Nature: a tree and a reed. And the immediate result of this repeated substitution is, of course, Marvell's most famous – and most vexed – version of the harmless fall:

> What wond'rous Life in this I lead!
> Ripe Apples drop about my head;
> The Luscious Clusters of the Vine
> Upon my Mouth do crush their Wine;
> The Nectaren, and curious Peach,
> Into my hands themselves do reach;
> Stumbling on Melons, as I pass,
> Insnar'd with Flow'rs, I fall on Grass.   (33–40)

Ever since William Empson's comments on this stanza,[27] critics have been disputing whether the speaker's experience here is sexual and fallen or paradisaically innocent;[28] their perplexity, I would claim, results from the perfectly logical – but completely unworkable – assumption that these antithetical alternatives are mutually exclusive.

Comparable displacements occur throughout Marvell's work. In *Upon Appleton House*, as we shall see, the various retreats, which are reflections, "in more decent Order tame" (766), of the fallen world they leave behind, become images of eternity – "*Paradice's only Map*" (768) – as well. In "The Nymph complaining," the fawn clearly begins its life as a "tame[r]" substitute (34) for Sylvio (a faun?). As the poem progresses, however, Sylvio is forgotten, and his surrogate becomes the object of the Nymph's desires. Simultaneously, the presentation of the fawn changes: it is transformed from an innocent image of sexual desire into a sexualized image of innocence.

An understanding of this paradoxical process helps us to understand "what Juliana does" in the Mower poems. In "The Mower's Song," the body of the poem presents the Mower's "Revenge" on Nature (20) as a displacement of his feelings towards his beloved.[29] But the repetitive refrain counters the movement of the poem by insisting, from the beginning, on the Mower's destruction of, separation from, and connection to the meadows;[30] and it further suggests that what Juliana does to the Mower can only be defined by reference to "what [he does] to the Grass." From the perspective of experience, the Mower's relation to Nature is a displacement of sexual desire; but from a "naive" point of view (which is created by means of this displacement), his desire for Juliana merely makes him aware of a separation that already exists. Since this separation is caused by self-consciousness and desire, the Mower's relationship to Juliana naturally intensifies his distance from innocence; but it also allows him to make his connection more secure. The movement of the three Juliana poems, in other words, serves to bring the naive Mower up to – and past – the condition of his extremely self-conscious creator. And that is all the progress in the world – and no progress at all.

We can trace this movement most easily by examining "Damon the Mower." At the beginning of this poem, a sophisticated, somewhat bored narrator invites us to witness Damon's complaint:

> Heark how the Mower *Damon* Sung,
> With love of *Juliana* stung!
> While ev'ry thing did seem to paint
> The Scene more fit for his complaint.
> Like her fair Eyes the day was fair;
> But scorching like his am'rous Care.
> Sharp like his Sythe his Sorrow was,
> And wither'd like his Hopes the Grass.   (1–8)

After this introduction, Damon's naive voice comes as something of a shock:

> Oh what unusual Heats are here,
> Which thus our Sun-burn'd Meadows sear!
> The Grass-hopper its pipe gives ore;
> And hamstring'd Frogs can dance no more.
> But in the brook the green Frog wades;
> And Grass-hoppers seek out the shades.
> Only the Snake, that kept within,
> Now glitters in its second skin.   (9–16)

Critical reactions to this stanza are quite varied and extremely instructive. They range from Patrick Cullen's assurance that Marvell is simply presenting us with a collection of "natural fact[s],"[31] to assertions that the details of the passage are meant to be read symbolically.[32] Paul Alpers, who examines Damon's "development of self-awareness" in the course of the poem,[33] takes a middle road. He points out that the passage is a reworking of Corydon's first words in *Eclogue* 2, and comments:

There are many common elements here…, [including] the speaker's sense of separation from other creatures. But the handling of these elements shows the difference between the two poems. Instead of appealing to his cold lover, Damon speaks of the "unusual heats" which he feels as external and internal realities. The loss of human companionship, which is the center of Corydon's lines, is not expressed at all: Damon compares his plight only to that of animals, whose relation to him is more metaphoric, less social than in Virgil… The plight of love, as Damon represents it, concerns individual feeling and sense of self.[34]

Alpers' remarks are illuminating and helpful. But they also illustrate the difficulties involved in discussing this passage and similar ones in Marvell's poetry. For surely Damon is not yet "compar[ing] his plight" or himself to anything at all; he does not even have a clearly defined self to which he can make comparisons. The "sense of separation" that was manifest in *Eclogue* 2 is assimilated here into natural description.[35] The only self-reference in the stanza is a vague first person plural (10), which, like the similar pronoun in "The Mower against Gardens," seems to include the Mower and the rest of creation. Here, as there, the speaker's lack of self-awareness results in the radical humanization of his surroundings. But what is missing from these lines is precisely what the introduction led us to expect: the explicit comparison of natural occurrences to human emotions.

While separation and symbolism are obscured by Damon's presentation of "natural fact," however, they are not obliterated by it. Even more clearly than in "The Mower against Gardens," Marvell is here creating a naive reality by turning symbols back on themselves. Damon makes use of words and images (e.g., the heats, the snake) that the narrator has already charged with symbolic significance; and we must actively desymbolize them if we wish to read the passage as "realistic." Furthermore, the very structure of the stanza reproduces, in external terms, the basic concerns of the introduction.[36] The attempt to create "a union in division," which lay behind the conventional mirroring of the opening lines, is expressed here by the insistent pairing of natural objects with each other: the grasshopper in line 11 is matched with the frogs in line 12, and this pair is, in turn, matched with its mirror-image in the following lines. The immediate effect of this repeated doubling is to emphasize the isolation of the snake; the reptile's "second skin," however, suggests the possibility of another kind of union, a union that is both different from those which preceded it (it is internal), and similar to them (like all unions, it is made possible by division). And this suggestion is emphasized and duplicated by Marvell's revisionary invocation of Virgil: in the passage from *Eclogue* 2 to which he alludes, Corydon's isolated condition was itself seen as alien to conventional pastoral – and as essential to it.

"Damon the Mower" is, in effect, a fugue on separation and connection.[37] The doubling that marks the first two stanzas is the characteristic locution of the poem. As Damon grows in self-consciousness, however, the values being doubled change. In the third stanza, the implications present in the figure of the snake are developed in the images of the inward-turning dog-star and sun; and Damon begins to see himself as separate from and analogous to the meadows: the heat, he declares, "burns the Fields and Mower both" (20). But he still describes himself as he describes other creatures – from the outside. It is not until the fourth stanza – immediately following his first mention of Juliana – that he begins to refer to himself as "I." At the same time, the undirected monologue of the earlier stanzas becomes a direct address, implying the existence of a "you." And it is only now that he consciously tries to create connections between himself and Nature:

> Not *July* causeth these Extremes,
> But *Juliana's* scorching beams.

> Tell me where I may pass the Fires
> Of the hot day, or hot desires,
> To what cool Cave shall I descend,
> Or to what gelid Fountain bend?
> Alas! I look for Ease in vain,
> When Remedies themselves complain.
> No moisture but my Tears do rest,
> Nor Cold but in her Icy Breast.   (24–32)

The progress that occurs in these lines seems quite logical. Romantic love makes Damon acutely aware of the separate existence of another; he therefore becomes aware of both his individual isolation and his desire for union. And, by the end of the stanza, he naturally replaces his earlier pairings with the coupling of himself and "her." We must remember, however, that Juliana "comes" only verbally here: the mention of her name produces the effect that "The Mower's Song" will ascribe, retrospectively, to her actual arrival. The difficulties critics have with the earlier stanzas arise in part from the fact that the progress of this poem is pointedly not narrative: a mower who has already met Juliana should not be in the naive state of the speaker of "The Mower against Gardens"; and there is no external reason why Damon should "fall in love" right now. In a much more extreme fashion than *Eclogue* 2 (in which Corydon's complaint begins and ends with Alexis), "Damon the Mower" presents the growth from "innocence" to experience as the result of singing a song; and it is one function of that song to attribute the movement towards experience to Juliana (it is a sign of experience to do so). But the poem simultaneously leads us beyond her.

In the lines that follow, the relationship between the lovers seems primary: Damon now addresses his words directly to his beloved. As increased consciousness of the other leads inevitably to increased consciousness of the self, however, the relation between Damon and Juliana is matched, and to some degree displaced, by the relation between Damon and the natural objects he has chosen as his "Presents" (presence),[38] and by the internal relations these objects themselves imply:

> How long wilt Thou, fair Shepheardess,
> Esteem me, and my Presents less?
> To Thee the harmless Snake I bring,
> Disarmed of its teeth and sting.
> To Thee *Chameleons* changing-hue,
> And Oak leaves tipt with hony due.   (33–38)

Damon's presents, I would suggest, are all images of the harmless fall. The "harmless," "disarmed" snake evokes both the idea in general and innocent desire in particular. The multihued chameleon just as readily suggests natural art. And Damon's final gift – "Oak leaves tipt with hony due" – is, I believe, an emblem of pastoral heroism; its significance is emphasized by its probable origin in Virgil's fourth eclogue:[39]

> at simul heroum laudes et facta parentis
> iam legere et quae sit poteris cognoscere virtus,
> ... durae quercus sudabunt roscida mella.   (26–27, 30)

> But when heroic praise, parental deeds
> You read and come to know what manhood is,
> ... rough-skinned oaks will sweat with honeydew.

Like Corydon in his flower passage, Damon is bringing together, in an imaginative vision of nature, the qualities that both he and the poet have been trying to join all along. Corydon's involvement in his own creation, we will recall, led him to realize its inadequacy, and to return, unhappily, to the external world. Damon comes to a similar realization; but rather than moving out of the realm of the individual imagination, he just keeps moving further in.

When he laments his inability to influence Juliana, he repeats the earlier pairing of himself and his presents, with the order and the emphasis reversed:

> Yet Thou ungrateful hast not sought
> Nor what they are, nor who them brought.   (39–40)

And, as he proceeds to explain who he is (stanza 6),[40] the suspensions of the preceding lines snap shut:

> I am the Mower *Damon*, known
> Through all the Meadows I have mown.   (41–42)

The origin of this well-known couplet has been generally overlooked. It derives, as we have seen, not from *Eclogue* 2, but from Theocritus' first idyll; it is a reworking of the central statement of Theocritus' pastoral – the self-definition of the heroic herdsman Daphnis:[41] "I am that Daphnis, he who drove the kine to pasture here, / Daphnis who led the bulls and calves to water at these springs" (120–21). By placing an allusion to Theocritus in the center of his poem – and by placing Daphnis' self-definition in the mouth of a character based ultimately upon Polyphemus[42] – Marvell is making the same paradoxical point the lines themselves make: he is asserting the equivalence of naive and sentimental, heroic and pastoral, self and world. And it is clearly Marvell's self-conscious self-enclosure that leads him back to Theocritus here: his vision of individual isolation prompts him to reimagine the limited rustic, not merely as the central character of his pastorals, but quite literally, as a pastoral hero. Like Daphnis, Damon is equating limitation with power: he is declaring that his "I" is heroic, and that his "here" is everywhere. And like Daphnis, he is seeing himself simultaneously from inside ("I") and out ("the Mower Damon"). But the "here" that Daphnis glorified was an identifiable external *locus*; Damon's place is entirely self-defined. Marvell's rustic is maintaining, in effect, that he *is* the world.[43] He has, of course, implicitly been saying this all along (he can say no other), but whereas self-consciousness was previously subordinated to external description, awareness of the self and awareness of the world are both perfectly explicit here – and perfectly conflated.

In the rest of the stanza, the Mower continues to bring together the antithetical ideas that his "Presents" had held in suspension:

> On me the Morn her dew distills
> Before her darling Daffadils.
> And, if at Noon my toil me heat,
> The Sun himself licks off my Sweat.
> While, going home, the Ev'ning sweet
> In cowslip-water bathes my feet.   (43–48)

Damon no longer sees natural objects as reflections of his relationship with Juliana; he now participates in a direct erotic relationship with Nature itself. What had been an imaginative displacement is transformed into reality, and innocence becomes the object of desire. Damon is, moreover, making an extraordinary claim here by not making one: he is not asserting that the world does anything special for him; he is merely declaring that it works as it always does – for him. And these lines may also have been suggested by *Idyll* 1; there, Daphnis' greatness is proven by the fact that wild animals behaved at his death as they always do – to mourn his loss: "For him the jackals howled, for him the wolves: the lion even / Came forth from the thicket to lament him when he died" (71–72).

Theocritus' paradox forms the pivot of the poem. After this stanza, we step through the looking-glass, and within becomes without. The qualities that were suppressed in the first part of the poem – interiority, self-assertion, and fiction – become progressively dominant, until we are confronted with an inverted image of the lines with which we began.

It is fairly obvious that this is occurring in stanzas eight and nine. As the "Ring" of the poem "contract[s]" around Damon (64),[44] internal realities assume priority over externals. In a characteristically Marvellian reversal, Damon now joins his "Labour to [his] Pain" (58–59);[45] and his *locus* seems to exist primarily inside of himself (66, 70).

But something similar occurs even earlier. In stanza seven, Damon boasts of his wealth:

> What, though the piping Shepherd stock
> The plains with an unnum'red Flock,
> This Sithe of mine discovers wide
> More ground than all his Sheep do hide.
> With this the golden fleece I shear
> Of all these Closes ev'ry Year.
> And though in Wooll more poor than they,
> Yet am I richer far in Hay.   (49–56)

His words clearly recall those of Corydon and Polyphemus. In a passage that echoes its prototype in *Idyll* 11, Corydon had boasted to Alexis:

> Mille meae Siculis errant in montibus agnae;
> lac mihi non aestate novum, non frigore defit.

canto quae solitus, si quando armenta vocabat,
Amphion Dircaeus in Actaeo Aracyntho.   (*Ecl.* 2.21–24)

A thousand lambs of mine roam Sicily's hills;
Summer or winter, I'm never out of milk.
I sing such songs as, when he called his herds,
Amphion of Thebes on Attic Aracynthus.

Early in the poem, as Alpers notes, similar allusions "[went] over Damon's head."[46] There is nothing particularly unusual about this situation: we do not normally expect shepherds (or any fictional characters, for that matter) to be conversant with the works upon which their words are modeled. In *Eclogue* 2 itself, however, the gap between naive character and sophisticated poet was pointedly problematical: Virgil's self-conscious concern with the powers and limits of poetic representation forced us to consider the questions raised by a bucolic monologue "interwoven with allusions to literature no herdsman could know."[47] And Marvell now revivifies Virgil's problematic by reversing it. For the oddity here is that Damon does seem to be familiar with the classical poets – or more precisely, with their characters: he seems to inhabit a fictional universe where Polyphemus, Corydon, and their many imitators also dwell. He is directly answering his predecessors' boasts here; and he appears to be arguing not so much for the hand of Juliana (his words are no longer addressed to her),[48] as for the right to replace "the piping Shepherd" as the hero of a pastoral poem. These lines have been cited as "the only unmistakable sign we have that Marvell deliberately intended an instructive shock when he chose the figure of the mower over that of the shepherd."[49] But the instruction we are given in the passage itself is more clearly attributable to the character than to his creator: the Mower seems perfectly well aware of the innovation he represents; and he asserts his superiority over the conventional herdsman on the grounds that he is at once the more sublimely heroic character (51–54), and the more ridiculously bucolic (55–56).[50]

As Damon grows in self-consciousness, then, his fictional world begins to displace the "reality" upon which it was modeled, and his self-absorbed brand of bucolic heroism similarly begins to supplant more traditional forms of pastoral. This movement is both imaged and intensified in the following stanza. Here, Damon presents us with internalized versions of two well-known figures for pastoral song – figures which, in their original form, already had as their focus the relation between persona and poet, image and thing. He first alludes to Corydon's celebration and questioning of the power of reflections:

> Nor am I so deform'd to sight,
> If in my Sithe I looked right;
> In which I see my Picture done,
> As in a crescent Moon the Sun.   (57–60)

> nec sum adeo informis: nuper me in litore vidi,
> cum placidum ventis staret mare. non ego Daphnin
> iudice te metuam, si numquam fallit imago.   (*Ecl.* 2.25–27)

> Nor am I ugly: once by the shore I saw
> Myself in the wind-calmed sea. I would not fear to
> Compete for you with Daphnis: mirrors don't lie.

[26b–27, *lit.*: I would not fear Daphnis, with you as the judge, if the image never lies.]

By claiming to equal the paragon of bucolic heroism, "if images never lie," Corydon had reflected Virgil's ambivalence about the adequacy of his creations to their models in poetry and fact. The insistent self-enclosure of Marvell's lines, however, makes Virgil's conception of art look comparatively external; and once more, the greater self-consciousness evident here leads us, paradoxically, back to Theocritus. In *Idyll* 6, Polyphemus had declared:

> For truly not ill-favoured is my face, as they pretend.
> Not long ago I looked into the sea, when it was calm,
> And beautiful my beard seemed, beautiful my one eye,
> If I have any judgment.   (35–37)

Like the naive Cyclops, Damon recognizes no external standard of judgment: he is himself the only model and arbiter of beauty. And, since the Mower's reflection is produced by his self-defining instrument, Corydon's questioning of the image returns, of necessity, to a questioning of the self. Once again, the speaker has become his own sole point of reference.

The second half of the stanza inevitably mirrors the first. Having used his instrument as his reflector, Damon now uses himself as his instrument; and this pairing gives added point to his repeated pun on "scythe":[51]

> The deathless Fairyes take me oft
> To lead them in their Danses soft;
> And when I tune my self to sing,
> About me they contract their Ring.   (61–64)

He alludes here to Colin Clout (himself an anglicized reflection of Corydon), and, specifically, to the episode in Book 6 of *The Faerie Queene* in which Colin had piped to the Graces and his beloved on Mount Acidale. That episode had culminated in Colin's recreating imaginatively the dancing beauties who had vanished in fact, repeating words spoken earlier by the narrator, addressing Gloriana directly, and assuming authorship of *The Faerie Queene* (10.25–28): for a brief moment in Spenser's epic, loss and consolation, reality and fiction, heroic author and bucolic character had become one.

Something even more radical – and more final – eventually occurs here. The poem proceeds until Damon appears to die of self-enclosure:

> While thus he threw his Elbow round,
> Depopulating all the Ground,
> And, with his whistling Sythe, does cut
> Each stroke between the Earth and Root,
> The edged Stele by careless chance
> Did into his own Ankle glance;
> And there among the Grass fell down,
> By his own Sythe, the Mower mown.   (73–80)

When this happens, as Elizabeth Story Donno notes, the Mower's figurative condition is translated into external fact: "The self-inflicted psychic wound of the lover becomes a literal wound."[52] This actualization of metaphor does not, however, signal a return to the external world; it is accomplished by a movement in the opposite direction. Damon is wounded when the scythe in which he had seen his reflection "glances" back at him.[53] He is defeated, in effect, by his own diminished image. The triumph of fiction seems now to be complete.

And Marvell then takes it one step further. The conclusion is a characteristically Marvellian extension of pastoral tradition. In *Eclogue* 2, Virgil had asserted the equivalence of reality and fiction by disappearing from the poem, and allowing Corydon to bring it to an end. When Damon speaks after the poet and corrects his false conclusion, it would therefore appear that the creation has grown past its creator, that the diminished image has replaced the thing itself.

When he "glances back" at the poet, Damon becomes a figure for the literalized metaphor; and like another such figure, Thestylis in *Upon Appleton House*, he proceeds, at this moment, "to make [the poet's] saying true" (407) – to literalize his metaphor. The glance of the scythe, he claims, is incommensurate to the "wound[s]" he suffers from Juliana's eyes; these cause him continually to "dye" a metaphoric death – a condition that, he feels, can only be cured by being actualized:

> Alas! said He, these hurts are slight
> To those that dye by Loves despight.
> With Shepherds-purse, and Clowns-all-heal,
> The Blood I stanch, and Wound I seal.
> Only for him no Cure is found,
> Whom *Julianas* Eyes do wound.
> 'Tis death alone that this must do. (81–87)

His words reproduce, on another level, the movement from metaphor to fact that occurred in the preceding stanza; and, once more, an apparent movement toward reality returns upon itself:

> For Death thou art a Mower too. (88)

The final line – the ultimate instance of "glancing back" in the the poem – is also Marvell's final bow to Virgil and Theocritus. It recalls the double ironies in both Corydon's conclusion – *invenies alium, si te hic fastidit, Alexin* (73, "You'll find another Alexis, if this one scorns you" [my trans.]) – and Polyphemus' assertion: "You'll find perchance another and a fairer Galateia" (76). Death, which is to rescue the Mower from both metaphor and himself, inevitably turns into "another and a fairer" image of Damon himself. Metaphor becomes truth here only because Damon's universe has become wholly metaphoric.

In the final stanza, then, the poem comes full circle, and traditional bucolic ideals are realized by actively pursuing their opposites. Fictions replace reality, not because their fictiveness is denied, but because it is openly asserted. And Damon achieves unity with his surroundings, not by absorbing his separate consciousness into externals, but by self-consciously absorbing the world into himself. The Mower and the poet even achieve a "comfortable natural passivity"[54] – through intellectual exertion. The triumph of his creation allows Marvell to "be laid ... [in] some shade,"[55] while Damon completes his poem; and Death's victory performs the same service for Damon: he is now able to to conceive of himself as a passive third person (85), defeated by another – who is himself.

The disappearance of Damon's "I" at the end brings us back to the beginning of the poem. The structure of the concluding lines, moreover, pointedly recalls that of the naive second stanza. The double pairing of animals there is matched by the double pairing of Damon and his cures (83–84); and the singularity of the snake is paralleled by the singularity of the alienated lover (85). Damon's new-found self-consciousness, however, now enables him to work out explicitly the implications that were present in the figure of the snake. The union in division that was suggested by the snake's "second skin" is fulfilled in the union of Damon and Death, who are connected through their mutual isolation:

> *Only* for him no Cure is found,
> ...
> 'Tis death *alone* that this must do:
> For Death thou art a Mower too.   (emphasis mine)

The malignant, self-renewing snake was also a common image of both death and immortality.[56] And eternal life in death is precisely what Damon attains here. The momentary death and resurrection he suffered earlier is now extended into eternity; he has, in effect, become both Daphnis and Thyrsis – a singer forever singing his own dirge.

This is even more obviously the case in "The Mower's Song," which is clearly identified as a dirge.[57] The paradoxically circular movement we have been examining in

"Damon the Mower" and its companion poems is, I would suggest, the movement of the sequence as as whole.[58] Each of the Juliana poems becomes progressively more explicit about its own progress, and progressively more insistent about attributing every step of that progress to Juliana: thus, while connections between the stanzas of "Damon the Mower" (and between the stages of Damon's development) are merely implied, "The Mower to the Glo-worms" assumes a logical structure in its final lines (when it describes the effects of Juliana's arrival), and "The Mower's Song" does so from its beginning; it presents itself as a chronologically organized narrative, and it is concerned, throughout, with cause and effect relationships. Each succeeding speaker seems more sophisticated: he is more clearly conscious, throughout his complaint, of his separation from innocence; and he is more fully aware of the paradoxical connections that he is creating to it. The lyrics thus arrive gradually at a logical, self-conscious view of the relation of innocence to experience; in so doing, however, they merely unpack what is already there in "The Mower against Gardens."

II

The static permanence that is imaged at the end of the Mower poems is the permanence of art. Marvell's naive characters tend to remain fixed in this state: they seem forever joined to innocence and forever separated from it; they live eternally, eternally "adorn[ing]" their own "Tomb[s]" ("The Mower's Song," 28).[59] This condition is not, of course, one that can be actualized in the lives of the poet and his readers. The Mower poems implicitly acknowledge this fact, and they also imply a relation to the greater world. But because this relation is not made explicit, they have sometimes occasioned criticism reminiscent of R. C. Trench's supposed objection to his friend Tennyson: "Tennyson," Trench was reported as saying, "we cannot live in Art."[60] Put this baldly, Trench's caveat sounds more than a bit silly (one would assume that Tennyson was perfectly aware of this limitation). But a similar objection, in a more sophisticated form, lies behind the moralistic responses of generations of anti-aesthetic aestheticians to figures such as Damon and Corydon; and, in an extremely self-conscious form, it also lies behind Sidney's ambivalence about lyric "pastime."[61] In his pastoral poems with sophisticated speakers, Marvell directly confronts – and acknowledges the validity of – the problems that Sidney had raised; and he explores the connections that exist between his creations and the external world. He does so, however, not by repudiating the self-conscious self-enclosure of the Mower poems, but by incorporating it into a more inclusive vision – or more accurately, by making explicit the "greater" vision that is already implicitly contained within the "lesser" lyrics.

For the remainder of this chapter, I would like to attempt to demonstrate the above assertion by examining Marvell's most inclusive – and most troublesome – poem, *Upon Appleton House*.[62] I will focus particularly on the progress of the speaker throughout the poem. While this progress has been noted by many readers, its implications have never been fully explored: it is quite similar – up to a certain point – to the (paradoxically nonprogressive) progress of the Mower poems.[63] The point at which it differs, is, of course, the point of return; but this conclusion, I will argue, is inescapably implied by what has gone before.

The opening stanzas of *Upon Appleton House* have disturbed critics from T. S. Eliot onwards. Marvell[64] begins by praising simplicity and sobriety in a manner that is anything but simple and sober:

> Within this sober Frame expect
> Work of no Forrain *Architect*;
> That unto Caves the Quarries drew,
> And Forrests did to Pastures hew;
> Who of his great Design in pain
> Did for a Model vault his Brain,
> Whose Columnes should so high be rais'd
> To arch the Brows that on them gaz'd.   (1–8)

The questions these lines raise will, of course, become more pressing as the poem continues; critical condemnations of the

"Forrain *Architect*" invariably end up sounding like descriptions of Marvell's poem.[65] Even at this point, however, the poetic excesses here are disconcerting: the involuted syntax (whose columns?) and fantastic imagery in these lines insistently reproduce the involuted excess that is being scorned. It will not do, moreover, merely to say that "the extravagance of the imagery demonstrates the absurdity of... architectural extravagance."[66] Similarly farfetched conceits appear in the following lines, which extol the virtues of natural simplicity; and "the extravagance of the imagery" reaches a height in the notorious seventh stanza, which describes Nun Appleton itself:[67]

> Yet thus the laden House does sweat,
> And scarce indures the *Master* great:
> But when he comes the swelling Hall
> Stirs, and the *Square* grows *Spherical*;
> More by his *Magnitude* distrest,
> Than he is by its straitness prest:
> And too officiously it slights
> That in it self which him delights.   (49–56)

As Donald Friedman notes, our difficulties with this stanza arise not merely from the absurdity of the image it contains, but from the juxtaposition of that image with the moral abstractions immediately preceding it:

> *Humility* alone designs
> Those short but admirable Lines,
> By which, ungirt and unconstrain'd,
> Things greater are in less contain'd.
> Let others vainly strive t'immure
> The *Circle* in the *Quadrature*!
> These *holy Mathematicks* can
> In ev'ry Figure equal Man.   (41–48)

Friedman comments:

The contrast between the "sweating" house that changes its shape in an effort to accommodate its master's fame and the "*holy Mathematicks*" of humility is informative because the conceit involving the house is one that Dr. Johnson might well have used to illustrate the excesses of the metaphysical imagination, while the latter is a fine example of Marvell's use of abstractions for morally didactic purposes. The difference between the two modes is a sign of the incoherence in

"Upon Appleton House" that draws the criticism of so many readers.[68]

The "incoherence" to which Friedman points is undeniably there; but it is not, I would argue, unconsciously produced: it is the inevitable result of "unpacking" – making more explicit and therefore more recognizable – the paradoxes that were at the heart of "The Mower against Gardens." In *Upon Appleton House*, as in all of Marvell's poetry, the human mind is viewed as creating a chasm between man and the rest of creation; all other creatures inhabit homes that are suited to their physical proportions: "No Creature loves an empty space; / Their Bodies measure out their Place" (15–16). Man's painful desires and ambitions, however, effectively displace him: he builds "unproportion'd dwellings" (10) in the image of his own aspiring mind; he blasphemously "thinks by Breadth the World t'unite / Though the first Builders fail'd in Height" (23–24).[69] The speaker here responds to this problem as the Mower initially did (albeit in a less radical fashion) – by trying to separate himself from it: he repeatedly refers to man in the third person, decrying "his" pains, desires, and ambitions, while he himself speaks in the communal, impersonal voice of an omniscient narrator. Upon a first reading, of course, we do not question the speaker's assumption of this voice: he is, after all, the narrator; and the denial of individual desire that is implicit in that role cannot become an issue until he, self-consciously, stops denying it. There is, however, a parallel denial in his description of his patron's house that should be immediately apparent: in an attempt to demonstrate that Appleton House is, indeed, a fit and "natural" home, he removes it as far as possible from the realm of active ambition and intellectual aggression. He repeatedly uses agentless passive constructions to describe its creation: while "others vainly strive" (45), we are told that Appleton House simply "was built upon the Place" (69), and that now, "All things are composed here / Like Nature, orderly and near" (25–26). When active verbs are used in connection with the construction of the house, their subjects are abstract virtues – e.g., "*Humility*" – and inanimate objects. As in ".The Mower against Gardens," the speaker's attempt to identify himself with what is not human results, necessarily, in the humanization of the qualities and objects with which he identifies.[70] The fantastic image of the sweating, swelling house is, in other words, the necessary corollary (as well as the obvious converse) of assertions like "*Humility* alone designs / Those short but admirable Lines" and "These *holy Mathematicks* can / In ev'ry Figure equal Man": it results from taking these assertions at face value, and following them through to their logical conclusions. Having been endowed by the narrator with all the intellect, desire, agency, and ambition that he himself wishes to disown, having been created – as it must be – in his own image, the house, impertinently, "glances back" at him; and, as it does so, it reproduces the central image of the first stanza – the image of man's swelling, vaulted brain.[71] Marvell is here again creating a latter-day version of the paradoxical "triumph" of the bucolic over the heroic: the contrast between stanzas six and seven enacts the paradoxes implicit in the statement that "Things greater are in less contain'd"; and it is because these paradoxes are not yet fully acknowledged that the poem appears incoherent.

Similar examples of "incoherence" appear throughout the introductory stanzas. In stanza four, Appleton House is described as tame and orderly – like Nature (25–26, quoted above). A few stanzas later, it is again described as being like Nature – that is, unconstrained and wild:

> But Nature here hath been so free
> As if she said leave this to me.
> Art would more neatly have defac'd
> What she had laid so sweetly wast.   (75–78)

These conflicting views of – and contradictory attitudes towards – the "wild" and the "tame" appear, as we have seen, throughout Marvell's poetry; they go back (at least) to Virgil, whose suspended view of his own creations allowed him to see them as both simple and complex. Here, however, they are presented in as disjunctive a manner as they were in the introductory paragraph of Sannazaro's *Arcadia*.[72] By the end of the poem, these conflicting perspectives will be brought together: in the conclusion, Appleton House is presented both as a tamer (i.e., diminished, simpler) image of the chaotic external world ("Your lesser *World* contains the same / But in more decent Order tame," 765–66), and as a tamer (i.e., sophisticated, more complex) metaphoric recreation of paradisaical simplicity ("*Paradice's only Map*," 768). From either perspective, it is clearly seen as an image – a product of the human mind – which is necessarily both connected to and distant from what it images; it therefore combines the simple with the complex, and recreates the wild within the tame. At the beginning of the poem, however, the narrator is attempting to identify the house simply as "simple," to associate it with Nature and distance it from both the chaos of the external world and the complexities of art. His attempt is, of course, notably unsuccessful. When the house is imagined as simple, natural, and tame (25–26), its status as an human artifact is implied by the word "composed"; and when – as a result of this initial perspective – the speaker is able to imagine the house as simple, natural, and wild (75–78), its "artiness" (naturally) becomes even more apparent: Nature is pictured "as if" she were sentient, sexual, and capable of speech (76); and the results of "her" actions are described in terms ("sweetly wast") that mirror the poet's description of artistic creation ("neatly ... defac'd") at the same time that they are opposed to it. The paradoxical connections that are made at the end are clearly suggested in these lines; and they are even more strongly implied in stanza nine, in which the house is described as both a reflection of man's ephemeral life ("an *Inn* to entertain / Its *Lord* a while, but not remain," 71–72) and as an image of eternity ("*a Mark of Grace*," 70). Because the narrator's distance from natural innocence is suppressed, however, his connection to it remains inadequately expressed.

Marvell is not, of course, creating a single-minded irony against the speaker here, any more than he was in "The Mower against Gardens." Even more obviously than in that poem, the speaker in *Upon Appleton House* is inseparable from Marvell himself. And he is quite obviously sincere in his praise of Fairfax's house, English architecture, and natural simplicity. But he is also acutely aware of the paradoxes that the desire for

innocence – the desire for the lack of desire – creates; and he is
exploring the self-contradictions that result from identifying
oneself with the "truth": the problematic situation he creates
for himself here is similar, in some respects, to the impasse that
was created in the *Arcadia* by Sidney's communal narrator (who
identified himself with a somewhat different truth). Marvell
does not resolve Sidney's dilemma in *Upon Appleton House* (or
anywhere else for that matter); he does, however, move to an
extreme self-consciousness of the problem, and of the im-
possibility of doing away with it; and that self-consciousness,
while exacerbating the problem, simultaneously becomes its
solution.

The paradoxes implicit in the beginning of the poem become
more apparent when the narrator recounts the history of the
house. The description of the nuns is Marvell's most searing
analysis of the desire for innocence. The nuns seek to excise
"wildness" from their lives, to do away with violence and sex
and to preserve intact the enclosed circles of their convent and
their virginity:

> 'Within this holy leisure we
> 'Live innocently as you see.
> 'These Walls restrain the World without,
> 'But hedge our Liberty about.
> 'These Bars inclose that wider Den
> 'Of those wild Creatures, called Men.
> 'The Cloyster outward shuts its Gates,
> 'And, from us, locks on them the Grates.   (97–104)

Their attempt, of course, is "fated" to fail; and its failure is
implicit in the attempt itself. Within the bounds of their
enclosure everything that is excluded comes back; the idea that
"you can't get rid of the damn thing" – that "greater" is,
necessarily, "in less contain'd" – is given explicit and disturbing
statement by the nuns themselves:

> 'So through the mortal fruit we boyl
> 'The Sugars uncorrupting Oyl:
> 'And that which perisht while we pull,
> 'Is thus preserved clear and full.   (173–76)

Inside the convent, the desire for innocence manifests itself clearly as desire:

> 'For such indeed are all our Arts;
> 'Still handling Natures finest Parts.
>   ...
> 'Each Night among us to your side
> 'Appoint a fresh and Virgin Bride;
> 'Whom if *our Lord* at midnight find,
> 'Yet Neither should be left behind.
> 'Where you may lye as chast in Bed,
> 'As Pearls together billeted.
> 'All Night embracing Arm in Arm,
> 'Like Chrystal pure with Cotton warm.[73]
>
> (177–78, 185–92)

And the aggression and violence that are shunned similarly reappear in a diminished, ineffective form: "Here we, in shining Armour white, / Like *Virgin Amazons* do fight" (105–06).

The nuns' reproduction of the fallen world they have left behind is the other side of their attempt to substitute that world for paradise. They are trying, in Sidney's terms, to "make a perpetual mansion of this poor baiting place of man's life" (*OA*, 5): they repeatedly substitute "within" for "without," the internal for the external, art for nature, and the human for the divine; in their most startling reversal, they present the Virgin Mary as the image of Isabella Thwaites:

> 'But much it to our work would add
> 'If here your hand, your Face we had:
> 'By it we would *our Lady* touch;
> 'Yet thus She you resembles much.   (129–32)

We are invited simply to condemn their words and actions, and most critics do so wholeheartedly. Rosalie Colie comments: " In the nun's persuasion of Isabella, the proper relation of morality to metaphor is inverted, showing thereby the inversion of the nun's moral ideas."[74] And Isabel MacCaffrey similarly remarks that the convent is an "instance of presumption and perversion of art": "Like the gardeners in 'The Mower against Gardens,' [the nuns] attempt to remake Nature in a human image." They exemplify "the human urge to imitate God's making, to evade limits and draw a map of salvation."[75] These comments contain obvious truths; but they present us with equally obvious difficulties. The "inversions" and "urges" that Colie and MacCaffrey describe (as the terms they use make clear) are the defining characteristics of Marvell's poetry. Similar inversions are implicit, as we have seen, in the opening stanzas of *Upon Appleton House*, and they will continue to appear – indeed, they will become more apparent – as the poem progresses. Critics who simply condemn the nuns are therefore driven either to condemn with equal fervor Fairfax's and/or the narrator's retreats,[76] or to insist Jesuitically on the determining importance of the differences between them.[77] These differences do exist, but they are created not by escaping the dilemmas explored here, but by acknowledging our necessary involvement in them. And while the narrator's exaggerated, parodic presentation of the convent makes explicit the paradoxes inherent in the desire for innocence, it simultaneously reproduces those paradoxes in another form: in his words, as in the nun's, there is an assumption "that something more than humane speaks" (144).[78]

I am not denying that the nuns are "wrong"; I am, however, suggesting that Marvell is presenting us with a situation in which it is impossible to be "right." It is, indeed, presumptuous to imagine the non-human in human terms; the only thing more presumptuous would be to imagine that one could do otherwise. The fact that the nuns – and implicitly all Catholics (those premier literalizers of metaphors) – are lying, is, in other words, intimately bound up with their insistence that their vision is literally true; and by distancing ourselves from them and claiming that we have access to the truth, we necessarily repeat their "error." Donald Friedman, one of the few critics who recognizes Marvell's (as yet unacknowledged) attraction to the nuns' position, and who refuses to condemn it "single-mindedly,"[79] argues that the attractiveness of the temptation underscores the difficulties involved in avoiding it; from the perspective of the poem as a whole, however, the "temptation" is unavoidable. Marvell is, of course, an advocate of the Reformation,[80] but he is also aware that in "reform[ing] the errours of the Spring," ("The Picture of little T. C.," 27) one inevitably re-forms them.

Fairfax's garden does just that: it reforms (and re-forms) the errors of both the nuns and the outside world. Marvell implies the connection between his patron's retreat and the convent in his swift transition from the description of the triumph of Fairfax's ancestor to a description of the general's own retirement; and the garden itself is clearly presented as the diminished image of the world that has been left behind:

> From that blest Bed the *Heroe* came,
> Whom *France* and *Poland* yet does fame:
> Who, when retired here to Peace,
> His warlike Studies could not cease;
> But laid these Gardens out in sport
> In the just Figure of a Fort.   (281–88)

Fairfax's retreat wittily embodies the idea that "you can't get rid of the damn thing." But because the inevitable return of the "heroic" perspective is implicitly acknowledged here (by both the narrator and Fairfax himself), it is not seen as completely undermining the innocence of the retreat;[81] rather, it allows the narrator to begin making connections he was unable to make before. At first he simply celebrates, in a playful manner, the peaceful mock-warfare of the garden. His celebration, however, leads inevitably to regret over the loss of peaceful England, which the garden is seen as imaging, and which, in turn, is seen as an image of Paradise:

> O Thou, that dear and happy Isle
> The Garden of the World ere while,
> Thou *Paradise* of four Seas,
> Which *Heaven* planted us to please,
> But, to exclude the World, did guard
> With watry if not flaming Sword;
> What luckless Apple did we tast,
> To make us Mortal, and The Wast?   (321–28)

By comparing prewar England to the Garden of Eden, and contrasting it to the "excluded" fallen world, the narrator implicitly marks his distance from it, and suggests that its loss was inevitable: permanent residence in Paradise is incontrovertibly "beyond a Mortal's share" ("The Garden," 61). At the same time, he begins to confront his own mortality and his own desire for immortal innocence. The direct address to a ravaged England introduces into the poem a more personal voice than we have heard before, and the pronoun "we" – which in its few earlier appearances had been used in a vague authorial manner ("We opportunely may relate / The Progress of this Houses Fate," 83–84) – now serves specifically to include the speaker within the ranks of mortal and erring Englishmen. The narrator, moreover, no longer claims direct access to innocent simplicity: he now uses the term "waste" to evoke, not the simple wilderness of Nature, but the "wild" chaos of the civil war. Paradise is clearly conceived here as that from which "we" are separated. The speaker then proceeds to use that separation itself to create connections:

> Unhappy! shall we never more
> That sweet *Militia* restore,
> When Gardens only had their Towrs,
> And all the Garrisons were Flowrs,
> Where Roses only Arms might bear,
> And Men did rosie Garlands wear?
> Tulips, in several Colours barr'd,
> Were then the *Switzers* of our *Guard*.
>
> The *Gardiner* had the *Souldiers* place,
> And his more gentle Forts did trace.
> The Nursery of all things green
> Was then the only *Magazeen*.
> The *Winter Quarters* were the Stoves,
> Where he the tender Plants removes.   (329–42)

This passage begins as many of Marvell's evocations of innocence do – with an exclamation of regret for the loss of that condition;[82] as the speaker progresses, however, the negative question with with he began is forgotten and the innocent state is more directly evoked. This movement from separation to (partial) connection is paralleled by – is, really, inseparable from – the technique that the narrator is using throughout the passage to recreate paradise. These lines are an especially clear example of the central mechanism of Marvell's poetry – the mechanism that we have previously examined in the Mower poems and termed the "harmless fall": Marvell arrives at "innocence" (here, at the original innocence) by taking a diminished image of the Fall (which is twice removed from innocence, because it is an image and because what it images is the Fall) and treating it as if it did not point elsewhere, as if it were not an image but "the thing itself." Isabel MacCaffrey comments on these lines: "Reality had not yet split into tenors and vehicles; there are no metaphors in paradise."[83] This is, indeed, the condition that the passage suggests; but Marvell can no more get rid of metaphors than he can get rid of guns – and both are persistently present in these lines and throughout the poem as a whole.[84] It is perhaps belaboring the obvious, but it seems necessary in the light of critical commentary to point out that imagining paradise as a place where "the only guns were flowers" is quite different from simply saying "there are [or even 'there were'] flowers." The latter is what the nuns and the narrator were attempting – but repeatedly failing – to say. The formulations here, in contrast, effectively admit that we are separated from innocence, and that our connections to it depend upon – are created out of – that separation. Much more explicitly than the picture of personified Nature "sweetly wast[ing]," this passage acknowledges its own artifice, its own status as metaphor and image, and its own inevitable involvement in the violence of the Fall. And it is precisely because this acknowledgment is present that the passage can function as a viable image of paradisaical innocence – of a condition where there are no metaphors, no desire, no wounds, and no guns – while the nuns' and the narrator's earlier imaginings cannot. Once again, Marvell has made separation both the means of connection and the point at which that connection is made.

Connection then becomes separation once more: just when the narrator has most fully planted us in paradise (with his use of the present tense, 244), he turns his trope around once more to create an image of the chaotic fallen world:

> But War all this doth overgrow:
> We Ord'nance Plant and Powder sow.   (343–44)

These lines so effectively evoke the horror of war that it is not usually noticed that they are no more "realistic" than the preceding ones. We do not, even in times of civil war, live in a world where "the only flowers are guns" any more than we live in its opposite: the vision in these lines reminds us of – and relies upon – the reality of flowers as surely as the picture of paradise had reminded us of the reality of guns. Thus, while the primary effect of the lines is to assert our distance from innocence, they also suggest our connection to it, and imply that we are equally distant from the pure "waste" of chaos. Both extreme "wild" conditions depend for their existence on the "tame" garden state, as, indeed, they must: the truly wild – whether it be pure innocence or pure chaos – is truly incomprehensible. And it is this "tame" state (quite literally, a state of mind), pointing both ways and suggesting both possibilities, that will eventually become emblematic of the human condition, which the narrator will term "amphibi[ous]" (774).

As the garden is "amphibious," so, too, is the narrator's attitude toward the retreat that garden represents. His own longing for a permanent return to innocence makes him wish that Fairfax had not retired to Nun Appleton:

> And yet their walks one on the Sod
> Who, had it pleased him and *God*,
> Might once have made our Gardens spring
> Fresh as his own and flourishing.
> But he preferr'd to the *Cinque Ports*
> These five imaginary Forts:
> And, in those half-dry Trenches, spann'd
> Pow'r which the Ocean might command.   (345–52)

The idea expressed here is fundamentally paradoxical: the possibility of enacting the retreat in the external world is cancelled out by the retreat itself. Marvell then complicates the paradox by reversing it; the virtues that one wishes to enact in

the external world can be cultivated only in a retreat from that
world:

> For he did, with his utmost Skill,
> *Ambition* weed, but *Conscience* till.
> *Conscience*, that Heaven-nursed Plant,
> Which most our Earthly Gardens want.
> A prickling leaf it bears, and such
> As that which shrinks at ev'ry touch;
> But Flowrs eternal, and divine,
> That in the Crowns of Saints do shine.   (353–60)

Both the ideas and the images in these lines inevitably remind us
of the attitude assumed by the nuns; and the figure of the
"prickling," shrinking leaf of conscience clearly suggests that
the desire to avoid (giving or receiving) wounds renders one
impotent in the world. The paradox that Marvell is contemplating here is, of course, a version of Sidney's dilemma: an
enactment of a "lyric" withdrawal destroys the virtues it seeks
to enact. By stating this dilemma the other way around,
however, Marvell allows the positive results of withdrawal to be
held in suspension with the negative ones. The retreat remains
an image (but only an image) of possibilities for life in the
external world and an image (but only an image) of eternity.

The connections that will be made at the end of *Upon Appleton
House* are, however, still only implicit here. The amphibious
nature of the garden passage parallels its amphibious position in
the poem; it functions, in many respects, similarly to the second
stanza of "The Mower to the Glo-worms" and the middle
stanzas of "Damon the Mower": on one hand, it points to and
comes out of the faux naiveté of the nuns, and the parallel
assumption of innocent possession of truth implicit in the
narrator's earlier impersonal voice; on the other hand, it points
to and results in the extraordinarily self-conscious creations of
the narrator's own retirement. During the description of
Fairfax's garden, we have witnessed the narrator's gradual
involvement in human losses and desires; it therefore seems
natural that after this description, he should fully emerge as a
specific "I" – "And now to the Abbyss I pass / of that

unfathomable Grass" (369–70) – and, eventually, undertake his own self-conscious retreat: "But I, retiring from the Flood, / Take Sanctuary in the Wood" (481–82).[85] And it further seems logical that as this passage to self-consciousness occurs, this still relatively tame and orderly poem should become amazingly "wild": the narrator is, effectively, creating "a little Wilderness" within "a Garden of [his] own" ("The Nymph complaining," 74, 71).

Even before this section, the parallels that existed between the retreats that the narrator described and the attitudes that he had assumed towards them implied that he was un-selfconsciously creating the idea of retreat in his own image; and this implication becomes explicit when the retreat he describes is his own. The necessary interrelation of perceiver and thing perceived is acknowledged in other other ways as well. Throughout this portion of the poem, Marvell proliferates interpretations of and metaphors for the events that he witnesses. His attitude towards his readings of reality is decidedly two-edged: he clearly presents himself as discovering meaning, pattern, and coherence behind a seemingly random, chaotic succession of events; at the same time, he continually calls our attention to the arbitrariness and artificiality of his own readings – through his self-conscious wit, through his frequent use of theatrical terms, and most especially, through the propensity of his metaphors to metamorphose into other metaphors.[86]

Both perspectives are evident in one of the most extraordinary sequences in the poem, a sequence that focuses – in both its content and its form – on the relation that exists between the human mind (and the mind of the artist, in particular) and the external world. Marvell begins by presenting us with an "innocent" view of this relation:

> This *Scene* again withdrawing brings
> A new and empty Face of things;
> A levell'd space, as smooth and plain,
> As Clothes for *Lilly* stretcht to stain.
> The World when first created sure
> Was such a Table rase and pure. (441–46)

The correspondence between human and divine creation that is the explicit subject of this passage is affirmed by the orderly, "natural" progression of the poet's metaphors. And both the theatrical terminology and artistic creation itself are rendered relatively innocent by the absence of human agency here, and by the poet's insistence on the natural "purity" with which we begin. The artist, we are given to believe, is simply enacting his natural role – and that role is a prelapsarian one. Marvell then proceeds to explode this belief in the following lines:

> Or rather such is the *Toril*
> Ere the Bulls enter at Madril.   (447–48)

Even before we have time to consider the content of these lines carefully, our confidence in the natural innocence of the poet's vision is shattered: one simply does not progress from the creation of the world to a bull-ring. The primary effect of this couplet is thus to call attention to the willful arbitrariness of Marvell's conceits, to their lack of necessary connection with any reality outside his own head; and our impression that the poet is speaking nonsense here is, paradoxically, supported by the "sense" that his lines do make: the bull-ring replaces the grand vision of creation with an image of meaningless, ritualistic play – play, moreover, that, far from being pure, is necessarily antagonistic to and destructive of nature, necessarily involved in violation, wounding, blood, and sacrifice.[87] Marvell then takes the paradoxes in these lines two steps further. First, he demonstrates that his seemingly arbitrary simile reflects external reality; reality, in effect, "glances back" at him and "make[s] his saying true" (407):

> For to this naked equal Flat,
> Which *Levellers* take Pattern at,
> The Villagers in common chase
> Their Cattle, which it closer rase;
> And what below the Sith increast
> Is pincht yet nearer by the Beast.   (449–54)

Before, however, one can fully formulate an idea like "the arbitrariness of the poet's conceits reflects the arbitrariness of

the external world," Marvell turns the appearance of incoherence into an assertion of coherence; he brings together all
the major images of the preceding lines in the final simile of the
stanza:

> Such, in the painted World, appear'd
> *Davenant* with th' Universal Heard.   (455–56)

These lines refer to a painting of creation (complete with cows)
that appears in William Davenant's epic *Gondibert*. Once more,
a relation between God's creation and that of the artist is
implied, but the relation is now, significantly, reversed: we
approach God's creation at two removes – by contemplating a
work of art within another work of art; and the fact that the
poem we are presently reading is itself (among other things) a
diminished image of the epic *Gondibert*[88] reproduces Marvell's
paradoxes on yet another level, and makes us realize (when our
heads stop spinning) how fully here "greater [is] in less
contain'd."

This is, admittedly, an abstruse passage. But although it has
been frequently discussed and debated, it does not occasion the
critical consternation that Marvell's swelling house does; the
difference, I believe, results from the fact that the whimsical wit
of these lines is clearly referable to a particular "I," while the
outrageousness of the earlier passage was simply presented as
abstract truth. Marvell's method in this complicated passage is
repeated in various forms throughout this section of the poem:
he repeatedly arrives at coherence through incoherence, stability through change, and an assertion of truth through the
admission of error.

The admission is indistinguishable from the assertion in one
of the central passages in this section:

> Out of these scatter'd *Sibyls* Leaves
> Strange *Prophecies* my Phancy weaves;
> And in one History consumes,
> Like *Mexique Paintings*, all the *Plumes*.
> What *Rome*, *Greece*, *Palestine*, ere said
> I in this light *Mosaick* read.
> Thrice happy he who, not mistook,
> Hath read in *Natures mystick Book*.[89]   (577–84)

Here, Marvell openly acknowledges that he is trying to do what he had initially criticized the presumptuous architects for attempting – "think[ing] by Breadth the World t'unite / though the first Builders failed in Height." He presents his own attempts, however, in a whimsical, self-mocking manner. Critical opinion on this stanza is, quite predictably, divided as to whether the speaker here is or is not "mistook," whether he has, in fact, discovered the secret of the universe, or is being held up as an object of scorn.[90] I am suggesting (equally predictably) that both perspectives are true – or, more precisely, that the speaker achieves access to truth by acknowledging his own inevitable mistakenness.

This is quite clearly the case a little later in the poem, when he unpacks the suspensions in the earlier stanza; as he is describing the meadows after the flood, he presents an idea as fanciful and mistaken:

> No *Serpent* new nor *Crocodile*
> Remains behind our little *Nile*;
> Unless it self you will mistake,
> Among the Meads the only Snake.   (629–33)

Then, as Christopher Ricks points out, he proceeds, in the next lines to "take the fancy as having an established life":[91]

> See in what wanton harmless folds
> It ev'ry where the Meadow holds.   (634–35)

The speaker is here, significantly, replacing a picture of pure innocence – of the world "newly washt" by the flood (628) – with an image of the harmless fall. But he does not do so by claiming access to the purity of truth; rather, he acknowledges the presence of the Fall in another way – by admitting that his "truth" contains within itself (and is created out of) its own mistake. His interpretation itself becomes another version of the harmless fall: it is both innocent and wantonly erring.

Similar passages recur throughout the poet's description of his own retirement. This portion of the poem is particularly rich in examples of the mechanism I have termed "glancing back": the poet's misreadings are frequently corrected by "reality," which then proceeds to "make his saying true." These incidents are usually interpreted as acknowledgments of the limits of imagination in general, and of the speaker's imagination in particular: Thestylis' exclamation (401–08), for example, has been described as "another reminder of the limits of fiction, and of its dependence upon an only partly controllable world of fact ... Once again, the determination of reality to cooperate in his fancies makes the poet seem a little irresponsible, or at least a little careless of his own premises."[92] Yet if this passage and similar ones remind us of the limits of fiction (and they do), they simultaneously assert its power; for the "reality" that repeatedly rebukes the poet is quite obviously a product of his own imagination. This is clearly true of Thestylis, who is his own character (his own diminished image) and who, insofar as she inhabits the external world, inhabits not "the world of fact" but the world of art (Virgil's second eclogue);[93] as in "Damon the Mower," Marvell approaches reality here, not by a direct route, but by traveling further into the realm of metaphor. And the comeuppance that he receives at the hands of Nature – the flood that "makes the Meadow truly be / (What it but seem'd before) a Sea" (467–68); "Chance's better Wit," which "with a Mask [his] studies hit[s]" (585–86) – seems to function in a similarly paradoxical fashion. Marvell's own wit in these passages serves pointedly to remind us of what is true in any work of art – that the "reality" the artist describes is, to a great extent, of his own making. The triumph of witty, theatrical "Chance" throughout this section seems, again, to be the triumph of the poet's diminished image;[94] Marvell is self-consciously making his choice destiny here, and as a result, he achieves the effect of making destiny his choice. And he becomes an "*easie Philosopher*" (561) in two senses: he is clearly a sophist, but his self-admitted sophistry allows him to assume a position of ease, of passive accord with natural innocence. From one perspective, he is clearly behaving like the nun who in "Words ... weav'd / (As 'twere by Chance) / Thoughts long conceiv'd" (95–96); unlike the nuns, however, he freely and frequently admits that he is "lying," and we are therefore more willing to accept his thoughts as "facts": our willingness to do so is evidenced not only by numerous critical remarks like the one quoted above, but by the multitude of readings that solemnly explain the religious, political, and/or historical allegory underlying the apparent chaos of *Upon Appleton House* – readings which may be open to criticism, but which are also based on justifiable responses to the claims of the text.[95]

As the passages that we have been examining suggest, the speaker's increase in self-consciousness is paralleled by his increasing acceptance of the other signs of the Fall. As the poem progresses, he presents us not only with more metaphors, but with more metaphors that evoke our fallen condition: the "allegorical history" that he constructs for us is marked by repeated discontinuities and violations, and it is imaged in terms of wounds, pricks, worms, and death. As these images and incidents recur, however, the poet begins to create continuity out of the repetition of discontinuity, and his equation of self-consciousness with innocent passivity is matched by other, similarly paradoxical equations. It is true, as Colie notes, that the most violent scenes in the poem are the descriptions of pastoral activity, but it is not, as she claims, surprising:[96] this is, after all, a "pure," unassuming pastoral lyric that finds within itself an epic history, and it moves to a self-conscious acknowledgment of the identity of lyric and epic, bucolic and heroic, stasis and motion – of enclosure and violation, "innocence" and the desires that result from the Fall.

This movement reaches a climax when the speaker asks to be permanently unified with Nature. In stanza 73, as we have seen, he attempts "the World t'unite" while simultaneously implying the mistakenness of his attempts. As he proceeds to imagine himself more fully into an innocent state, he also confronts more directly the fallen pain, artifice, and desire upon which his imaginings are based. In stanza 75, for example, he quite clearly presents his own desire for innocence as desire:

> Then, languishing with ease, I toss
> On Pallets swoln of Velvet Moss.
> While the Wind, cooling through the Boughs,
> Flatters with Air my panting Brows,
> Thanks for my Rest, ye *Mossy Banks*, ...   (593–97)

And the paradoxes suggested by this (characteristically) eroti-
cized picture of innocent union reappear, in another form, in
the concluding lines of the stanza, in which the speaker claims
– by means of an extremely witty and involuted conceit – that
he has been separated from his wit:

> And unto you *cool Zephyr's* Thanks,
> Who, as my Hair, my Thoughts too shed,
> And winnow from the Chaff my Head.   (598–600)

In the following stanza, he unpacks these paradoxes even
further, as he presents us with an anatomy of his own harmless
fall:

> How safe, methinks, and strong, behind
> These Trees have I incamp'd my Mind;
> Where Beauty, aiming at the Heart,
> Bends in some Tree its useless Dart;
> And where the World no certain Shot
> Can make, or me it toucheth not.
> But I on it securely play,
> And gaul its Horsemen all the Day.   (601–08)

The opening couplet makes it clear that the idea that one can
separate the self from the mind ("I...my Mind") is precisely
that – an idea conceived by a self that is inseparable from the
mind ("methinks"). And the self-contradiction implied here is
the focus of the stanza as a whole. The first four lines
acknowledge that the speaker's safety and "innocence" are
achieved by displacing desire onto innocent nature: the
potentially dangerous "Dart" lodges itself in a tree, and is thus
rendered effectively harmless ("ben[t]," "useless"). Having
been blunted, however, fallen desires inevitably assert themselves once more: the image of the wounding dart reappears,
pointedly, in the vision of the speaker's own triumph over the
world; as he "gaul[s] its Horsemen," he pierces them (with his
spurs), and repeats the customary action of their "arrows or
shot."[97] Much more clearly than either Fairfax or the
Amazonian nuns (whose mock-militaristic postures his own
attitude recalls), and much more openly than he ever has before
(in his earlier images, thorns were frequently retracted, wounds
were often banished or mourned),[98] the speaker here acknowledges his own involvement in the wound that Earth felt. He

presents us with a triumph that is necessarily also a defeat, with a vision of innocent "security" that contains within itself its own violation, its own "*Traitor-worm*" (554). The disruption that threatens his vision is inseparable from the desires that create it.

Then, in lines that are both predictable and endlessly surprising, he pushes self-consciousness one final step further, openly confronts his self-division, and creates a vision of a defeat that is also a triumph:

> Bind me ye *Woodbines* in your 'twines,
> Curle me about ye gadding *Vines*,
> And Oh so close your Circles lace,
> That I may never leave this Place:
> But, lest your Fetters prove too weak,
> Ere I your Silken Bondage break,
> Do you, *O Brambles*, chain me too,
> And courteous *Briars* nail me through.   (609–16)

This extraordinary stanza is, in many respects, similar to the end of "Damon the Mower": here, as there, the boundaries of self-consciousness are reached – and passed – when the speaker imagines his permanent defeat by his own diminished image. The trees and bushes, on whom his desire has been displaced, are asked to "glance back" at him, to imprison him in their embrace, and finally, to wound him with their pricks. The (courteously) aggressive sexual energy with which they are endowed is quite clearly his own: it derives from his fantasy of "gauling" the world, and it is transferred by means of his (courteously) urgent apostrophe. Here, as in "Damon the Mower," this final movement into the realm of self-conscious metaphor and self-divided desire allows the speaker to assume a posture of passivity. And, in a similar manner, he brings together life and death, permanence and interruption, violation and enclosure. The penetrating thorns, which earlier had been opposed to the purity of pastoral enclosure, are now invoked for the purpose of preserving that enclosure (indeed, since the encircling enclosure has become less pure [609–14], and the thorns less threatening, the two images seem continuous). Like Damon, the speaker imagines escaping wounds by being wounded, and living eternally by submitting to death.

In a sense, Marvell is only doing here what he has been doing throughout the poem – attempting to create innocence out of fallenness. The poet's extreme self-consciousness about his own image-making process, however, reverses his earlier images at the same time that it extends them. This is not, of course, a harmless fall but a mock-crucifixion – and it is logical that it should be so: while the harmless fall creates "paradise" by pretending to erase our distance from innocence, the crucifixion presents us with an explicit image of undoing the effects of the Fall by consciously submitting to them; the paradoxes that the speaker creates here are those which Christ embodied when He redeemed humanity from sin by shouldering the burden of the Fall, and triumphed over death by enduring it. Simply to say this, however, is shockingly to confuse "within" and "without" – to make Christ a type of the bucolic hero, to say, as the nuns do, that divinity resembles man very much.[99] From one perspective, this is undeniably what the passage does suggest; at the same time, however, it repeatedly acknowledges the ludicrous "mistookness" of its claim: the same self-conscious wit that creates Christ in the image of the poet also points, at every moment, to the distance between them. Marvell's vision is clearly presented as self-generated, unfulfilled, and unfulfillable – and it is not, as some readers maintain, simply "ecstatic";[100] it is also very funny: what he imagines here is, explicitly, a mock-crucifixion, and his mockery, like everything else, is self-directed. He is, after all, atoning for the fact that he has been imaginatively wantoning with Nature by imagining that Nature is wantoning with him – and finally deflowering him (and the "courteous" briars that he imagines would not, one supposes, hurt much more than retracted thorns). Because the poet's "mistake" is self-evident, he is also able to "make his saying true." Looked at in a certain light (admitting that we see through a glass, darkly, or, in Marvell's terms, that "till prepar'd for longer flight, / [the Soul] Waves in its Plumes the Various Light"[101]), the idea that our images of the Passion are intertwined with and created out of our own passions is not a theologically unacceptable one; and it appears, in various forms, throughout Marvell's poetry: it is central to "The

Nymph complaining," it is clearly present in stanza 4 of "The Garden,"[102] and it is explicitly treated as a problem in "The Coronet." All of Marvell's lyrics suggest (and *Upon Appleton House*, in particular, insists) that the only thing we can do about our distance from innocence is to acknowledge it; and by doing so (to turn Marvell's paradoxical equations around once more), we best approximate the action of shouldering the burden of the Fall.

And thus become "innocent." The reasoning in the preceding two paragraphs is circular because the effect of Marvell's image is.[103] Theoretically, one could go on like this forever, oscillating endlessly between unity and self-contradiction, innocence and involvement in the Fall, truth and fiction, seriousness and humor, the eternity of the moment and the consciousness of the pressures of time. But, as a matter of fact, we can't. When "Damon the Mower" ends at a similar point, it does so by implicitly conceding its own status as fiction, as lyric, as – to use Sidney's term – "pastime." Because *Upon Appleton House* is a much more openly self-conscious poem – a poem that is more explicit about the circumstances of its own creation, a poem in which both the narrator and his subjects are "real" – this concession must be made more explicit as well. The poem cannot rest "within" its most extreme lyric moment: as we have seen, this moment itself derives its power from the narrator's knowledge that permanent residence there is "beyond a Mortal's share"; and as he attempts to nail down the "here and now" that he will inhabit forever, he inevitably moves further "without":

> Here in the Morning tye my Chain,
> Where the two Woods have made a Lane;
> While, like a *Guard* on either side,
> The Trees before their *Lord* divide;
> This, like a long and equal Thread,
> Betwixt two *Labyrinths* does lead.
> But, where the Floods did lately drown,
> There at the Ev'ning stake me down.   (617–24)

His "here" is transformed into (and balanced by) its mirror image, "there," and his eternally ephemeral lyric moment becomes the endlessly recurring cycle of a natural day.[104] In the following lines, the self-enclosed paradoxes of the crucifixion stanza similarly unwind once more into suspensions, as, in a series of images that both proceed from those paradoxes and reverse them, Marvell imagines both himself and the world reborn after the flood; and his mock-crucifixion becomes, once again, an "innocent" harmless fall (629–34). Finally, he puts away his pointlessly pointed imaginings – "My Hooks, my Quills, / and Angles, idle Utensils"[105] – as "Toyes" when Maria approaches (649–50, 654).

But he never stops playing. The final movement of the poem clearly serves to return the speaker to external reality. But because the whole force of the poem up to this point, and of the crucifixion stanza in particular, has been to insist on the necessary interconnection of "within" and "without," of withdrawal and return, of enclosure and violation, this move-ment does not – cannot – simply contradict the poet's vision in the grove; rather, like the immediately preceding lines, it simultaneously corrects that vision and enacts it in another way. Upon Maria's arrival, the paradoxical equations of the cruci-fixion stanza are further unpacked and externalized as sus-pensions: the poet acknowledges that his images are only images, that they are bounded by reality, and that they do point "without"; but this acknowledgment is made – as it must be – from within the images themselves. For the reality that the poet returns to is self-consciously presented as his own creation. The suspended moment that Maria ushers in, which temporarily halts the movement "betwixt the Day and Night" (670), clearly places the fleeting stasis of the mock-crucifixion within the context of the natural cycle; and, in so doing, it continues the process of externalization begun in lines 616–24. Maria herself (the human embodiment of suspension) is even more obviously an imaginative construct as well as a real little girl. As Harry Berger points out, Marvell repeatedly emphasizes the "disparity between young Mary Fairfax and the symbolic Maria."[106] If she is an image of the Virgin as (eventual) mother, she is still an image of the Virgin, and critics who attempt to separate the poet's idealized portrait from the nun's idealization of Isabella inadvertently point up the difficulty in doing so completely. Rosalie Colie, for example, comments that "the nuns had promised Isabella, falsely, that she should work miracles... [but] Maria does so *in fact*" (emphasis mine); at another point, she remarks, "In contrast to her ancestress, Maria is not 'like' the Virgin; she is a separate, independent virgin Mary."[107] There are, of course, important differences between the poet's image and that of the nuns, but these differences are referable precisely to the poet's self-reflexive vision in the grove, and they are inseparable from the self-consciousness with which he now presents his ideas. As Berger notes, his praise of Maria "echoes with images from [his own] sylvan retreat – the *antick cope*, the prelate of the grove, the 'double Wood of ancient Stocks'"; the lines describing her skill at languages, in particular, seem to "echo... the poet as '*easie Philosopher*.'"[108] As well they might. Marvell was, of course, Mary Fairfax's tutor: she is, in a very real sense, his own creation, his own diminished image; and the controlling idea of this section – the conceit that the pupil has surpassed and is now correcting her teacher – is a self-conscious reimagining of the "glancing back" that has permeated the poem and that reached a climax in the crucifixion stanza.

It is, of course, significant that the poet's diminished image here is neither purely "natural," nor purely "artificial," but a human child who contains and combines both of these antithetical, mirroring perspectives. Marvell is clearly acknowledging the bonds that connect him to human society; but again, this acknowledgment proceeds from and reflects his earlier, self-enclosed fantasies: acceptance of humanity and of the human imagination is, after all, what the crucifixion image, in a number of ways, is fundamentally about. And the poet's displacement of his impulses here onto a creature who is a more innocent version of himself (as houses, birds, trees, and bushes are not)[109] allows him to present explicitly – and to accept – the relation between nature and the human intellect that has been implicit throughout the poem. Maria, we are told, creates the "Gardens, Woods, Meads, [and] Rivers" around her in her own image (689–96); and they, in turn, glance back at her: "Therefore what first *She* on them spent, / They gratefully again present" (697–98).

Correction and reflection are even more clearly intertwined in the description of Maria's future. Because Maria *is* a more innocent version of the poet, she cannot be completely innocent; like the poet, she exists in time, and must eventually move further "without":

> Hence *She* with Graces more divine
> Supplies beyond her *Sex* the *Line*;
> And, like a *sprig of Misleto*,
> On the *Fairfacian Oak* does grow;
> Whence, for some universal good,
> The *Priest* shall cut the sacred Bud;
> While her *glad Parents* most rejoice,
> And make their *Destiny* their *Choice*.   (737–44)

M. J. K. O'Loughlin, who has supplied us with an excellent analysis of this stanza, sees it as contrasting sharply with the crucifixion image:

The crucifixion in the grove is important to recall here, for its insistently voiced private seclusion from time is precisely the opposite of the liberating deliverance which animates the public engagement with time symbolized by the cutting of the "sacred bud" from the tree. It is a perfect expression of the poet's georgic vision of the necessary interplay of private contemplative ease with active public involve- ment. The cutting off of the misletoe is itself a practical horticultural example of the destruction necessary for transplanting. With its delicate suggestion of the defloration which must precede burgeoning it is also a poignantly intimate image of the nature of Mary's future engagement as another "blooming" Thwaites.[110]

But as O'Loughlin's analysis itself makes evident, it is impossible to contrast the two stanzas without suggesting that the poet's vision of fruitful defloration here grows out of his earlier image: if his evocation of Maria's future seems more "poignant" than his earlier description of Isabella's marriage, and his celebration seems more earned, it is because he has imagined himself being "cut." And the relationship of simultaneous correction and reflection that exists among all these images clearly reproduces, on yet another level, the paradoxical equivalence of destruction and creation, connection and discontinuity, enclosure and violation that is at the heart of each one.

Moreover, although Marvell's lines point to a future that will be characterized by a "public engagement with time," he does not attempt to present such an engagement directly; and in the next lines, he turns away from his vision to return to a "Mean time" in which a still virginal Maria still inhabits an Edenic estate (744–60).[111] What is at stake here is not simply Marvell's obvious unwillingness to return to external reality,[112] but his awareness of his inability ever to do so completely – of the inability of any human mind to reproduce directly any "wild" reality, be it chaotic or divine. Maria is a creature of the "Mean time," in other words, because, "till prepar'd for longer flight," we all are. And it is by conflating Nun Appleton with its most innocent human representative that Marvell is finally able explicitly to present Fairfax's home as an image – and only an image – of both Paradise and the chaotic fallen world:[113]

> 'Tis not, what once it was, the *World*;
> But a rude heap together hurl'd;
> All negligently overthrown,
> Gulfes, Deserts, Precipices, Stone.
> Your lesser *World* contains the same.
> But in more decent Order tame;
> *You Heaven's Center, Nature's Lap.*
> *And Paradice's only Map.*   (761–68)

Then – one last time – an abstract formulation is answered by the self-assertive, idiosyncratic wit that is both its converse and its necessary corollary:

> But now the *Salmon-Fishers* moist
> Their *Leathern Boats* begin to hoist;
> And, like *Antipodes* in Shoes,
> Have shod their *Heads* in their *Canoos.*
> How *Tortoise like*, but not so slow,
> These rational *Amphibii* go?
> Let's in: for the dark *Hemisphere*
> Does now like one of them appear.   (769–76)

This stanza clearly both recalls and revises the opening lines of the poem. Here, as there, the poet's whimsical imagery effectively removes his pronouncements from the realm of absolute truth and serves to suggest that his ideas find their source in his own self-enclosed imagination. But this suggestion does not simply undermine his intended meaning, as it did in the opening lines; it simultaneously "make[s] his saying true." For the self-enclosed self-assertiveness that is implied by the form of this stanza is also its explicit subject; not only is everything turned on its head here,[114] everything turns on the head: the speaker openly acknowledges that he is creating the universe in the image of man ("like one of them") and, specifically, in the image of that part of man which he had despised before – his swelling, vaulted, head.[115] Because self-consciousness is self-consciously (and self-amusedly) accepted here, the speaker is able to hold mistakenness and truth in suspension, and to bring together the conflicting mirroring perspectives of the preceding lines: he joins chaos and paradise in the human imagination (where, of course, they have implicitly been joined throughout the poem), and answers the questions he posed at the beginning by seeing the fallen universe itself as a fit, proportionate home for man. In a similar manner, he brings together "within" and "without," and manages to create a communal voice out of involution and self-enclosure: he addresses his readers with a "we" that clearly derives from and includes his "I," and he affirms his connection to simpler, more externalized forms of art and (ultimately) to simple, external nature by concluding this most unconventional of all pastoral poems with a conventional pastoral image of natural suspension.

Marvell's suspended ending is, of course, Virgilian in origin. And, as we have seen, his preoccupation with the artistic imagination also connects him with Virgil. But the manner in which he arrives at his suspensions and the attitude he assumes towards them once again recall Theocritus. Theocritus' attitude toward the products of the human imagination was very much of a piece with his attitude toward all aspirations, desires, and follies: throughout the *Idylls*, we will recall, there was really no question that images do, constantly, lie; recognizing this fact,

however, in no way lessened our need for them, or permitted us
to escape from our necessary involvement with them. Similarly,
in *Upon Appleton House*, there is no question that the poet is – that
his readers are, that all mortals are – continually "mistook";
but our inability to "get rid of the damn thing" is, once more,
accepted with amused equanimity. As a result, our limitations
and constraints themselves become enabling here, at the same
time that they are clearly recognized as killing. In other words,
while Marvell is acutely aware that "we cannot live [with]in
Art," he is equally aware – and he makes his readers aware –
that we cannot, very well, live "without" it.

Farewell to pastoral: The Shepherd's Week

Break off, I pray, ye Muses, break off the pastoral song.
... O Muses, fare you well,
And again farewell. Another day a sweeter song I'll sing you.
Theocritus, Idyll 1

Surgamus: solet esse gravis cantantibus umbra,
iuniperi gravis umbra; nocent et frugibus umbrae.
ite domum saturae, venit Hesperus, ite capellae.

Arise: the shade weighs heavily on singers,
The shade of junipers, and shade harms crops.
Go home well fed, my goats: go: Vesper comes.
Virgil, Eclogue 10

Tomorrow to fresh woods, and pastures new.
Milton, "Lycidas"[1]

Let's in.   Marvell, *Upon Appleton House*

Marvell's self-conscious exploration of pastoral paradoxes makes his poetry a convenient stopping place for this study: it provides us both with a sense that pastoral has, in effect, ended where it began, and with a very clear consciousness of the arbitrariness of such "beginnings" and "endings." If much of his poetry seems to be a farewell to pastoral, it is well to remember that this is a space that has always been occupied by pastoral poetry – and it is a space that pastoral will continue to inhabit. The self-contradictory constructions that Marvell appears to push to their limits reappear, in different forms, not only in contemporary works like *Paradise Lost* – in which prelapsarian nature is created by an art supremely self-conscious of its own limitations[2] – but also in modern poems such as (to cite only one of the more obvious examples) Robert Frost's exercise in pastoral *praeteritio*, "The Need of Being Versed in Country Things." After the seventeenth century, however, the poet's relation to pastoral conventions and models begins to change significantly. During the Restoration and the eighteenth century, the relation between the modern pastoral poet and his classical predecessors becomes a topic for explicit critical debate.[3] It is, indeed, amid an eighteenth-century quarrel about the proper mode of poetic imitation – a quarrel not unlike the Hellenistic debate between Callimachus and the Homeric poets – that one of the most curious post-Marvellian versions of pastoral, John Gay's *The Shepherd's Week*, is born. Since this work seems to mark the end of conventional pastoral even more surely than Marvell's lyrics, I would like to look at it briefly by way of a coda.

The basic technique of *The Shepherd's Week* is to place literary (generally Virgilian) allusions in a exaggeratedly "low" British rustic setting. The resultant incongruities are heightened by the addition of pseudo-Spenserian names and "scholarly" notes, and by the creation of a language which, Gay assures us,

is ... such as is neither spoken by the country Maiden nor the courtly Dame; nay, not only such as present Times is not uttered, but was never uttered in Times past; and, if I judge aright, will never be uttered in Times future. ("Proeme," 69–73)[4]

Even in their mildest form, the effect of these juxtapositions can be quite disconcerting, as when a list of trees beloved to the gods from Virgil's *Eclogues* becomes, in the mouth of one of Gay's bumpkins, rustic food for thought:

> *Leek* to the *Welch*, to *Dutchmen Butter*'s dear,
> Of *Irish* Swains *Potatoe* is the Chear;
> *Oats* for their Feasts the *Scottish* Shepherds grind,
> Sweet *Turnips* are the Food of *Blouzelind*,
> While she loves *Turnips*, *Butter* I'll despise,
> Nor *Leeks* nor *Oatmeal* nor *Potatoe* prize.
>
> ("Monday," 83–88)[5]

And frequently, the transformations that Gay effects are outrageously bawdy – their explicit sexuality being justified (*pace* the "insipid Delicacy" of certain neo-classicists), by an ironic appeal to the example of Theocritus, who "rightly, throughout his fifth *Idyll*, maketh his Louts give foul Language and behold their Goats at Rut in all Simplicity" ("Proeme," 14, 19–22).[6] The two prizes in a Virgilian song-contest, for example, are an "*Oaken Staff*" and a "*Tobacco Pouch* that's lin'd with Hair, / Made of the Skin of sleekest fallow Deer... [and] ty'd with Tape of reddest Hue"; when the judge concludes that both singers are equally loutish, they both are given the staff ("Monday," 33, 35–37, 120).

Since its appearance, the target of the satire in *The Shepherd's Week* has been a subject of some critical debate. For years, the most popular theory was that supported by Alexander Pope's statement that "the world owed Mr. *Gay's Pastorals*" to a quarrel between Ambrose Philips and himself.[7] Philips had written a group of pastoral poems, which, claiming descent from Theocritus, Virgil, and Spenser, attempted to accommodate pastoral traditions to contemporary British surroundings and customs. While Pope had initially praised Philips' efforts, he was angered at the appearance of a series of essays in the *Guardian* that proposed a set of criteria for judging pastoral poems – drawing almost all of its examples from Philips' works and ignoring Pope's neo-classical pastorals. Pope countered with a ironic essay of his own, which, under the guise of praising Philips, took him to task for ignoring literary decorum in an attempt to create a specious simplicity. *The Shepherd's Week*, he suggests, is a further salvo in the war against Philips.

Gay does appear to have drawn inspiration from the Pope–Philips quarrel, and the desire to ridicule Philips' poems and the assumptions behind them is clearly present in his own pastorals; but it is insufficient to account for even their most superficial effect. For if the proximity of self-consciously literary Virgilian allusions makes the more contemporary rustic details in *The Shepherd's Week* seem especially ludicrous, the reverse is equally true: indeed, at least one critic has suggested that Gay's primary target was Virgil himself.[8] Ultimately, Gay's satire seems aimed neither at contemporary rustic "realism" nor at neo-classical artifice but at the gap between the two – at, in other words, the juncture of the literary and the real, the sophisticated and the naive, the high and the low, the present and the past upon which most pastoral poetry depends.

Gay's interest in targeting pastoral incongruity is particularly evident in his "Prologue"; he begins:

> Lo, I who erst beneath a Tree
> Sung *Bumkinet* and *Bowzybee*,
> And *Blouzelind* and *Marian* bright,
> In Apron blue and Apron white,
> Now write my Sonnets in a Book,
> For my good Lord of *Bolingbroke*.   (1–8)

This is, of course, a version of epic poet's conventional farewell to pastoral. It has its origin in four lines traditionally prefixed to the *Aeneid*:

> Ille ego, qui quondam gracili modulatus avena
> carmen, et egressus silvis vicina coegi
> ut quamvis avido parerent arva colono,
> gratum opus agricolis; at nunc horrentia Martis...

I am he who once tuned my song on a slender reed, then, leaving the woodland, constrained the neighbouring fields to serve the husbandmen, however grasping – a work welcome to farmers: but now of Mars' bristling [arms and the man I sing].[9]

These lines were copied repeatedly by English poets, perhaps most relevantly by Spenser, at the beginning of the *Faerie Queene*:[10]

> Lo I the man, whose Muse whilome did maske,
>   As time her taught, in lowly Shepheards weeds,
>   Am now enforst a far vnfitter taske,
>   For trumpets sterne to chaunge mine Oaten reeds,
>   And sing of Knights and Ladies gentle deeds.   (I.Proem.i)

Gay's parody here is clearly part of the burlesque of Spenser that runs throughout his work; but it is also clearly more than that: by beginning his pastoral poem with the traditional farewell to pastoral, Gay effectively suggests that a pastoral poem is a contradiction in terms – that "pastoral" and "poetry" are antitheses, and that the birth of the poet marks, of necessity, the death of the shepherd. And, indeed, that is what his lines literally say: the speaker's former life as a rustic, singing under the shade of a tree, "now" comes to an end when he writes and publishes his "Sonnets in a Book." The *locus* of the speaker's early songs – as well as the journey he later undertakes to the city and the patron he finds there – further identifies him with Tityrus, the settled shepherd in Virgil's first eclogue.[11] But the effect of the journey he describes is to rob that "Tityrus" of his naiveté, to transform him, not even into Meliboeus (Virgil's displaced shepherd), but into Virgil – or more precisely, into Gay.

The rest of the "Prologue" traces the speaker's progress between those two points: upon hearing a false report of the queen's death, he breaks his reed – an action that traditionally signaled the end of pastoral song[12] – and travels to the court, which he likes much better than the country. He would like to stay, and to devote himself to praising court ladies rather than simple shepherds, but he is persuaded by Bolingbroke, who admires his rustic "Madrigals," to return "Home" and prepare his songs for publication (82, 85); they should appear, he is told,

> With Preface meet, and Notes profound,
> Imprinted fair, and well y-bound.   (83–84)

And, of course, he no longer needs his reed because he has become a recognized pastoralist, with a publisher, an editor, and a patron. It is this point, significantly, that the citified country poet – now explicitly identified in Bolingbroke's speech as "Gay" (80)[13] – takes on (what has become) the mask of the shepherd, asking us not to take time from important affairs of state, "while our *Bowzybeus* sings ... Verse of simple Swain" (90–91).[14]

The ironies and incongruities that Gay plays upon here are not, of course, new to pastoral, as his numerous allusions implicitly acknowledge. But the view of classical pastoral in *The Shepherd's Week* is filtered through so many layers of later imitations, transformations, and rewritings, and is so heavily swathed in irony, that the primary effect of most of Gay's allusions is not to create connections but to sever them. Gay crashes the oppositions upon which pastoral is based so violently against one another that they effectively explode – and, as they do, almost every extant pastoral tradition is buried in laughter. The convention of sympathetic nature is repeatedly skewered: a singer's lament is, for example, introduced with the comment, "Her Piteous Tale the Winds in Sighs bemoan, / And pining Eccho answers Groan for Groan" ("Thursday," 4–5). And the feelings of every reader who has endured one pastoral song-contest too many are effectively expressed when Gay's judge tells his singers to shut up:

> Your Herds for want of Water stand adry,
> They're weary of your Songs – and so am I.
>
> ("Monday," 123–24)[15]

And then something else occurs. Particularly in the final eclogues, a different tone begins to emerge. Here, as several critics have noted, Gay drops his ironic approach for long stretches of verse in which he evokes, in a relatively straight-forward manner, the charms of rural simplicity.[16] In "Friday," the dying Blouzelinda's distribution of her meagre possessions generates genuine pathos:

> Mother, quoth she, let not the Poultry need,
> And give the Goose wherewith to raise her Breed,
> Be these my Sister's Care – and ev'ry Morn
> Amid the Ducklings let her scatter Corn;
> The sickly Calf that's hous'd, be sure to tend,
> Feed him with Milk, and from bleak Colds defend.
> Yet e'er I die – see, Mother, yonder Shelf,
> There secretly I've hid my worldly Pelf.
> Twenty good Shillings in a Rag I laid,
> Be ten the Parson's, for my Sermon paid.
> The rest is yours – My Spinning-Wheel and Rake,
> Let *Susan* keep for her dear Sister's sake;
> My new Straw Hat that's trimly lin'd with Green,
> Let *Peggy* wear, for she's a Damsel clean.
> My leathern Bottle, long in Harvests try'd,
> Be *Grubinnol's* – this Silver Ring beside:
> Three silver Pennies, and a Ninepence bent,
> A Token kind, to *Bumkinet* is sent.
> Thus spoke the maiden, while her Mother cry'd,
> And peaceful, like the harmless Lamb, she dy'd.   (113–32)

And "Saturday" contains a similarly lengthy and finely observed depiction of a country fair (71–90). These passages, are, of course, surrounded both by Gay's ironic humor and by his characters' return to more prosaic matters: the description of Blouzelinda's death, for example, ends with the note that "In Ale and Kisses they forget their Cares, / And *Susan Blouzelinda's* Loss repairs" ("Friday," 163–64). But the pathos here seems at least as powerful as the irony that contains it (if not more so), and that irony itself – with its two-edged reassertion of the primacy of the practical, the mundane, and the physical – now seems more recognizably pastoral.

Indeed, the entire *Shepherd's Week* has often been praised, both in the eighteenth century and afterwards, for the accuracy of its portrait of rural life.[17] Thomas Purney (1717) lauded Gay's powers of representation; and Robert Shiels (1753) found both "the characters and [the] dialogue ... natural and rurally simple."[18] Dr. Johnson commented that *The Shepherd's Week* overcame its origins in the Pope–Philips controversy:

The effect of reality and truth became conspicuous, even when the intention was to shew them groveling and degraded. These Pastorals became popular, and were read with delight, as just representations of rural manners and occupations, by those who had no interest in the rivalry of the poets, nor knowledge of the critical dispute.[19]

And Oliver Goldsmith declared: "Gay has hit the true spirit of pastoral poetry. In fact, he more resembles Theocritus than any other English pastoral writer whatsoever."[20] Gay, of course, explicitly invokes Theocritus only to distance himself ironically from his "ancient *Dorick*" predecessor ("Proeme," 20). Nevertheless, as Dr. Johnson's comment implies, *The Shepherd's Week* is, finally, Theocritean despite itself (and, ultimately, *because* it is despite itself), not so much in its "rusticity," nor even in its incongruities, as in its bemused recognition that "you can't get rid of the damn thing" – that ironic distancing and nostalgic recall are inevitably intertwined, that "the natural" is created by (but is also inseparable from) the most extreme forms of artifice and play.[21] The particular form this recognition takes is characteristic of the eighteenth century – a period whose poets repeatedly approach established genres through "mock" forms.

And the mockery here is strong enough to signal an end to conventionally allusive pastoral: once this can be done, it is very difficult to take one's allusions straight. But the very adaptability of the Theocritean mechanism is also a sign of its ongoing vitality. While clearly constituting a farewell to pastoral, then, Gay's work just as clearly evidences the continuing relevance of a genre that has always called into question categories of the "literary" and the "literal," of inside and out, of continuity and change – a genre that has, after all, been ending since (before) it began, ever since Theocritus, despite himself, effectively initiated a new form of poetry by having his shepherd-singer implore the Muses to "break off the pastoral song."

Notes

Introduction   "*Remedies themselves complain*": *pastoral poetry, pastoral criticism*

1 For the classic statement of the idealist position, see Renato Poggioli, *The Oaten Flute: Essays on Pastoral Poetry and the Pastoral Ideal* (Cambridge, MA: Harvard University Press, 1975). For a recent study of Renaissance "antipastoralism" (which complicates the traditional view somewhat but still proceeds from similar assumptions), see Peter Lindenbaum, *Changing Landscapes: Anti-Pastoral Sentiment in the English Renaissance* (Athens, GA: University of Georgia Press, 1986). Paul Alpers' analyses of pastoral provide an excellent critique of the premises underlying these approaches: see, in particular, *The Singer of the Eclogues: A Study of Virgilian Pastoral* (Berkeley: University of California Press, 1979); "What is Pastoral?" *Critical Inquiry* 8 (1982): 437–60; "Convening and Convention in Pastoral Poetry," *New Literary History* 14 (1982/83): 277–304; "Theocritean Bucolic and Virgilian Pastoral," *Arethusa* 23 (1990): 19–47; "Schiller's *Naive and Sentimental Poetry* and the Modern Idea of Pastoral," in *Cabinet of the Muses: Essays on Classical and Comparative Literature in Honor of Thomas G. Rosenmeyer*, ed. Mark Griffith and Donald J. Mastronarde (Atlanta, GA: Scholars Press, 1990), 319–31.

2 Of the critics that I discuss below, Annabel Patterson has been particularly eager to dissociate herself from the new historicism: see, esp., her comments in "'The Very Age and Body of the Time His Form and Pressure': Rehistoricizing Shakespeare's Theater," *New Literary History* 20 (1988): 91–95; the polemic in this article is softened somewhat when it is reworked in her more recent book, *Shakespeare and the Popular Voice* (Cambridge: Basil Blackwell, 1989).

3 Montrose's ideas on pastoral are contained most succinctly in "'Eliza, Queene of shepheardes,' and the Pastoral of Power,"

English Literary Renaissance 10 (1980): 153–82, and "Of Gentlemen and Shepherds: The Politics of Elizabethan Pastoral Form," *ELH* 50 (1983): 415–59. See also "Celebration and Insinuation: Sir Philip Sidney and the Motives of Elizabethan Courtship," *Renaissance Drama*, n.s., 8 (1977): 3–35; "'The perfecte paterne of a Poete': The Poetics of Courtship in *The Shepheardes Calender*," *Texas Studies in Literature and Language* 21 (1979): 34–67; "The Elizabethan Subject and the Spenserian Text," in *Literary Theory/Renaissance Texts*, ed. Patricia Parker and David Quint (Baltimore: Johns Hopkins University Press, 1986), 303–40.

4 George Puttenham, *The Arte of English Poesie* (1589), quoted in Montrose, "Of Gentlemen and Shepherds," 444, 452.

5 As Patterson has noted in *Pastoral and Ideology: Virgil to Valéry* (Berkeley: University of California Press, 1987), he repeatedly privileges the Aprill Eclogue of *The Shepheardes Calender*, effectively "reinstat[ing] the idealism of... earlier twentieth-century criticism" (130); he also tends to ignore (in "Eliza, Queene of shepheardes," 166–68) or to downplay (in "The Elizabethan Subject," 321) the frame of the eclogue, which calls our attention to the absence of Colin Clout, the composer of Eliza's encomium.

6 Montrose, "Eliza, Queene of shepheardes," 172. See also his comments on the "purified" eroticism of the Aprill Eclogue in "The perfecte paterne of a Poete," 39–40.

7 Montrose, "Of Gentlemen and Shepherds," 433. In this essay, Montrose criticizes Raymond Williams' sharp distinction between the "primary activities" represented in Virgil's *Eclogues* and the aestheticized "forms" of Renaissance pastoral (418–19), but he proceeds to recuperate this distinction in a more complex manner.

8 See, e.g., Montrose's reflections on the fact that his "pursuit of knowledge and virtue is necessarily impure," in "Professing the Renaissance: The Poetics and Politics of Culture," in *The New Historicism*, ed. H. Aram Veeser (New York: Routledge, 1989), 30. In the same volume, both Stanley Fish ("Commentary: The Young and the Restless," 305–07) and Frank Lentricchia ("Foucault's Legacy: A New Historicism?" 237–38) comment incisively on new historicist confessions of impurity; Fish concentrates on Montrose's statements, while Lentricchia quotes and analyzes Stephen Greenblatt's exemplary assertion, "I do not shrink from these impurities – they are the price and perhaps among the virtues of this approach" (*Renaissance Self-Fashioning: From More to Shakespeare* [Chicago: University of Chicago Press, 1980], 5).

9 Montrose, "Eliza, Queene of shepheardes," 154.

10 For the argument that there can be no consequences, see Stanley

Fish, *Doing What Comes Naturally: Change, Rhetoric, and the Practice of Theory in Literary and Legal Studies* (Durham, NC: Duke University Press, 1989), esp. ch. 14, "Consequences," and ch. 19, "Critical Self-Consciousness, or Can We Know What We're Doing?" See also W. J. T. Mitchell, ed., *Against Theory: Literary Studies and the New Pragmatism* (Chicago: University of Chicago Press, 1985).

11 Patterson also discusses pastoral in her earlier books, which proceed from similar assumptions: see *Marvell and the Civic Crown* (Princeton: Princeton University Press, 1978), and *Censorship and Interpretation: The Conditions of Writing and Reading in Early Modern England* (Madison: University of Wisconsin Press, 1984), esp. the Introduction and ch. 1, "'Under...pretty tales': Intention in Sidney's *Arcadia*."

12 Patterson, *Pastoral and Ideology*, 5. In a review of Patterson's book, Richard Jenkyns also points to the problem here, and remarks that "on this basis a contrast is developed between the politicised pastoral of the first Eclogue and the aestheticised pastoral of the second" ("Pastoral and Misprision," *Essays in Criticism* 39 [1989]: 67). Significantly, a number of other problems in translation and interpretation that Jenkyns cites in his review seem to be similarly attributable to Patterson's desire to find two completely opposable, self-identical categories within pastoral. Thus, she translates a passage from Servius comparing Virgil and Theocritus so that it appears to make a much greater distinction between the two poets than it actually does (*Pastoral and Ideology*, 33). And she insists that a 1649 illustration by Cleyn depicting the characters from *Eclogue* 1 in its foreground depicts *Eclogue* 2 instead; it thus helps to make "the entire sequence" seem "equally and vaguely idyllic" (182).

13 Patterson, *Pastoral and Ideology*, 11.

14 She does, however, allow for an attenuated connection, noting that "even this poem, with its reduction of *otium* to solipsism, ends with the self-injunction to 'at least do something useful,' and so points against itself to the limited instrumentality of Eclogue 9" (*Ibid.*, 5).

15 The repeated efforts of recent critics to distance themselves from what is seen as the "self-reflexive aestheticism" of this eclogue are paralleled in interesting ways by the attempts of earlier critics and translators to distance themselves from its homoerotic content. See Gregory W. Bredbeck, *Sodomy and Interpretation: Marlowe to Milton* (Ithaca: Cornell University Press, 1991), 197–213, for a discussion of a number of strikingly self-defeating attempts to suppress homoerotic elements in Theocritus and Virgil. In "The Mirror and the Tank: AIDS, Subjectivity, and the Rhetoric of Activism,"

in *Homographesis: Essays in Gay Literary and Cultural Theory* (New York: Routledge, 1994), 93–117, Lee Edelman provides a fascinating commentary on our cultural investment in reifying, connecting, and identifying with the active, the masculine, the heteroerotic, the serious, and the "political," and in distancing the feminine, the passive, the homoerotic, the playful – the "narcissistic." See also Bruce R. Smith, *Homosexual Desire in Shakespeare's England: A Cultural Poetics* (Chicago: University of Chicago Press, 1991), 79–115, for an argument that the association of pastoral (and of *Eclogue* 2 in particular) with homoeroticism had a somewhat different force among the educated elite in Renaissance England.

16 Ann Berthoff, *The Resolved Soul: A Study of Marvell's Major Poems* (Princeton: Princeton University Press, 1970), 178, n. 38.

17 Leah S. Marcus, *The Politics of Mirth: Jonson, Herrick, Milton, Marvell, and the Defense of Old Holiday Pastimes* (Chicago: University of Chicago Press, 1986), 258. Throughout her study of *Upon Appleton House*, Marcus' perspective makes her especially alive to some of Marvell's paradoxes, while blinding her to others. She is, for example, keenly aware of the presence of particular instances of military violence in the poem, but she cannot connect these to the problems of linguistic and sexual violation that the poem also explores. And while she notices that "the supposedly antithetical realms of 'innocent' country retirement and 'corrupt' action at the nation's center keep collapsing into each another" (241), she seems unaware that similar "collapses" occur between antitheses that she herself constructs (e.g., between the present and the past). Thus, she comments that the "virtues [of Nun Appleton] are founded upon a clean break with the past" (242), and maintains that the poem ultimately bids a "final farewell" to the "ideal of perpetual retreat" (259), without noting (as the poem does) that such statements clearly reintroduce the ideals they attempt to leave behind.

18 She comments that critics who have found crucifixion imagery and "somber significance of sacrifice" in the poem are clearly "disregarding decorum, to say nothing of Marvell's wit" (Berthoff, *The Resolved Soul*, 186).

19 Patrick Cullen, *Spenser, Marvell, and Renaissance Pastoral* (Cambridge, MA: Harvard University Press, 1970), 193.

20 David M. Halperin, *Before Pastoral: Theocritus and the Ancient Tradition of Bucolic Poetry* (New Haven: Yale University Press, 1983); Halperin does, however, emphasize the "originality" and the oppositional force of Theocritus' bucolic *epos*.

21 Cf. Patterson's comments on the importance of the *Arcadia* as "a symbol of a certain type of fiction – the romance – fiction with ideological content, whose very fictionality held an interesting and provocative relation to its engagement with history" (*Censorship and Interpretation*, 24).

22 See Derrida's complex analysis of the multiple meanings of this term in "Plato's Pharmacy," in Jacques Derrida, *Dissemination*, trans. Barbara Johnson (Chicago: University of Chicago Press, 1981), 61–171.

23 In *Idyll* 11, the poet, addressing a doctor, describes the Muses as the only *pharmakon* ("medicine") for love (1, 17); the ambiguities in the term are brought out as the idyll continues. See also *Idyll* 2 (15), where the word refers to the drugs (and/or spells) of an infatuated, would-be sorceress (*pharmakeutria*). Virgil imitates *Idyll* 2 in *Eclogue* 8; compare, esp. *Id.* 2.14–16 with *Ecl.* 8.69–71.

24 Montrose, "Of Gentlemen and Shepherds," 415. Montrose is actually speaking only of "modern theories of pastoral"; he is commenting on the way in which "the study of pastoral may have become a metapastoral version of pastoral" (415). I am suggesting that most pastoral poetry is itself already "metapastoral"; cf. Harry Berger's suggestive comments on "strong pastoral" in "The Origins of Bucolic Representation: Disenchantment and Revision in Theocritus' Seventh *Idyll*," *Classical Antiquity* 3 (1984): 1–39.

1 *Bringing it all back home: bucolic and heroic in Theocritus'* Idylls

1 For notable exceptions to this approach, see Berger, "Origins," and Alpers, "Theocritean Bucolic."

2 Callimachus was well-known for his belief "that the day of full-scale epic poems on the Homeric model was over, and that what the times demanded was small-scale treatment and elaborate finish" (Gow, *Theocritus*, I, xxii). He was traditionally thought to have engaged in a famous quarrel with Apollonius of Rhodes over this matter. While recent scholarship suggests that the rivalry between the two poets may be apocryphal, the controversy itself certainly existed; see Kathryn J. Gutzwiller, *Theocritus' Pastoral Analogies: The Formation of a Genre* (Madison: University of Wisconsin Press, 1991), 144–45.

3 As David Halperin has demonstrated in *Before Pastoral*, "pastoral" functioned as a purely descriptive (rather than generic) term in classical times. Halperin argues that continuities exist among all the *Idylls*, and that Theocritus' poetry is an oppositional form of

epic (properly termed "bucolic"). Halperin's researches lend support to the conclusions I reach in this study; I would, however, argue for clearer connections between Theocritus and later poets than he allows. In order to suggest and explore these connections, I have chosen to retain the term "pastoral" as a general term for the mode, and to focus, in this chapter, on Theocritus' rustic idylls (1, 3–7, 10–11). I believe that these poems contain, in solution, the paradigmatic elements of Theocritus' poetic project – elements that are later separated out and codified (while still problematized) by pastoral poets. Cf. Gutzwiller's interesting discussion of genre formation and definition in *Theocritus' Pastoral Analogies*.

4 For further discussion of Theocritus' relation to epic, see Adam Parry, "Landscape in Greek Poetry," *Yale Classical Studies* 15 (1957): 3–29; Gilbert Lawall, *Theocritus' Coan Pastorals: A Poetry Book* (Cambridge, MA: Harvard University Press, 1967); Gianfranco Fabiano, "Fluctuation in Theocritus' Style," *Greek, Roman, and Byzantine Studies* 12 (1971): 517–37; John Van Sickle, "Epic and Bucolic," *Quaderni Urbinati di Cultura Classica* 19 (1975): 45–72.

5 Thomas G. Rosenmeyer, *The Green Cabinet: Theocritus and the European Pastoral Lyric* (Berkeley: University of California Press, 1969), 97.

6 *Ibid.*, 22–23.

7 *Ibid.*, 267.

8 *Ibid.*, 97.

9 *Ibid.*, 111–12, 265 (on *Id.* 1); 174 (on *Id.* 3); 137–38, 139, 140, 163, 188 (on *Id.* 5); 86, 191 (on *Id.* 7); 25, 56, 142, 254 (on *Id.* 10); 87–88, 102–3, 139, 165, 254 (on *Id.* 11).

10 Charles Segal, *Poetry and Myth in Ancient Pastoral: Essays on Theocritus and Virgil* (Princeton: Princeton University Press, 1981), 44, 46. Despite my disagreements with Segal, I have found his uniformly sensitive readings very helpful.

11 Elsewhere, he invokes "a profound cleavage in the nature of reality" (*Ibid.*, 45), "universal antitheses in the nature of art" (45) "an underlying harmony" (93, 219), "a cosmic order" (219), and "the larger compass of nature's rhythms" (219).

12 *Ibid.*, 225, 222.

13 See Berger's acute analysis of Segal's criticism in "Origins," 7 ff.

14 Segal, *Poetry and Myth*, 222.

15 Berger ("Origins," 9 ff.) declares his sympathy for the "ironic" approach adopted by Gary Miles in "Characterization and the Ideal of Innocence in Theocritus' *Idylls*," *Ramus* 6 (1977): 139–64. He complicates this approach considerably, however, in the course of his own analysis.

16 Segal, *Poetry and Myth*, 45.

17 These (and similar) dichotomies appear in the writings of critics as diverse as Berger ("Origins" and *Revisionary Play: Studies in the Spenserian Dynamics* [Berkeley: University of California Press, 1988], 277–89 ff.), Annabel Patterson (*Pastoral and Ideology*), and Bruce Smith (*Homosexual Desire in Shakespeare's England*, 88–89; in the pages that follow, Smith does introduce more complexity into his discussion).

18 In these lines (105–10), Daphnis seems to be simultaneously (1) reminding Aphrodite of her own ill-fated love affairs, (2) implying that the goddess is more suited to bucolic life than he is, and (3) suggesting that herdsmen can be – and have been – heroes (cf. *Id.* 3.40–51). For further discussion of the problems here (and of the various traditions surrounding Adonis and Anchises), see Gow, *Theocritus*, II, 23–24.

19 See Miles, "Characterization," 151.

20 See Segal, *Poetry and Myth*, 41, and Halperin, *Before Pastoral*, 220.

21 By explicitly juxtaposing *ad sidera* with *in silvis* (and *hinc*), Virgil effectively unpacks Theocritus' lines.

22 Theocritus' desire to focus *only* on Daphnis' self-assertive individualism is, I believe, the primary reason for his lack of clarity about the external circumstances of the herdsman's death.

23 Segal (*Poetry and Myth*, 41–42) notes Daphnis' frequent use of and association with words meaning "everything," "every," and "all"; see lines 81, 83, 102, 110, 134.

24 William Empson, *Some Versions of Pastoral* (1935; New York: New Directions, 1974), 115.

25 For an excellent analysis of the cup as an emblem for Theocritus' poetry, see Halperin, *Before Pastoral*, 161–89.

26 Cf. Rosenmeyer's comments on the function of refrains – and of repetition in general – in pastoral (*The Green Cabinet*, 94–97, 118–19). See also Gutzwiller's (somewhat differently focused) discussion of both the traditional form and the originary force of the refrain of *Idyll 1* (*Theocritus' Pastoral Analogies*, 103).

27 I have omitted Trevelyan's (modern) quotation marks.

28 Segal, *Poetry and Myth*, 41, 32.

29 Cf. Segal's interpretation of the idyll (*ibid.*, 85–106).

30 The similarity between the attitude Battos adopts here and Daphnis' stance in *Idyll 1* ("[He] still endured / His bitter love, aye, he endured it even to the fated end," 92–93) forces us to wonder to what extent Daphnis endured his lot because it was fated (cf. 141), and to what extent it was "fated" because he "endured" it. Insofar as the latter is true, the quality of

endurance, which is conventionally considered "bucolic," begins to take on a somewhat "heroic" cast, while the capacity and willingness to change one's fate seem relatively "bucolic." Cf. *Id.* 2.164: "And I will endure my misery still, even as I have borne it."

31 See Rosenmeyer on the antihierarchical nature of Theocritean figures and tropes, *The Green Cabinet*, 247–67.

32 For significantly different translations of these lines, see Gow, *Theocritus*, 1; Anna Rist, trans., *The Poems of Theocritus* (Chapel Hill: University of North Carolina Press, 1978); Anthony Holden, trans., *Greek Pastoral Poetry* (Harmondsworth: Penguin, 1974); Daryl Hine, trans., *Theocritus: Idylls and Epigrams* (New York: Atheneum, 1982). Gow provides an useful analysis of the translator's difficulties here (*Theocritus*, II, 84).

33 Segal, *Poetry and Myth*, 98.

34 Hills (or mountains) have "heroic" implications in *Idd.* 1.115, 123–25; 7.45, 51, 74, 148–53; 11.25–27; cf. Segal, *Poetry and Myth*, 202, 225–26. The wound of a thorn is clearly associated with the pains of love in *Id.* 10.4.

35 Rosenmeyer, *The Green Cabinet*, 279; see also 247–82.

36 Cf. Gutzwiller's discussion of the simultaneously "mimetic" and "analogic" nature of the *Idylls* in *Theocritus' Pastoral Analogies*.

37 Segal, *Poetry and Myth*, 100.

38 In addition to the examples given throughout this chapter, one might consider the following two series: the goatherd, the boy with the cage for cicadas, the cicadas (*Idyll* 1); Daphnis and Damoetas, Polyphemus, Polyphemus' dog (*Idyll* 6; here, the concern with "mirror images" is made explicit [35–41]).

39 For an analysis of our simultaneous experience of distance from and identification with the Cyclops, see Edward W. Spofford, "Theocritus and Polyphemus," *American Journal of Philology* 90 (1969): 22–35.

40 John Van Sickle, "The Fourth Pastoral Poems of Virgil and Theocritus," *Atti e Memorie dell' Arcadia*, ser. 3a, vol. 5, fasc. 1 (1969): 146.

41 Satyrs and Pans, of course, represent "bucolic" qualities, rather than the conventionally heroic ones exemplified by Herakles; the fact that Battos holds them up as a standard of excellence (in words that recall Korydon's reference to Herakles) is therefore itself an instance of the bucolic perspective displacing – and in the process effectively becoming – a heroic model.

42 See, in this context, Rosenmeyer's comments on the progressive actualization of the *locus amoenus* in *Idyll* 7 (*The Green Cabinet*, 187–88).

43 As a result of Cheiron's invitation, the centaurs became drunk, a battle ensued, and Cheiron himself was wounded; Polyphemus' drunkenness resulted, of course, in his blinding. It is significant that neither of these incidents is explicitly mentioned: the limits of Theocritean pastoral will not permit a direct confrontation with the tragedies of the heroic world (cf. *Idylls* 6 and 11; all other versions of the Polyphemus–Galateia story seem to have included the encounter with Odysseus [Gow, *Theocritus*, II, 118]). But while the "heroic" feelings in this passage are somewhat muted, they are still stronger than those expressed earlier in the idyll; and they are further emphasized by the reappearance of steep mountains here. For other interpretations of the significance of this moment, see Segal, *Poetry and Myth*, 154–55; Miles, "Characterization," 158; Rosenmeyer, *The Green Cabinet*, 191; Berger, "Origins," 8.

44 Cf. Halperin's discussion of the role of love in the *Idylls* in *Before Pastoral*, 243.

45 Rosenmeyer, *The Green Cabinet*, 81.

46 These ambiguities are given a distinctively pastoral cast in the narrator's conclusion, "Well, thus it was that Polyphemus shepherded (*epoimainen*) his love / With song ... (80–81); cf. Alpers, *Singer*, 123.

47 It therefore seems appropriate that the two speakers are (working) reapers rather than shepherds. But the attitudes they assume are clearly continuous with those expressed by Theocritus' other rustics. Bucaeus is a typical foolish, lovelorn swain (cf. *Idyll* 3), and Milon represents a version of the bucolic perspective at its most extreme: he is, in effect, the first critic to denounce a recognizable form of pastoral as "antipastoral."

48 I follow Gow, who explains that when Milon addresses his partner as "Bucaeus," he is clearly calling him by name, and that "Battos" (which Trevelyan uses) was supplied by the scribes of the manuscripts from *Idyll* 4 (*Theocritus*, II, 193). It is, of course, significant that the lovesick reaper is given a name that means "cowherd."

49 See Alpers, "Theocritean Bucolic," 25, and Berger, "Origins," for somewhat different perspectives on the myth of origins that this poem provides.

50 Simichidas was traditionally identified with Theocritus – an identification that lost much of its force when more recent critics realized that the narrator's position was "ironized." I would suggest that the combination of irony and identification evident in the presentation of Simichidas is in fact typical (in differing degrees) of all Theocritus' representations, and does not *ipso facto* undermine Simichidas' status as a self-representation – although it

does problematize the notion of self-representation itself. For further discussion of this problem, see Rosenmeyer, *The Green Cabinet*, 63; Segal, *Poetry and Myth*, 167–75; Berger, "Origins," 15 ff.; Alpers, "Theocritean Bucolic," 23. See also my discussion in chapter 4 of *Upon Appleton House*, in which Marvell's similarly problematic representation of himself as the narrator occasions a host of similar critical arguments.

51 "First" (50) is Trevelyan's addition, but it captures the spirit of the line: Gow explains that "I will begin" is understood, but that "Lycidas breaks off in favour of a less self-assertive expression of his intention" (*Theocritus*, II, 144). "Worked out" (51) translates *exeponasa*, the root of which is *ponos*, "toil"; on *ponos* in *Idyll* 7, see Segal, *Poetry and Myth*, 229, and Berger, "Origins," 16–19.

52 See Segal, *Poetry and Myth*, 119–23; cf. Halperin's comments on Theocritus' use of the "traditional hierarchy" of herdsmen in *Idyll* 1 (*Before Pastoral*, 182).

53 Berger, "Origins," 17.

54 Compare this passage (and the speeches of Theocritus' more ordinary men) with the end of the "Lament for Bion"; note the changes in the mood of the verbs:

> But I weep for this sorrow and lament thy death. And if I could, I too as Orpheus, as once Odysseus, and ere them Alcides, would have gone down to Tartarus and entered the halls of Pluteus to see thee, and if for Pluteus thou makest music, to hear what thy music is. Nay, come sing to the Maid some song of Sicily and make her sweet rustic melody. She too is Sicilian and sported on the shores of Etna. She knows the Dorian strain. Not unrewarded shall thy music be, and as of old she gave Eurydice to Orpheus' sweet harping, back, Bion, to thy hills she will send thee too. And if my piping also anything availed, before Pluteus I myself would sing. (114–26; A. S. F. Gow, trans., *The Greek Bucolic Poets* [Cambridge: Cambridge University Press, 1953].)

See also Milton, "L'Allegro," 145–50.

55 Berger, "Origins," 34.

56 See Hesiod, *Theogony*, 22–23. As numerous critics have noted, the entire idyll is an adaptation of Hesiod's initiation; see, e.g., Van Sickle, "Epic and Bucolic," 60. But Simichidas' allusion to the *Theogony* seems, in particular, to be a self-conscious imitation of a "heroic" model (as well as of Lycidas' speeches).

57 Simichidas' final lines may be compared to Korydon's advice to Battos (4.56–57): he does not hope that "unlovely things" will be eliminated, merely that they may be "kept afar." Segal remarks that "the familiar situation of the desperately unhappy, suffering lover [Molon] is still present at the end of his song" (*Poetry and*

Myth, 140), and criticizes Simichidas as a result. Note also the appearance of the heroic word "alone" in this context (125; "*eis* = in effect *monos*," Gow, *Theocritus*, II, 162).

58 Berger, "Origins," 15, n. 28, provides a list of the numerous negative critical evaluations of Simichidas.

59 For a different interpretation of this incident, see Berger, "Origins," 25.

2 Si numquam fallit imago: *Virgil's revision of Theocritus*

1 This line can also be translated "From that time, Corydon has been Corydon [i.e., peerless] to us"; Servius interpreted it in this manner. See Robert Coleman, ed., *Vergil: Eclogues* (Cambridge: Cambridge University Press, 1977), 22, and T. E. Page, ed., *P. Vergili Maronis Bucolica et Georgica* (London: Macmillan, 1931), 155. Page points out that the line is a revision of *Id.* 8.92, "Thenceforth among the shepherds Daphnis became the first," in which, he explains, "[first] is equivalent to Virgil's second *Corydon.*"

2 "Whither by noon, Simichidas, are you toiling along thus, / When even the very lizard in the stone wall is asleep, / And the tomb-crested larks no more are flitting to and fro?" (21–23).

3 Alpers, *Singer*, 121; see also Brooks Otis, *Virgil: A Study in Civilized Poetry* (Oxford: Clarendon Press, 1963), 124.

4 This awareness is most explicit in *Eclogue* 1 (see, e.g., lines 3, 49–50, 55 ff., 62, 67 ff.); but it is present, to varying degrees, in all the *Eclogues*.

5 See, e.g., 2.49, 5.31 (*intexo*); 2.72 (*detexo*); 9.41, 10.72 (*texo*). For similar images (mingling, mixing, etc.), see 2.45, 4.15–16, 19–20, 5.3, 8.13. Alpers defines this process as "suspension" in *Singer*, 97–98.

6 See particularly *Eclogues* 6 and 8, in which the poet begins by calling attention to the limits of his pastoral song.

7 Virgil's use of *mecum* here (rather than *mihi*) is somewhat problematic; editors often suggest that the word implies that the cicadas provide Corydon with "company": see Coleman, *Vergil*, 93–94, and Page, *Bucolica*, 103–04. Page also notes that "the word is thrown forward to mark the antithesis with the preceding line." The stressed first syllable of the word, I believe, makes this antithesis seem stronger, and permits Virgil to create and then undermine an impression of total isolation (thus replicating in miniature the effect of the passage as a whole).

8 Coleman (*Vergil*, 93–94) and Page (*Bucolica*, 104) go to great

lengths to emphasize the "shrill," "oppressive," "restless" sound of the cicadas; but Coleman also comments on "the traditional esteem in which their sound was held" (94) and cites (among other examples) *Idd.* 1.148, 7.138–39.

9 Coleman comments that *Idyll* 7 is specifically recalled here by "the presence of Lycidas, the encounter on a journey and numerous echoes in detail (at 1, 32–36, 42, 59–61, 64) which keep the Greek poem constantly in our minds" (*Vergil*, 273); the attempt to replace a superior singer is further reminiscent of the similar attempt in *Idyll* 4, although the similarity is not often noted.

10 In the first set of "matched" traditional and contemporary songs (23–25, 26–29), we are asked to look to the future, and to await the resolution of some activity or event (Tityrus' return, Mantua's survival, and the completion of the song). In the second set (39–43, 46–50), our attention is focused on the "here-and-now," as the speakers create different versions of the pastoral *locus amoenus* (in the last passage, this focus on the present is seen as assuring future well-being).

11 Before the song is repeated, Virgil once again opposes and balances its individual and communal aspects; Lycidas declares: *numeros memini, si verba teneram* (45, "I recall the tune, if only I can the words"). Cf. Wordsworth, "The Solitary Reaper."

12 Cf. Alpers, *Singer*, 240.

13 I use this term (and "sentimental," below) in Schiller's sense; see Friedrich von Schiller, *Naive and Sentimental Poetry and On the Sublime*, trans. Julius A. Elias (New York: Frederick Ungar, 1975). Schiller explains that, while "naive" poetry is an imitation of actuality, "sentimental" poetry derives its force from a sense of felt separation from the actual; it is self-conscious and self-reflexive, concerned with representing ideas rather than "simple" reality. Theocritus, of course, can be considered "naive" only in comparison to Virgil and later pastoralists: he is himself a "sentimental" poet.

Schiller's opposition is clearly problematic; it serves as the basis for modern idealizing approaches to pastoral (see Alpers, "Schiller's *Naive and Sentimental Poetry*"). But like the opposition between "pastoral" and "antipastoral," it also clearly responds to contradictions that pervade the mode: I have found Schiller's categories – and his notion of the "sentimental," in particular – quite useful in thinking about the problems that are posed by the self-conscious metaphoricity of much pastoral poetry (especially the poetry of Virgil and Marvell).

14 Michael C. J. Putnam, in *Virgil's Pastoral Art: Studies in the Eclogues* (Princeton: Princeton University Press, 1970), points out that

"Virgil is using a familiar word from Cicero for the rhetorically uncouth" (85). *Condere*, as Page notes, "is regularly used of 'putting together' or 'composing' a poem" (*Bucolica*, 103; cf. *Ecl.* 6.7, 10.50).

15 Eleanor Winsor Leach, *Vergil's Eclogues: Landscapes of Experience* (Ithaca: Cornell University Press, 1974), 147. Leach concludes that "the song is inappropriate to the singer because it serves Vergil's purpose rather than Corydon's; it is a *reductio ad absurdum* of the pastoral tradition that preceded the *Eclogue* book" (150). Harry Berger presents a more persuasive version of this argument in an unpublished essay on the *Eclogues* (hereafter cited as "*Eclogues*").

16 Marvell, "The Mower against Gardens," 24.

17 This opposition is set up in the first two words of the poem, *formosum pastor*; see Coleman's comments on the word order of the first line (*Vergil*, 91). See also my discussion, below, of *formosus* ("finely formed," "beautiful") and *sordidus* ("dirty," "mean," "despicable"), the terms in which, I believe, Corydon conceives the opposition.

18 See, e.g., Leach, *Vergil's Eclogues*, 146–52; Berger, "*Eclogues*," 28–32; Patterson, *Pastoral and Ideology*, 5 ff.; and W. R. Johnson, *The Idea of the Lyric: Lyric Modes in Ancient and Modern Poetry* (Berkeley: University of California Press, 1982), 163–66. Johnson feels that the failure here is ultimately Virgil's.

19 Putnam notes that this phrase is "ambiguous": "The *studium* is Corydon's fruitless passion for Alexis, but the fact remains that both these words frequently appear in technical rhetorical vocabulary as well" (*Virgil's Pastoral Art*, 86). Cf. Leach, *Vergil's Eclogues*, 146. The coincidence of art and desire that the phrase suggests will be viewed in a more positive light as the poem progresses (largely because Corydon himself realizes that it exists), and, as a result, this early criticism begins to take on an added resonance similar to that of Shakespeare's line, "the truest poetry is the most faining" (*As You Like It*, 3.3.16–17; I quote from William Shakespeare, *The Complete Works*, ed. Alfred Harbage *et al.* [Baltimore: Penguin, 1969], because the spelling in this edition suggests the pun in the line).

20 In Theocritus' poetry, Daphnis' status was, of course, largely dependent on the fact that, unlike Corydon (but like his comic opposite and equivalent Polyphemus), he claimed to be self-defining (see ch. 1, above).

21 *Idyll* 6 is explicitly concerned with mirror-images, and this concern is evident in the lines following those I have quoted (37–40). But Theocritus does not have the investment in – or the resultant

anxiety about – the veracity of these images that Virgil does; and Polyphemus is not even aware that this is an issue.

22 See Patterson's different interpretation of the resonance of this phrase in *Pastoral and Ideology* (5).

23 In line 19, Corydon laments, *despectus tibi sum, nec qui sim quaeris, Alexi* ("You scorn me, never asking who I am"); he then begins to explain (and, in the process, to construct) "who he is." Cf. "Damon the Mower," 39–40 ff.

24 William Empson, *Seven Types of Ambiguity*, 3rd edn. (New York: New Directions, 1966), 114.

25 As Virgil's editors often note, the precise opposite of *sordidus* is *nitidus* ("shining, bright, clear"; fig., "cultivated, polished, refined"); see Coleman, *Vergil*, 98, and Page, *Bucolica*, 106. Page also points out that *sordidus* can have positive connotations (e.g., "natural") as well as negative ones.

26 Cf. Putnam, *Virgil's Pastoral Art*, 103–06; Alpers, *Singer*, 122.

27 Alpers, *Singer*, 122–23.

28 In discussing the multiple meanings of these lines, Putnam points out that "*detexere*, which means, literally, to finish off by weaving ... can also be synonymous for 'write,' usually defining the completion of a work, whether prose or verse" (*Virgil's Pastoral Art*, 113).

29 *Idyll* 11, in contrast, ends with Theocritus speaking in his own voice.

30 The identity of Perimede is uncertain; she is mentioned in conjunction with Medea by Propertius. See Gow, *Theocritus*, 11, 39.

31 Cf. Putnam, *Virgil's Pastoral Art*, 280–81.

32 The word that Alpers renders as "incantations" (*cantando*) can be translated literally, "by singing."

33 The two invocations are not, however, exactly alike. The moon is much more clearly humanized; Simaitha addresses it as a partner in a conversation: "Bethink thee of my love and whence it came, O holy Moon." It seems significant that this address begins after her actual human companion has left; she declares: "Now that I am alone, whence am I to bewail my love?" (64). She is, in fact, incapable of imagining herself "alone."

34 Virgil himself does appeal to the Muses (as well as to Pollio, earlier):

> Haec Damon; vos, quae responderit Alphesiboeus,
> dicite, Pierides: non omnia possumus omnes.   (62–63)

> Thus, Damon; what Alphesibee replied
> Sing, Muses: all things lie not in our power.

But his appeal also explicitly focuses on the question of the powers and the limitations of the artist.

35 The difficulties we experience in separating the sorceress' fantasies from reality are essentially the same as those we face if we attempt to ascertain who speaks the final line – is it spoken by a "real" person or a fictional character? And similar difficulties recur throughout the eclogue. After Virgil's description of the morning (14–16), for example, the first singer begins with an invocation of Lucifer (17); it seems clear, at this point, that the invocation should be assigned to the speaker himself, but the following lines make it equally clear that it is spoken by the character he is impersonating.

36 For a different interpretation of these lines, see Patterson, *Pastoral and Ideology*, 5.

3 *Pastime and passion: the impasse in the* Old Arcadia

1 Unless otherwise noted, all references to Sidney's *Arcadia* in this chapter are to the *Old Arcadia*. I am not, of course, suggesting that the original version of Sidney's romance had a significant influence on contemporary pastoral; manuscripts of the *Old Arcadia* were not discovered until this century. In her introduction, Jean Robertson comments that "it seems likely" that Spenser saw some portion of the work during his residence at Leicester House (*OA*, xix); she later adds that "the only works of fiction that show any signs of their authors' having seen a manuscript of the *Old Arcadia* are the pastoral tales of Lodge and Greene" (xxxvii). I discuss the relation between the *Old Arcadia* and the revised text in more detail below.

2 *Apology*, 104, 100.

3 Sannazaro and Montemayor were, of course, only the most influential (from Sidney's perspective) of the continental pastoralists. See Walter R. Davis, "A Map of Arcadia: Sidney's Romance in Its Tradition," in Walter R. Davis and Richard A. Lanham, *Sidney's Arcadia*, Yale Studies in English, vol. 158 (New Haven: Yale University Press, 1965), 7–44, for a concise (if somewhat oversimplified) history of the development of the Renaissance pastoral romance. For two recent, contrasting views of Sidney's relation to the pastoral tradition, see Lindenbaum, *Changing Landscapes*, and Robert E. Stillman, *Sidney's Poetic Justice: The Old Arcadia, Its Eclogues, and Renaissance Pastoral Traditions* (Lewisburg, PA: Bucknell University Press, 1986).

4 *Apology*, 133.

5 It was Virgil, of course, who first placed pastoral in Arcadia (see

Ecl. 7.4; 10.13–15, 31–33). But Sannazaro's romance both transformed the Arcadian setting and popularized it among Renaissance pastoralists; see Rosenmeyer, *The Green Cabinet*, 231–46, and Coleman, *Vergil*, 22, 207–09. For more detailed analyses of Sannazaro's work, see David Kalstone, *Sidney's Poetry: Contexts and Interpretations* (Cambridge, MA: Harvard University Press, 1965), ch. 1; William J. Kennedy, *Jacopo Sannazaro and the Uses of Pastoral* (Hanover, NH: University Press of New England, 1983); and David Quint, *Origin and Originality in Renaissance Literature: Versions of the Source* (New Haven: Yale University Press, 1983), ch. 3.

6 The final two eclogues were probably written somewhat later than the first ten; see Quint, *Origin and Originality*, 49 ff., for an interesting discussion of the critical and textual problems they pose.

7 All quotation of Sannazaro's *Arcadia* follows the text of *Opere di Iacopo Sannazaro*, ed. Enrico Carrara (Turin: Tipografia Torinese, 1952); English translations are from Jacopo Sannazaro, *Arcadia & Piscatorial Eclogues*, trans. Ralph Nash (Detroit: Wayne State University Press, 1966).

8 Kalstone, *Sidney's Poetry*, 34.

9 See Nash's comments in Sannazaro, *Arcadia and Piscatorial Eclogues*, 12.

10 Kalstone comments: "Though lovers complain, Sannazaro's governing response appears to be 'i sospiri si convertirono in dolce suono' [153] – sighs transform themselves into sweet sound" (*Sidney's Poetry*, 23).

11 Sannazaro is clearly aware of the paradoxes in classical pastoral. In Virgil's eighth eclogue, for example, a shepherd had ended a list of *adynata* with the impossible condition that "Tityrus [Virgil's "accepted" persona] / In woods be Orpheus and on waves Arion" (*sit Tityrus Orpheus, / Orpheus in silvis, inter delphinas Arion*, 55–56); one of Sannazaro's shepherds, Ergasto, transforms this into the similarly "unimaginable" condition that "Ergasto [will] outdo Tityrus in rhyme" (*Ergasto vincerà Titiro in rime*, *Ecl.* 4.63), thereby confronting us with a tradition of pastoral succession that is based on each singer's acknowledgment of his inability to replace his predecessors. But the primary reaction that Sannazaro elicits here is admiration for his own cleverness; it is not essentially different from the response he calls forth in the *Piscatorial Eclogues* when he changes Virgil's *non ego Daphnin / iudice te metuam* (2.26–27; "I would not fear to / Compete for you with Daphnis") to *Non ego delphinis* [dolphins], *te judice*... (*Ecl.* 5.107 in *Arcadia & Piscatorial Eclogues*).

12 Davis, "A Map of Arcadia," 22–23.

13 See, e.g., *OA*, 9, 41, 46, 84, 91. For a different interpretation of Sidney's preoccupation with "pastime," see Patterson, *Censorship and Interpretation*, 24–43.

14 *OED*, "pastime," 2.

15 Cf. the *Apology*, 100.

16 In the narrative, by contrast, rusticity is represented by Dametas and his family of louts. I do not, of course, mean to suggest that the shepherds' songs in the eclogues are simply idyllic; for a complex analysis of how they reflect the problems of the romance as a whole, see Richard C. McCoy, *Sir Philip Sidney: Rebellion in Arcadia* (New Brunswick, NJ: Rutgers University Press, 1979), 47–54. See also Stillman's extended discussion in *Poetic Justice*.

17 His lament is balanced by the speeches of Pyrocles ("Cleophila"), which enumerate the constraints of a courtier's life. The arguments that both speakers advance are complicated – and reinforced – by the fact they are implicitly discussing the advantages and limitations of their different disguises. In this eclogue, the princes conclude that the "shepherd's" lot, while unsatisfactory, is preferable.

18 Ringler, *Poems*, 419.

19 Sannazaro's principal model is the "Lament for Bion" (attributed to Moschus), which is itself indebted to Theocritus' first idyll. The traditional apotheosis of the departed seems to owe its existence to Virgil's "unpacking" of Theocritus in *Eclogue* 5: whereas in *Idyll* 1, Daphnis lives again as Thyrsis laments his passing, in *Eclogue* 5, Daphnis is first mourned and then apotheosized by two different singers. See also Quint, *Origin and Originality*, 52–60.

20 After describing his mother's eternal life in heaven, Sannazaro's singer concludes:

> Ove, se 'l viver mio pur si prolunga
>   tanto che, com'io bramo, ornar ti possa
>   e da tal voglia il ciel non mi disgiunga,
> spero che sovra te non avrà possa
>   quel duro, eterno, inecitabil sonno
>   d'averti chiusa in così poca fossa;
> se tanto i versi miei prometter ponno.   (*Ecl.* 11.154–160)

> Whereupon – if my life be yet prolonged
>   so far that I can adorn you as I wish,
>   and Heaven not disjoin me from such will –
> that harsh unwakable and eternal sleep
>   I trust will not have power over you
>   to keep you close, within so narrow trench:
> if thus much promise my verse have power to make.

His final line imitates the conclusion of the "Lament for Bion."

21 In the *Old Arcadia*, the singers of this poem, Strephon and Klaius, are identified as "two gentlemen" who have taken on the shepherd's "trade of life" for the love of Urania, "thought a shepherd's daughter, but indeed of far greater birth" (328). In the revised version, they have become real shepherds who are, however, said to be "beyond the rest by so much, as learning commonlie doth adde to nature" (27). Their new status is characteristic of the *New Arcadia*: while the distinctions between courtier and shepherd are still fairly rigid here, they are noticeably less so than in the *Old Arcadia*. This difference, I believe, results from Sidney's shift in focus in the revised version: he no longer identifies the dilemmas he is exploring so closely with pastoral, and he is less interested in the problems that the genre itself presents.

22 The context forces us to remember the word's meaning as a noun ("a phrase or verse recurring at intervals, esp. at the end of each stanza of a poem or song," *OED*) which Sidney probably saw as related to its more usual verbal meaning, "restrain." Cf. the song-contest between Plangus and Boulon, in which Sidney similarly seems to activate both meanings of the word (146.30; see also Boulon's conclusion, 152.1–12).

23 McCoy offers an interesting and illuminating perspective on the courtiers' (and Sidney's) self-division in *Sir Philip Sidney*; see also A. C. Hamilton, *Sir Philip Sidney: A Study in His Life and Works* (Cambridge: Cambridge University Press, 1977), 45.'

24 For a somewhat different interpretation of the connection between Philisides and the rebels see Robert E. Stillman, "The Politics of Sidney's Pastoral: Mystification and Mythology in *The Old Arcadia*," *ELH* 52 (1985): 802.

25 The ambiguous, reflecting pronouns here emphasize the inter-reflection that exists between the two characters.

26 In an unpublished essay, Christopher P. Motley discusses Sidney's reliance on overhearing, and contrasts the responses of the characters in the *Arcadia* to songs (overheard and otherwise) with those of the characters in the *Diana* ("Crossing the Threshold: Public Form and Private Meaning in Sidney's *Arcadia*," 22–25). I am indebted to Motley's perceptions.

27 All references to the *Diana* follow the text of Judith M. Kennedy, ed., *A Critical Edition of Yong's Translation of George of Montemayor's Diana and Gil Polo's Enamoured Diana* (Oxford: Clarendon Press, 1968).

28 This song – which also mentions reflection – explicitly balances "staying" and "parting"; and the narrative that follows calls our

attention to the temporary halting of movement that is occurring: "After *Sylvanus* had made an ende of *Dianas* amorous song, he saide to *Syrenus* ... When faire *Diana* was singing this song, ... I came to the place where she was. *Syrenus* interrupting him at these wordes, saide, Stay a little *Sylvanus* ..." (23). Compare the different force of the "interruptions" in Sidney's text.

29 It seems likely that Sidney is playing on this motif when he describes Gynecia remembering an appropriate "old song" – which she had no leisure to sing (123).

30 Here, as before, the princes' emotions are externalized in a frightening fashion: Gynecia "rise[s] up" and fixes the prince with "her piercing lover's eye" and Pyrocles attempts, unsuccessfully, to "withdraw" (183). The confusion of sexual roles, which terrifies Pyrocles in these scenes, becomes appealing in his scenes with Philoclea.

31 In *As You Like It*, Shakespeare makes the distinctions between the two types of overhearing we have been considering clear. In the scenes at court, overhearing is connected to individual motives and plots, and to the movement of the drama: Duke Frederick learns of Rosalind's affection for Orlando through the report of an overheard conversation, and he is thus aided in his search for his runaway daughter (2.2); Orlando learns of Oliver's plot against him in a similar manner, and he decides to leave court as a result (2.3). When movement is suspended in the forest of Arden, however, overhearing – though frequent – has no serious consequences in the "real world": it serves primarily to uncover emotions shared by all the characters ("Alas, poor shepherd, searching of thy wound, / I have by hard adventure found mine own," 2.4.44–45).

32 Neil Rudenstine, *Sidney's Poetic Development* (Cambridge, MA: Harvard University Press, 1967), 47–52.

33 See the *Apology*, 106–11, 125.

34 In the initial debate between Pyrocles and Musidorus, for example, Pyrocles admits that he has been defeated by his cousin's rational arguments; he ultimately triumphs, however, by first tearfully appealing to Musidorus' affection for him and then swooning (24–25). Musidorus' witty comment on one of Pyrocles' speeches seems particularly significant in this context: "I give you leave, sweet Pyrocles, ever to defend solitariness so long as, to defend it, you ever keep company" (16). Similarly, after listening to Philoclea's (admirable) arguments against suicide, Pyrocles is "not so much persuaded as delighted by her well conceived and sweetly pronounced speeches" (298); he accedes to her point of

view only when she threatens to kill herself. See Nancy Lindheim's excellent discussion of this scene in *The Structures of Sidney's Arcadia* (Toronto: University of Toronto Press, 1982), 137–38. In his Eclogues, Sidney makes it particularly clear that his characters' responses to songs depend on their feelings about the singers.

35 Musidorus similarly "reveals" his identity to Pamela by present-ing himself – even more obviously – as the hero of a romance (103–06); he asks her, in effect, to "pitie the tale of [him]" (*AS* 45.14).

36 Cf. Ronald Levao, *Renaissance Minds and Their Fictions: Cusanus, Sidney, Shakespeare* (Berkeley: University of California Press, 1985), 189. As Levao points out, Sidney emphasizes this situation by telling us that "Cleophila" would "often ... speak to the image of Philoclea (which lived and ruled in the highest of her inward part) and use vehement oaths and protestations unto her" (*OA*, 212). Pyrocles also makes a speech to himself which is addressed first to "Pyrocles," then to "Love," then to "Pyrocles" again, and finally to "Philoclea" (97); and Philoclea similarly switches abruptly from "O Philoclea" to "O prince Pyrocles" when she is privately lamenting her lover's apparent betrayal (210). In all these passages, and in his comments on the young lovers' relationship, Sidney appears to be remembering – and gently mocking – pastoral love songs like *Idyll* 11 and *Eclogue* 2.

37 The harmony of the "Pygmalion" scene itself is disrupted first by Gynecia and then by Phagonian rebels; see McCoy, *Sir Philip Sidney*, 114–15. See also Elizabeth Dipple, "Harmony and Pastoral in the *Old Arcadia*," *ELH* 35 (1968): 309–28, for a discussion of the movement in the *Arcadia* "from literary stasis to the dynamic flux of realistic examination, from the timeless world of pastoral to the world of hopelessly flawed character and action" (320).

38 Rudenstine bases his characterization on "the particular kinds of rhetorical heightening" in the passage, which, he argues, "are precisely those Sidney associated most intimately with lyric poetry"; he feels that Sidney is demonstrating – and celebrating – the fact that Pyrocles is "no longer respond[ing] in terms of Musidorus' heroic code, but ... react[ing] in a way that can only be called poetic" (*Sidney's Poetic Development*, 20). I would agree that poetry as well as love is being tested here, but I believe that Sidney's evaluation of that test is less positive than Rudenstine's analysis suggests.

39 Throughout the *Old Arcadia*, Sidney appears to be playing on the words "contentation," "contention," and "contentment": the similarities among them (like the double meaning of "refrain")

seem to suggest to him the ways in which pastoral consolations are inevitably involved with their antitheses. Many instances of their use are excised from the revised version (compare, e.g., *OA*, 3.1–14 with its revision *NA*, 19).

40 Interestingly, the scribe of one of the manuscripts of the *Old Arcadia* misread "contention" here as "contentation"; in another manuscript, "contentation" is corrected to "contention" (see Robertson's textual note, *OA*, 46). The phrase does not appear in the *New Arcadia*.

41 Consider, for example, the following description:

> Cleophila, seeing how greedily the lion went after the prey she herself desired [i.e., Philoclea], it seemed all her spirits were kindled with an unwonted fire; so that, equalling the lion in swiftness, she overtook him as he was ready to have seized himself of his beautiful chase, and disdainfully saying "are you become my competitor?" – strake him so great a blow upon the shoulder that she almost cleaved him asunder. (47)

42 The parenthetical phrase (which, significantly, focuses on reflection) also imitates the interruption; cf. the parallel phrase in Musidorus' "enactment" of this scene, below.

43 C. S. Lewis has condemned this scene as incredible: "We cannot suspend our disbelief in a Musidorus who commits indecent assaults" (*English Literature in the Sixteenth Century Excluding Drama* [Oxford: Clarendon Press, 1954], 332). I would argue, on the contrary, that it is one of Sidney's greatest successes: we are compelled, simultaneously, to abhor Musidorus' actions and to see them as the inescapable consequence of desires with which we have sympathized; the impasse that Sidney creates for his readers here parallels the one that Musidorus himself experiences.

44 Lindheim, *The Structures of Sidney's Arcadia*, 33–41. Lindheim is speaking about the *New Arcadia*, but many of her comments suggest that she believes that a similar, less successfully realized idea underlies the original version.

45 *Ibid.*, 34, 40.

46 McCoy, *Sir Philip Sidney*, 27; cf. Franco Marenco, "Double Plot in Sidney's Old 'Arcadia,'" in *Essential Articles for the Study of Sir Philip Sidney*, ed. Arthur F. Kinney (Hamden, CT: Archon Books, 1986), 287–310.

47 Ringler, *Poems*, 418, quoted in McCoy, *Sir Philip Sidney*, 45.

48 See, e.g., Patterson, *Censorship and Interpretation*, 34; Hamilton, *Sir Philip Sidney*, 35; Robertson, *OA*, 430; and Lindenbaum, *Changing Landscapes*, 29–30.

49 Sannazaro also creates other self-representations (e.g., Ergasto);

but his various personae (unlike Sidney's) are not relegated to clearly separated fictional domains.

50 McCoy, *Sir Philip Sidney*, 45.

51 For an argument (unpersuasive, to my mind) that Sidney's narrator should be considered "unreliable," see Richard A. Lanham, "The Old *Arcadia*," in Davis and Lanham, *Sidney's Arcadia*, 181–405.

52 Rudenstine, *Sidney's Poetic Development*, ch. 7, title.

53 The obvious parallels between the princes and Philisides are matched by those between the princes and Sidney; both Rudenstine (*Sidney's Poetic Development*, 16–22) and McCoy (*Sir Philip Sidney*, 54 ff.) have noted that Pyrocles' speeches are often strikingly similar to Sidney's letters (as well as to his other writings). And Sidney's narrator does, of course, evince especial affection for Philoclea (see esp. *OA*, 108). At least one early reader seems to have identified Philoclea with Stella (whom she physically resembles): Sir John Harington "headed his transcript of *AS* x 'To the beauty of the world'" (Robertson, *OA*, 419), using a phrase that describes Philoclea in the *Old Arcadia* (9).

54 Sidney does identify himself with other characters as well (e.g., Philanax; cf. Patterson, *Censorship and Interpretation*, 34–35). It could, in fact, be argued that most of the major characters are, to a certain extent, self-reflections; the number of names beginning with "Phil" is remarkable, even considering the Greek setting. Cf. *Astrophil and Stella*, in which Stella (= *sidus*, star), as well as Astrophil, is clearly imagined as a reflection of the author.

55 As Sidney later makes clear (328 ff.), Philisides, like the other "stranger shepherds" (245), is actually a gentleman in exile.

56 Cf. "Dametas'" and Musidorus' blazons – and the action that follows them.

57 This is a characteristic pun; cf. the "slackness" of the narrator's "pen" to "come to [Philoclea's] woes" (108). A comparable pun (suggesting a similar dilemma) is present, I believe, in Sidney's famous discussion of the "infected will" and the "erected wit" in the *Apology* (101): if the wit cannot affect the will and the world, it is clearly impotent, and the writer's pen is slack; insofar as the wit is truly potent ("erected" in all senses), and enacts its visions in the external world, it necessarily becomes infected by that which it attempts to cure (for "wit" and "will" as "penis," see Stephen Booth, ed., *Shakespeare's Sonnets* [New Haven: Yale University Press, 1977], 177, 466; on "pen," see 270). An understanding of this dilemma, I believe, does much to explain Sidney's tendency to make phallic jokes at moments of high seriousness.

58 All quotation of *The Faerie Queene* follows the text of J. C. Smith (Oxford: Clarendon Press, 1909), rpt. in Edmund Spenser, *The Faerie Queene*, ed. A. C. Hamilton (London: Longman, 1977).

59 He had often implicitly connected the "good fortune" of his characters with self-conscious artistic manipulation (see particularly Calepine's adventure with the baby, the bear, and the wife of Sir Bruin [canto 4]). In his description of Melibee's relation to Pastorella, he explicitly links these two ideas: the old shepherd, we are told, was not really her father, "but as old stories tell / Found her by fortune, which to him befell" (9.14).

60 See also Harry Berger's analysis of the simile and the episode as a whole in "A Secret Discipline: *The Faerie Queene*, Book VI," in *Form and Convention in the Poetry of Edmund Spenser*, ed. William Nelson (New York: Columbia University Press, 1961), 35–75, rpt. in Berger, *Revisionary Play*, 215–42.

61 See, e.g., Stephen J. Greenblatt, "Sidney's *Arcadia* and the Mixed Mode," *Studies in Philology* 70 (1973): 278; Margaret E. Dana, "The Providential Plot of the *Old Arcadia*," *Comparative Literature* 25 (1973): 54–57; Jon S. Lawry, *Sidney's Two Arcadias: Pattern and Proceeding* (Ithaca: Cornell University Press, 1972), 149; Hamilton, *Sir Philip Sidney*, 55–56; McCoy, *Sir Philip Sidney*, 124 ff.; Levao, *Renaissance Minds and Their Fictions*, 206–07. Ever since Fulke Greville (in *The Life of the Renowned Sir Philip Sidney*, ed. Nowell Smith [Oxford: Clarendon Press, 1907], 13–15), there have, of course, been readers who have wholly agreed with Euarchus' perspective. Marenco's interpretation of the romance in "Double Plot," for example, implies such agreement, although he avoids discussing the ending; see also Davis, "A Map of *Arcadia*," 160 ff. The continued controversy surrounding the trial scene and conclusion, however, provides sufficient evidence of the discomfort these events occasion.

62 See Hamilton, *Sir Philip Sidney*, 49.

63 Heliodorus, *An Aethiopian History*, ed. Charles Whibley, trans. Thomas Underdowne (1895; New York: AMS Press, 1967).

64 Critical discussions of the conclusion often inadvertently use or suggest Musidorus' antithetical terms; see esp. Peter Lindenbaum, "Sidney's *Arcadia*: The Endings of the Three Versions," *Huntington Library Quarterly* 34 (1970/71): 208; Elizabeth Dipple, "Unjust Justice in the *Old Arcadia*," *Studies in English Literature* 10 (1970): 93; McCoy, *Sir Philip Sidney*, 136.

65 See his early debate with Musidorus (25) and his argument with Philoclea in Book 3 ("with a dreadful shutting of his eyes, he fell down by her bedside, having had time to say no more than 'Oh,

whom dost thou kill, Philoclea?'" 235). The swoon similarly functions as a death-and-resurrection image in the *Diana* (see esp. 239, also 186–87, 196–97).

66 As numerous critics have pointed out, Sidney comments on Gynecia: "So uncertain are mortal judgements, the same person most infamous and most famous, and neither justly" (416). The difficulty is that no such acknowledgment is made in regard to the princes; Gynecia's actions are not – and have never been – the real problem. Cf. McCoy, *Sir Philip Sidney*, 135–36.

67 See Lanham, "The Old *Arcadia*," 375; Greenblatt, "Sidney's *Arcadia*," 278; Dana, "Providential Plot," 56–57; Dipple, "Unjust Justice," 100–01; Stillman, *Poetic Justice*, 225.

68 Both Robertson (*OA*, lxii), and Ringler (*Poems*, 378–79) assume without question that this is the case.

69 The conflation of distance and immediacy here, apparent in any case (because of the directness of the statement, the content, the many monosyllables, the first appearance of the first person singular in the sonnet), would be even more obvious in a Renaissance text without quotation marks: the distance that has been established allows Sidney explicitly to blur the line between Astrophil and Desire, and implicitly to identify Astrophil's desire with his own. Throughout *Astrophil and Stella*, Sidney often similarly achieves the greatest personal immediacy at moments of the greatest distance. In *AS* 1, for example, a conclusion comparable in some respects to that of 71 is attributed to Astrophil's "Muse." And in *AS* 45, the distancing that takes place at the end (12–14) permits Astrophil to speak more simply and directly than he did in his earlier lines, and to address Stella for the first time in the sonnet; his statement of self-alienation seems, paradoxically, to include more "selfness" than the rest of the poem (it certainly includes more instances of the first person singular). These conflations are facilitated, I believe, by the absence of a narrator in most of *Astrophil and Stella*, and by the lack of a decisive conclusion (to either the sequence or any individual poem).

70 McCoy, *Sir Philip Sidney*, 132–37.

71 Robertson argues against the view that "these changes were the result of bowdlerization by the Countess of Pembroke"; she believes that they accurately represent Sidney's intentions in the revised version (*OA*, lxii).

72 Ringler notes that except for a single appearance "in a new guise as an Iberian knight," Philisides disappears from both the manuscript version and the 1590 edition of the *New Arcadia*; the editors of the 1593 edition, however, "replaced Philisides in the

eclogues by printing OA9 and OP [Other Poems] 5 for the first time and by restoring his name to OA31 and OA66, which does not accord with Sidney's own plans for the revised version of his work" (*Poems*, 418).

73 The final sentence, however, has become a rhetorical question, "Who can set confidence there ...?" (319).

74 Sidney seems to alter some incidents for the specific purpose of making them accord to this pattern. Thus, in the *Old Arcadia*, Musidorus had helped Pyrocles disguise himself (26–27), but in the revised version, he is attracted to a strange woman – whom he then discovers to be Pyrocles (75–77). And the narrator similarly omits to inform us that the shepherds' pastorals were disrupted before he describes their idyllic setting (118–19; cf. *OA*, 45–46). The new incidents that Sidney adds frequently have "surprise endings."

75 See also Lindenbaum, *Changing Landscapes*, 111–35. Lindenbaum's acute discussion of the play anticipates some of the points I make here; his analysis is somewhat hampered, however, by his assumption that Shakespeare's perspective is fundamentally "anti-pastoral."

76 Traditional readings of this episode, which see it simply as a rejection of pastoral, typically fail to note how central acknowledgments of absence and death have always been to pastoral assertions of presence and continuity. For a different interpretation, see Patterson, *Pastoral and Ideology*, 131–32.

4   *Complaints themselves remedy: Marvell's lyrics as problem and solution*

1 I use both this term and "naive," below, in Schiller's sense (*Naive and Sentimental Poetry*). As I have noted above (ch. 2, n. 13), Schiller's influential formulations are both highly problematic and extremely useful in helping one to conceptualize the contradictions inherent in pastoral self-consciousness – contradictions that are made particularly pressing by Marvell's intensely self-reflexive revision of the mode.

2 Rosalie L. Colie, "*My Ecchoing Song*": *Andrew Marvell's Poetry of Criticism* (Princeton: Princeton University Press, 1970), 40–41.

3 Christopher Ricks uses a similar phrase – "self-infolded self-division" – to describe a "characteristic figure of speech in Marvell"; see "Its Own Resemblance," in *Approaches to Marvell: The York Tercentenary Lectures*, ed. C. A. Patrides (London: Routledge & Kegan Paul, 1978), 113, 108.

4 For a different account of the significance of this progress, see

Donald M. Friedman, *Marvell's Pastoral Art* (Berkeley: University of California Press, 1970), 136–38.

5 *Ibid.*, 137.

6 Similar problems are apparent in Virgil's original formulation of this idea. In *Eclogue* 1, Tityrus castigates himself for comparing Rome to the small town he inhabits; as he decries the foolishness of "compar[ing] great things and small," however, he inadvertently demonstrates his inability to do otherwise:

> Vrbem quam dicunt Romam, Meliboee, putavi
> stultus ego huic nostrae similem, quo saepe solemus
> pastores ovium teneros depellere fetus.
> sic canibus catulos similis, sic matribus haedos
> noram, sic parvis componere magna solebam.
> verum haec tantum alias inter caput extulit urbes
> quantum lenta solent inter viburna cupressi.   (19–25)

> The city they call Rome, my Melibee,
> I like a fool thought like our own, where shepherds
> Drive down the new-weaned offspring of their sheep.
> Pups are like dogs, kids are like mother goats
> I knew, and thus compared great things and small.
> But she, among cities, holds her head aloft
> As cypresses among the creeping shrubs.

While there is a greater difference between "cypresses" and humbler plants than there is between "dogs" and "pups," there is also a fundamental similarity; and Tityrus' final simile is still drawn – as it must be – from his own bucolic experience. His inability to escape the limits of that experience is underscored by the repetition of the verb *soleo* ("to be accustomed," 20, 23, 25).

7 Of the many critical comments on Marvell's habit of literalizing metaphors – of which this is a roundabout example – Rosalie Colie's ("*My Ecchoing Song*") are the most extensive. Colie's primary interest is in Marvell's ability to "enliven ... what was so conventional as to be a cliché or near-cliché, forcing the reader to take the conventional image seriously, to give a sharp look at an old custom" (79). I would not dispute that Marvell does, in fact, accomplish this end; but I believe that his relation to art and metaphor is more complex than the above statement leads one to believe. See also Ann Berthoff, "Note 1," in *The Resolved Soul*, 201–04, and Cynthia Chase, "A Stroke of the Scythe: Marvell's Mower Eclogues as Anamorphosis," *Enclitic* 5 (1981): 55–64.

8 Jim Swan ("History, Pastoral and Desire: Andrew Marvell's Mower Poems," *International Review of Psycho-Analysis* 3 [1976]:

194–205, 200) comments on the "double focus" apparent in the phrases "Country Comets" and "living Lamps"; he believes that it represents an "attempt to assert the existence of bonds where in fact there are conflicts and separations" (200). The parallel structure of the poem makes us aware of a similar doubleness inherent in the name "Glo-worms"; the assonance within the word, moreover, mirrors the alliteration in the preceding epithets.

9 Elizabeth Story Donno, ed., *Andrew Marvell: The Complete Poems* (Harmondsworth: Penguin, 1972), 262. The "foolish Fires" are, of course, literally *ignes fatui*, or will-o'-the-wisps; they are figures of all misleading or illusory goals.

10 Cf. Swan's comments on the "urban" perspective of this stanza in "History, Pastoral and Desire," 194.

11 Note that even Colin Clout – who might be cited as an exception to the rule – is considerably more sophisticated than the Mower: he is decisively distanced from other, more naive rustics, and clearly presented as the poet's pastoral persona.

12 The word that Alpers renders above as "tune" is, of course, *meditaris*. J. B. Leishman convincingly demonstrates that "The Mower to the Glo-worms" repeatedly draws upon Philemon Holland's 1601 translation of Pliny, which contains a description of "yong Nightingales [who] studie and meditate how to sing, by themselues"; see Leishman, *The Art of Marvell's Poetry* (London: Hutchinson, 1966), 151–52, and J. Newsome, ed., *Pliny's Natural History: A Selection From Philemon Holland's Translation* (Oxford: Clarendon Press, 1964), 114. It seems unlikely, however, that Marvell, who clearly knew Virgil well, could have used "meditate" in this context without being aware of the echo of *Eclogue* 1; cf. Milton, "Lycidas," 66. See also Donno, *Andrew Marvell*, 262.

13 Cf. Marvell's fascination with "Infant Love" ("The Unfortunate Lover," 2; "Young Love," 1). See also Swan's comments on speech and silence, "History, Pastoral and Desire," 201–02.

14 Virgil was, in fact, frequently called "Tityrus" during this period; and the stable shepherd's viewpoint in *Eclogue* 1 was commonly identified with that of the poet. Apollo's address to the poet in *Eclogue* 6 – *pastorem, Tityre, pinguis / pascere oportet ovis, deductum dicere carmen* (4–5, "A shepherd, Tityrus, / Should feed fat sheep, recite a fine-spun song") – lent support to this identification.

15 For an analysis of these conflicting approaches, see Alpers, "Convening and Convention," 277–78.

16 See Colie, "*My Ecchoing Song*," 40–41, quoted above.

17 Swan, "History, Pastoral and Desire," 195. Swan aptly applies

the Mower's condemnation of fallen man's "double mind" to the speaker of "The Mower to the Glo-worms"; he comments upon that poem: "[the speaker] *has only this language of an already displaced mind with which to tell how his mind was displaced to begin with*" (195; emphasis his). He does not, however, seem to feel that his comments (or the Mower's strictures) apply to the speaker of "The Mower against Gardens" himself. Generally, critical disagreements about this poem center around the question of whether Marvell endorses the Mower's speech. Several critics feel that Marvell establishes an ironic distance between himself and his character, but their conception of irony (and of distance) is extremely "single-minded"; see, e.g., Harold Toliver, *Marvell's Ironic Vision* (New Haven: Yale University Press, 1965), 104–06, and Bruce King, "'The Mower Against Gardens' and the Levellers," *Huntington Library Quarterly* 33 (1970): 237–42.

18 Isabel G. MacCaffrey, "The Scope of Imagination in *Upon Appleton House,*" in *Tercentenary Essays in Honor of Andrew Marvell,* ed. Kenneth Friedenreich (Hamden, CT: Archon Books, 1977), 226.

19 Friedman, *Marvell's Pastoral Art,* 124. Friedman analyzes in detail the sexualization of Nature discussed below; but although he finds the Mower's imagery "exaggerat[ed]" and sometimes "absurd" (125), he does not feel that it undermines the ostensible argument of the poem.

20 In this respect, the Mower's position is a latter-day version of the self-contradictory, antiheroic perspective exemplified by Milon in *Idyll* 10; see ch. 1, above.

21 Friedman, *Marvell's Pastoral Art,* 126.

22 Marvell's lines bring out – as similar Renaissance images do not – the full implications of tree-carving in Virgilian pastoral. In *Eclogue* 10, Gallus imagines himself forcing Nature to echo his own erotic pains and pleasures:

> certum est in silvis inter spelaea ferarum
> malle pati tenerisque meos incidere amores
> arboribus: crescent illae, crescetis, amores.   (52–54)
>
> In woods and lairs of beasts I choose to languish,
> Carve my love sufferings on the tender trees:
> As they grow up, so you will grow, my loves.

He thus self-consciously insures the truth of the poet's earlier declaration, *respondent omnia silvae* (8, "woods answer all").

23 Friedman comments on this stanza: "'*Fauns* and *Faryes*' are natural only in a very unusual sense; they are not real, but only the effective symbols of what is best in nature – innocence, [etc.]" (*Marvell's Pastoral Art,* 128).

24 Colie, "*My Ecchoing Song*," 37.

25 See, e.g., King, "The Mower Against Gardens," and Frank Kermode, Introduction, *Andrew Marvell: Selected Poetry* (New York: Signet, 1967), xvi–xx.

26 The poem is thus a complete inversion (not simply, as Kermode believes, the "antithesis") of "lascivious garden poetry" like Randolph's *Upon Love Fondly Refused for Conscience' Sake* (*Andrew Marvell*, xviiii–xix).

27 Empson, *Some Versions*, 131–32.

28 For a good survey of earlier criticism, see Swan, "At Play in the Garden of Ambivalence: Andrew Marvell and the Green World," *Criticism* 17 (1975): 297–99.

29 Patrick Cullen comments on the poem: "The only way [the Mower] can mow Juliana the way she mows him is vicariously, and so ... [he] transforms the grass into an image of Juliana ... Like a punished child, he kicks the cat" (*Spenser, Marvell, and Renaissance Pastoral*, 196).

30 The literal content of Marvell's refrain thus, inevitably, reproduces the formal properties of all refrains: it contradicts the poem's progress and, in a number of ways, creates connection and stasis out of separation and change (e.g., the parallel between the Mower and the grass depends on their both being "mown"). Marvell repeats this equation of the literal with the metaphoric, on another level, by using a refrain, which is traditionally associated with actual dirges, in a song about metaphoric death. And he reproduces it once more by effectively conflating the two principal types of pastoral refrains – those which contain grief by insisting on the artifice of the song, and those which perform the same function by insisting repetitively on the fact of grief itself. These two varieties had frequently overlapped in earlier pastorals (e.g., *Idyll* 1), but here, they are indistinguishable: the Mower's grief is caused by, and is identical with, his symbolic vision. As in all of Marvell's poems, art is here both the problem and the solution, and if "Remedies themselves complain" ("Damon the Mower," 30), it is equally true that complaints (plaintive songs) themselves remedy. For a "naive" version of this paradox, see Theocritus, *Idyll* 11, esp. lines 1, 17, 80.

31 Cullen, *Spenser, Marvell, and Renaissance Pastoral*, 192. Cullen does seem to believe that the Mower is projecting his feelings onto the landscape here. His primary concern is to cleanse the animals in this stanza – especially the snake – of any symbolic significance whatsoever, and particularly of any associations with the Fall. He believes that Edenic analogues are irrelevant to the "comic and amorous" Juliana poems (194), and that the frequent appearance

of the word "fall" in these poems is not significant. His comment on Damon's fall later in this poem illustrates the perils of attempting to apply such a position to Marvell: "The falling in grass has no thematic relevance to the original Fall," he declares; "the similarity is verbal, not real" (193).

32 See, e.g., Friedman, *Marvell's Pastoral Art*, 130–31; for a more extreme example, see Elaine Hoffman Baruch, "Theme and Counterthemes in 'Damon the Mower,'" *Comparative Literature* 26 (1974): 246.

33 Alpers, "Convening and Convention," 291.

34 *Ibid.*, 288.

35 Corydon tells Alexis:

> nunc etiam pecudes umbras et frigora captant,
> nunc viridis etiam occultant spineta lacertos,
> Thestylis et rapido fessis messoribus aestu
> alia serpyllumque herbas contundit olentis.
> at mecum raucis, tua dum vestigia lustro,
> sole sub ardenti resonant arbusta cicadis.   (8–13)

> Now even cattle seek out shade and coolness,
> Green lizards hunt for shelter in a thornbush;
> Thestylis pounds thyme, garlic, and pungent herbs
> For reapers weary in the consuming heat.
> But with me shrill crickets, as I trace your steps
> Under the burning sun, sound through the trees.

His emphatic self-reference in line 12 is missing from "Damon the Mower"; like his references to other human beings, it is replaced by the description of animals. Because Damon has very little self-consciousness at this point, he has very little consciousness of others (and vice-versa); note that there is nothing in his words that explicitly indicates that he is concerned with "the plight of love."

36 The second stanza (like the initial portions of the other Mower poems) is thus reminiscent of passages that frequently occur towards the ends of Theocritus' *Idylls*: these passages seem to present us with a picture of the concrete bucolic present; but they contain suppressed symbolism whose content (and whose very existence) makes us aware of a separation that the surface of the poetry denies.

37 Baruch bases her analysis in "Theme and Counterthemes" upon an extended comparison between the poem and a fugue; she believes that, throughout the poem, "a religious theme is pitted against naturalistic and pastoral counterthemes, and the three themes … are played one against the other" (243). For a detailed

discussion of the importance of musical concepts in Marvell's poetry, see Donald M. Friedman, "Marvell's Musicks," in *On the Celebrated and Neglected Poems of Andrew Marvell*, ed. Claude J. Summers and Ted-Larry Pebworth (Columbia: University of Missouri Press, 1992), 8–28.

38 *OED*, "presence," 4: "With possessive, denoting the actual person (or thing) that is present…; hence sometimes nearly = embodied self, objective personality."

39 Berthoff also cites *Eclogue* 4 as the source of this image (*The Resolved Soul*, 137, n. 17). If we do recall Virgil's golden-age prophecy here, we may also recall that the poet foretold the death of serpents (24), and described sheep who would naturally change their hues, rendering the dyer's art obsolete:

> nec varios discet mentiri lana colores,
> ipse sed in pratis aries iam suave rubenti
> murice, iam croceo mutabit vellera luto;
> sponte sua sandyx pascentis vestiet agnos.   (42–44)

> Wool will not learn to counterfeit his hues,
> Since in the fields the ram himself will blush
> All purple, or transmute his fleece to gold;
> Spontaneous dyes will clothe the feeding lambs.

Eclogue 4 is, I believe, Virgil's most daring attempt at interweaving "heroic" and "bucolic" perspectives.

40 In *Eclogue* 2, Corydon complains: *despectus tibi sum, nec qui sim quaeris, Alexi* (19, "You scorn me, never asking who I am"). His explanation – and investigation – of "who he is" culminates in the suspensions he creates in his imagined offering; Damon's explanation proceeds from this point.

41 David Kalstone senses Daphnis' presence in the poem: he comments in passing that Damon revives the hero's "god-like claims" ("Marvell and the Fictions of Pastoral," *English Literary Renaissance* 4 [1974]: 182; cf. 175). But he does not point to any particular lines, and he does not really develop his insight. Because the importance of *Idyll* 1 here has been ignored, critics (including Kalstone, 182) generally view Damon's final alliance with death as a more radical departure from pastoral tradition than it actually is.

42 Polyphemus, the model for Corydon, is in many respects Daphnis' diametric opposite; in the *Idylls*, however, opposing points of view are ultimately equated. Marvell's conflation of the two characters is therefore another instance of his returning to Theocritus by bringing together perspectives that Virgil had suspended; note

that when Corydon boasts of his beauty, he *compares* himself to Daphnis (*Ecl.* 2.25–27). See also Virgil's "suspended" version of Daphnis' statement in *Eclogue* 5 (43–44).

43 The result of this self-reflexiveness is that Damon's lines seem simultaneously more sophisticated and more comically naive than Daphnis' statement. Cf. Empson's comment on this stanza: "In these meadows [Damon] feels he has left his mark on a great territory, if not on everything, and as a typical figure he has mown all the meadows of the world; ... I suppose he is not only the ruler but the executioner of the daffodils – the Clown as Death" (*Some Versions*, 128–29).

44 See Colie's remarks on "contraction" in "Damon the Mower" ("*My Ecchoing Song,*" 34) and in Marvell's other poems (118–23).

45 John Carey comments on similar reversals throughout Marvell's work; see "Reversals Transposed: An Aspect of Marvell's Imagination," in *Approaches to Marvell,* ed. Patrides, 136–54. He feels they evidence "the frustrating nature of reality" (139): "In the subtle trap which life ... becomes for Marvell, actions are constantly turning against themselves" (142). See also Ricks' remarks on "the self-inwoven simile" in "Its Own Resemblance," 108–34.

46 Alpers, "Convening and Convention," 290.

47 Leach, *Vergil's Eclogues,* 147.

48 As the poem continues, we become gradually more certain that he is talking to himself.

49 Friedman, *Marvell's Pastoral Art,* 133.

50 Alpers comments on "the heroic meaning of 'discover,'" and notes that the stanza contains "the first wordplays that we can think of attributing to [Damon]: one heroic ('the golden fleece') and the other pastoral ('richer far in Hay')" ("Convening and Convention," 294). Since "hay" is both a traditional symbol of worthlessness (see Colie, "*My Ecchoing Song,*" 130) and a pleasant country dance, it exemplifies both the absurd and the attractive aspects of the bucolic perspective. On the heroic implications of this stanza, see also Kalstone, "Marvell and the Fictions of Pastoral," 181, and Friedman, *Marvell's Pastoral Art,* 145, n. 53.

51 See Friedman, *Marvell's Pastoral Art,* 133. The pun now seems earned, as it did not in the first stanza.

52 Donno, *Andrew Marvell,* 261; see also Chase, "A Stroke of the Scythe," 56–57.

53 The pun on "glance" is emphasized by the mirroring, implied pun on Latin *acies* ("a sharp edge," "sharpness of vision"), which Colie notes as an example of Marvell's etymological "unfiguring" ("*My Ecchoing Song,*" 84). Cf. "The Picture of little T. C.," 20.

54 Colie, "*My Ecchoing Song*," 41, quoted above. For a different account of the relation between violent exertion and "natural passivity" in Marvell's pastoral, see John Rogers' recent essay, "The Great Work of Time: Marvell's Pastoral Historiography," in *Celebrated and Neglected Poems*, ed. Summers and Pebworth, 207–32. Throughout his essay (which treats *Upon Appleton House* and "The Nymph complaining" as well as the Mower poems), Rogers is admirably alert to many of the conflicts this opposition creates in Marvell's poetry; but like most critics, he believes that the opposed attitudes he outlines are ultimately separable.

55 See "The Picture of little T. C.," 24–25: "Let me be laid, / Where I may see thy Glories from some shade." In these lines, significantly, Marvell addresses his character directly for the first time in the poem.

56 Cullen comments on the second stanza: "I cannot think that the serpent's Edenic symbolism of evil is any more relevant here than its symbolism of immortality (like the Phoenix, the snake, emerging from its dead form, was often taken as a symbol of immortality)" (*Spenser, Marvell, and Renaissance Pastoral*, 192). I agree with the explicit content of his statement, if not with its implications; and I would add that the traditional romance association of death and resurrection with separation and reunion is also relevant here. Cf. Sidney's more conventional use of this image in Dicus' dirge for Basilius; note the series of oppositions here (man/nature, death/renewal, etc.) that Marvell's poem joins together:

> Time ever old and young is still revolved
> > Within itself, and never taketh end:
> > But mankind is for ay to nought resolved.
> The filthy snake her aged coat can mend,
> > And getting youth again, in youth doth flourish;
> > But unto man, age ever death doth send.   (*OA*, 347.10–15)

57 See n. 30, above.

58 My suggestions here depend, of course, on the hypothesis that the order in which the poems appeared in the 1681 folio reflects the poet's intentions. See Friedman, *Marvell's Pastoral Art*, 120 ff., for another reading that assumes the poems are "progressive."

59 This line, of course, mirrors the final description of the statues that "adorn the Gardens" in "The Mower against Gardens" (41); cf. "The Nymph complaining," in which the consciousness of loss similarly ends by producing completely externalized, memorializing art. See also the end of "The unfortunate Lover" (a poem in which Marvell distances his subject from himself by somewhat

different means): "And he in Story only rules, / In a Field *Sable* a Lover *Gules*" (63–64; note the ambiguity in "only").

60 Quoted in Christopher Ricks, *Tennyson* (New York: Macmillan, 1972), 92.

61 To do Sidney justice, we should remember that it was not at all clear that Sannazaro was aware of the limitations of art, and that none of Sidney's predecessors in the pastoral romance had fully confronted the problems that are posed by the *Old Arcadia*. Sidney is, moreover, extremely alive to the contradictions that are implicit in his own position. For comparisons of Marvell and Sidney from somewhat different perspectives, see Berthoff, *The Resolved Soul*, 182 ff., and MacCaffrey, "The Scope of Imagination," 226.

62 Many of the general statements I will make about this poem apply to "The Garden" as well.

63 For a different interpretation of the speaker's role, see Charles Molesworth, "Marvell's 'Upon Appleton House': The Persona as Historian, Philosopher, and Priest," *Studies in English Literature* 13 (1973): 149–62.

64 I believe (for reasons that I will develop in the course of this chapter) that Marvell's intentions regarding the narrator of *Upon Appleton House* are best honored not by observing the conventional, clear distinction between "poet" and "speaker," but by blurring it; I therefore intend to do so, repeatedly, in the following pages.

65 MacCaffrey, for example, declares:

The violence perpetrated upon the landscape manifests the architect's conceit, in two senses of the word. It is an extreme instance of imagination's metamorphosing power: caves become quarries, forests pastures, in the interests of a "great Design" which has forgotten its origin in the patterns of created nature. ("The Scope of Imagination," 227)

Throughout her essay, MacCaffrey attempts (unsuccessfully, I believe) to separate conclusively the "true art" of Marvell's poem from the "false art" that is exemplified by the "Forrain *Architect*" and the nuns.

66 Colie, "*My Ecchoing Song*," 230. Colie's remarks on the reader's confusion here are quite illuminating; like MacCaffrey, however, she is attempting to argue for an absolute distinction between "false conception[s] and ... real ones" (230).

67 T. S. Eliot cited this stanza as an example of Marvell's descent from imagination to fancy: "Obviously, an image which is immediately and unintentionally ridiculous is merely a fancy ... [The description of the house] whatever its intention, is more absurd than it was intended to be" ("Andrew Marvell," in *Selected Essays* [New York: Harcourt, Brace & World, 1950], rpt. in *Andrew*

Marvell: *A Collection of Critical Essays*, ed. George deF. Lord [Englewood Cliffs, NJ: Prentice-Hall, 1968], 22).

68 Friedman, *Marvell's Pastoral Art*, 218.

69 The verb "thinks" clearly has a double force here: the fact that man "thinks" at all is the root of the problem; cf. Friedman, *Marvell's Pastoral Art*, 215.

70 It is both significant and logical that at the same time that this humanization is occurring, human beings are described as inanimate objects:

> A Stately *Frontispiece of Poor*
> Adorns without the open Door:
> Nor less the Rooms within commends
> Daily new *Furniture of Friends*. (65–68)

For a somewhat different approach to the problems in this passage (and in other similarly "disquieting" passages throughout the poem), see Heather Dubrow, "The Country-House Poem: A Study in Generic Development," *Genre* 12 (1979): 153–79.

71 Cf. Colie, "*My Ecchoing Song*," 230. The image here is, of course, simultaneously one of an impregnated female body; it is one of Marvell's most compressed evocations of the idea that "man's" attempts to imagine himself out of himself (into the innocent, the physical, the natural, the feminine) are violations that inevitably reproduce what they try to leave behind.

72 Sannazaro's unquestioning faith in the powers of art – and the relatively "pure" formalism that resulted from this faith – led him to see this disjunction as unproblematic, and to present it, simply, as a suspension (see ch. 3, above). It is logical – in Marvell's terms – that the speaker's attempt to identify himself with "Nature" here results in a perspective that is the image (as well as the opposite) of Sannazaro's. In the course of *Upon Appleton House*, the speaker will move, progressively, to more and more self-conscious apprehensions of the ways in which form and content, art and nature, the complex and the simple are necessarily opposed – and connected.

73 Shakespeare frequently presents the desire for innocence in strikingly similar terms; see esp. *A Midsummer Night's Dream*, 3.2.203–14, and *The Winter's Tale*, 1.1.62–75: in each of these speeches a character evokes, longingly, a vision of an idyllic pastoral youth in which s/he experienced a painless, timeless, "innocent" union with another character of the same sex. Cf. *The Two Gentlemen of Verona*, 2.4.62–63; *As You Like It*, 1.3.71–76.

74 Colie, "*My Ecchoing Song*," 225.

75 MacCaffrey, "The Scope of Imagination," 228.

76 Condemnations of the narrator are fairly frequent: examples can be found in George deF. Lord, "From Contemplation to Action: Marvell's Poetic Career," in *Andrew Marvell*, ed. Lord, 65–66; M. J. K. O'Loughlin, "This Sober Frame: A Reading of 'Upon Appleton House,'" in *Andrew Marvell*, ed. Lord, 134–38; Patterson, *Marvell and the Civic Crown*, 103–06; and James Turner, *The Politics of Landscape: Rural Scenery and Society in English Poetry 1630–1660* (Oxford: Basil Blackwell, 1979), 76–78. Readers who feel that Marvell is ultimately critical of Fairfax's retirement include Lord, "From Contemplation," 62, and Marcus, *The Politics of Mirth*, 240–63.

77 For example, "There would be nothing wrong with [the nun's] argument if Fairfax were the speaker. The sub[t]lety of her seduction of Isabella consists in misapplying the truth about Christian retirement to a bad cause" (John M. Wallace, *Destiny his Choice: The Loyalism of Andrew Marvell* [Cambridge: Cambridge University Press, 1968], 244–45).

78 "Speaks" literally means "speaks of" (i.e., "gives indications of") in this line; but the word (like "thinks," 23) is clearly a loaded one here.

79 Friedman, *Marvell's Pastoral Art*, 221; Friedman also discusses the critical problems such a condemnation inevitably poses (248, n. 30). See also Michael Schoenfeldt's acute remarks in John Klause, Ann Baynes Coiro, and Michael C. Schoenfeldt, "The Achievement of Andrew Marvell: Excerpts from a Panel Discussion," in *Celebrated and Neglected Poems*, ed. Summers and Pebworth, 245.

80 He did, however, briefly convert to Catholicism when he was 17; and his youthful flirtation with the religion of ritual seems to have some relevance here.

81 In *The Politics of Mirth*, Leah Marcus comments acutely on the manner in which Fairfax's retreat – and all the retreats in the poem – are "invad[ed]" by "history" (246) and implicated in "the 'fallen' world of political conflict" (241). Because her model of pastoral is an idyllic one, however, she sees Marvell's awareness of our inability to escape the effects of the Fall as necessarily undermining the retreats he describes (see, e.g., 244–46) and as resulting ultimately in a vision that is "something other, quite new" (241). I am suggesting, on the contrary, that both the fundamental paradox that is being explored here and the attitude that Marvell assumes towards that paradox are as old as Theocritus' hills.

82 Cf. "The unfortunate Lover," "The Mower's Song," and "The Nymph complaining."

83 MacCaffrey, "The Scope of Imagination," 230.

84 It is really impossible here (or in any of Marvell's poetry) to separate the poet's evocations of physical violence from his evocations of artistic creation and sexual desire: these impulses and activities are continually represented as intertwined, and they are all, repeatedly, imaged by piercing wounds; all three are seen as reflections of the wound that Earth felt.

85 Before he undertakes his retreat, he returns, several times, to the first person plural (370 ff., 435); and when he describes his wooded sanctuary from the outside, he does so in an impersonal manner ("When first the Eye this Forrest sees," 497). Once he has passed "within" (505), however, he uses the first person singular consistently. Frank J. Warnke discusses the implications of this shift from a somewhat different perspective in "The Meadow-sequence in *Upon Appleton House*: Questions of Tone and Meaning," in *Approaches to Marvell*, ed. Patrides, 234–50.

86 Cf. Friedman's comments on Marvell's "far-fetched analogies" and rapidly shifting metaphors (*Marvell's Pastoral Art*, 234).

87 Cf. Marcus, *The Politics of Mirth*, 252, and Jim Swan, "'Betwixt Two Labyrinths': Andrew Marvell's Rational Amphibian," *Texas Studies in Language and Literature* 17 (1975): 555.

88 John Wallace argues that *Upon Appleton House* was conceived, in part, as "an answer to *Gondibert* and its famous preface" (*Destiny his Choice*, 240); he believes that Marvell intends to criticize both Davenant's soaring ambition and his "insistence on active rather than a contemplative virtue" (241). While Wallace clearly overstates his case, he does point out many interesting parallels between the two poems.

89 Both the imagery and the ideas here recall stanza 6 of "The Garden"; the final couplet may also be compared to Virgil's central conditional statement, *si numquam fallit imago*, and to Marvell's version of that statement in "Damon the Mower": "If in my Sithe I looked right" (58).

90 Compare, for example, the following comments:

> The light by which the poet "reads" all this is like that of Moses, who chronicled the beginning of all created things, who gave the world its geography, its cosmosgraphy, and its morality. Also, the light on the forest floor makes a mosaic from which the "one History" can be read, the character of truth cast before the poet in the mixed wood of his experience. (Colie, "*My Ecchoing Song*," 234–35)

> [The speaker's] character is vegetative and his philosophy dilletantish, making grossly exaggerated claims for random or trivial concurrences. Not even Ralph Austen believed that all the bible and all the philosophers

were hidden in the trees. Marvell regarded Mexique paintings as trash, and castigates Clarendon's "Palace Mosaic"; he also hated prelates. (Turner, *The Politics of Landscape*, 76)

91　Ricks, "Its Own Resemblance," 116.
92　MacCaffrey, "The Scope of Imagination," 234.
93　Many readers have recognized that Marvell is alluding here to *Eclogue* 2; but even critics who are specifically concerned with Marvell's relation to Virgil tend to view Thestylis as "real." Annabel Patterson argues in *Pastoral and Ideology*:

By identifying himself with Corydon and by identifying Thestylis with an actual and brutal rusticity, Marvell took elegant cognizance of a double dialectic: that between pastoral leisure and rural labor, as in the Virgilian original, and that between Cavalier contempt for the rustic laborer and the voice of genuine social protest, most clearly heard in the programs of the Levellers and Diggers. (155–56)

Patterson's desire to separate the poles of her dialectic decisively from each other leads her to ignore the extent to which "pastoral leisure and rural labor" are presented as reflecting (as well as opposing) each other in *Eclogue* 2 itself, and the extent to which Marvell is clearly complicating and intensifying Virgil's paradoxes by self-consciously presenting "actual and brutal rusticity" as the product of the retired artistic imagination.

94　Cf. Harry Berger, Jr., "Marvell's 'Upon Appleton House': An Interpretation," in *Southern Review* 1 (1965), rpt. in *John Donne and the Seventeenth-Century Metaphysical Poets*, ed. Harold Bloom (New York: Chelsea House, 1986), 201. This essay is combined with Berger's other articles on Marvell to form a chapter ("Andrew Marvell: The Poem as Green World") in Berger, *Second World and Green World: Studies in Renaissance Fiction-Making*, (Berkeley: University of California Press, 1988).

95　Seminal allegorical readings include those of Maren-Sofie Røstvig in *The Happy Man: Studies in the Metamorphosis of a Classical Ideal 1600–1700*, rev. edn. (Oslo: Norwegian University Press, 1962), 174–90, and Don Cameron Allen in *Image and Meaning: Metaphoric Traditions in Renaissance Poetry*, enlarged edn. (Baltimore: Johns Hopkins University Press, 1968), 187–225; for an argument that these critics and their successors are wrong to see any political or religious allegory in the latter part of the poem, see Berthoff, *The Resolved Soul*, 171–97. The problems posed by the "allegory" in *Upon Appleton House* quite clearly duplicate those posed by the "symbolism" of the Mower poems, and by all of Marvell's versions of the harmless fall. Marshall Grossman offers a complex and suggestive approach to these problems in "Authoring the Boundary: Allegory, Irony, and the Rebus in 'Upon Appleton House,'" in "*The muses common-weale*": *Poetry and Politics in the Seventeenth Century*, ed. Claude J. Summers and Ted-Larry Pebworth (Columbia: University of Missouri Press: 1988), 191–206. See also Grossman, "Literary Forms and Historical Consciousness in Renaissance Poetry," *Exemplaria* 1 (1989): 248–64, for a related discussion (focusing on "The Garden") of the problems involved in constructing "literary history."

96 Colie, "*My Ecchoing Song*," 244, 267.

97 *OED*, "gall," $v.^1$, 5.

98 Cf. the descriptions of the "prickling leaf" of conscience (357–58), the death of the rail (393–400), and the shrinking thorns that refuse to harm the nightingale (513–20).

99 Cf. the last line of "Damon the Mower." Critics who believe that Marvell is viewing his speaker with single-minded irony generally use this passage as their central piece of evidence; critical supporters of the speaker generally either deny the presence of the crucifixion here (e.g., Berthoff, *The Resolved Soul*, 186; Margoliouth, *Poems and Letters of Andrew Marvell*, 290), or attempt to ignore the stanza's (pleasantly) masochistic sexual overtones.

100 For an example of this kind of reading, see Warren L. Cherniak, *The Poet's Time: Politics and Religion in the Works of Andrew Marvell* (Cambridge: Cambridge University Press, 1983), 36–37.

101 "The Garden," 55–56.

102 Donald Friedman first called my attention to the references to the crucifixion in the following lines:

> When we have run our Passions heat,
> Love hither makes his best retreat.
> The *Gods*, that mortal Beauty chase,
> Still in a Tree did end their race.   (25–28)

103 To actually reproduce the effect of the image, however, I should be able to make two contradictory statements, not successively, but at exactly the same time.

104 Swan makes a related point about the imagery of this stanza: "No sooner does the narrator call on the vines to 'lace' their 'circles' close, than he thinks of a labyrinth and a thread leading the way out" ("Betwixt Two Labyrinths," 563).

105 The final epithet is intentionally oxymoronic (a "utensil" being, etymologically, something that is useful), and it encapsulates the paradoxes that Marvell is presenting us with here.

106 Berger, "Marvell's 'Upon Appleton House,'" 208. While my interpretation of the conclusion differs somewhat from Berger's, I am indebted, throughout this section, to his perceptive analysis.

107 Colie, "*My Ecchoing Song*," 270, 246.

108 Berger, "Marvell's 'Upon Appleton House,'" 209.

109 The difference in gender is of course significant: "Maria" is (and is pointedly presented as) the poet's (necessarily violated) image of innocence, rather than the thing itself.

110 O'Loughlin, "This Sober Frame," 140.

111 For a discussion of Marvell's fascination with the "Mean time," see MacCaffrey, "The Scope of Imagination," 241.

112 On this aspect of the poem, see Berger, "Marvell's 'Upon Appleton House,'" 210–11.

113 As Berger points out, the opening lines of this stanza can be read two ways: "(1) 'The world is no longer the rude heap it once was'; (2) 'The world is no longer what it once was; now it is a rude heap and the paradisaic order of a Former Age is all negligently overthrown'" (*Ibid.*, 193). I am, obviously, treating the second reading as primary: I believe that the tone of the stanza and the poem as a whole leads us to do so; but I also believe that we are led (here and throughout the poem) to see how the first reading is "contain'd" in the second.

114 Through the numerous inversions in this stanza, the speaker tacitly – and wittily – admits that his perspective (like that of the nuns) necessarily involves an "inver[sion]" of "proper relation[s]" (see Colie, "*My Ecchoing Song*," 225, quoted above).

115 Cf. Colie, "*My Ecchoing Song*," 237. Marvell's repetition of the word "like" (770, 772, 776) further emphasizes the (necessarily self-reflexive) image-making process here: to be really precise, one would have to say that the speaker is self-consciously (re)creating the universe in the image of images of the mind of man.

Epilogue   *Farewell to pastoral*: The Shepherd's Week

1 Quotation of Milton's shorter poems follows the text of John Milton, *Complete Shorter Poems*, ed. John Carey (London: Longman, 1971); quotation of *Paradise Lost* follows Alastair Fowler's edition (London: Longman, 1971).

2 See esp. the description of paradise beginning "But rather to tell how, if art could tell…" (4.236 ff.); and cf. Virgil, *Ecl.* 2.27, *si numqam fallit imago*.

3 For a detailed account of eighteenth-century criticism of pastoral,

see J. E. Congleton, *Theories of Pastoral Poetry in England, 1684–1798* (Gainesville: University of Florida Press, 1952). Patterson provides an interesting account of the political stakes in the critical debates in *Pastoral and Ideology*, 193–262. She also provides some striking examples of explicit Virgilian imitation dating from later centuries (including a poem by Frost), but her book itself testifies to their rarity.

4 All citation of *The Shepherd's Week* follows the text of John Gay, *Poetry and Prose*, ed. Vinton A. Dearing and Charles E. Beckwith, 2 vols. (Oxford: Clarendon Press, 1974), I.

5 Cf. Virgil, cited by Gay in his note:

> Populus Alcidae gratissima, vitis Iaccho,
> formosae myrtus Veneri, sua laurea Phoebo;
> Phyllis amat corylos; illas dum Phyllis amabit,
> nec myrtus vincet corylos, nec laurea Phoebi.   (7.61–64)

> Poplars delight Alcides, vines please Bacchus,
> Myrtles fair Venus and his laurel Phoebus;
> Phyllis loves hazels and while Phyllis loves them,
> Myrtle nor Phoebus' laurels shall match hazels.

6 As Nigel Wood notes, in Restoration and eighteenth-century criticism, Theocritus began to be set against the more decorous and "literary" Virgil: while the Greek poet's "clownish" simplicity was often admired, it also caused him to be viewed, in some quarters, as "the black sheep of the classical canon." See Wood, "Gay and the Ironies of Rustic Simplicity," in *John Gay and the Scriblerians*, ed. Peter Lewis and Nigel Wood (London: Vision Press, 1988), 103.

7 Alexander Pope, *The Correspondence of Alexander Pope*, ed. George Sherburn, 5 vols. (Oxford: Oxford University Press, 1956), I, 137. Pope specifically attributed his irritation with Philips to the latter's withholding of subscription money for Pope's translation of Homer. For accounts of the Pope–Philips quarrel (and differing interpretations of its relation to *The Shepherd's Week*), see Wood, "Gay and the Ironies of Rustic Simplicity," 94–121; John Irwin Fischer, "Never on Sunday: John Gay's *The Shepherd's Week*," *Studies of Eighteenth Century Culture* 10 (1981): 191–203; Patricia Meyer Spacks, *John Gay* (New York: Twayne, 1965), 30–40; Adina Forsgren, *John Gay: Poet "Of a Lesser Order"* (Stockholm: Lagerström, 1964), 106–13; William Henry Irving, *John Gay: Favorite of the Wits* (New York: Russell & Russell, 1962), 82–90; William D. Ellis, Jr., "Thomas D'Urfey, the Pope–Philips Quarrel, and *The Shepherd's Week*," *PMLA* 74 (1959): 203–12; and

Hoyt Trowbridge, "Pope, Gay, and *The Shepherd's Week,*" *Modern Language Quarterly* 5 (1944): 79–88.

8 Irving, *John Gay,* 82–90.

9 I follow the text and translation of H. Rushton Fairclough, trans., *Virgil,* 2 vols. (Cambridge, MA: Harvard University Press, 1974), I.

10 Milton also imitates "Virgil's" opening at the beginning of *Paradise Regained,* when he bids farewell to *Paradise Lost* (here conceived in pastoral terms): "I who erewhile the happy garden sung ..." (1).

11 Cf. Wood, "Gay and the Ironies of Rustic Simplicity," 112; see also my discussion of Marvell's revision of this eclogue in "The Mower to the Glo-worms" (ch. 4, above).

12 See Spenser, *The Shepheardes Calendar,* "Januarye," 72.

13 The prose "Proeme" is signed "thy Loving Countryman JOHN GAY" (89–90), but the first time the speaker of the poem is named is when Bolingbroke praises his verse. Anne McWhir, who discusses the question of Gay's persona(e) in "The Wolf in the Fold: John Gay in *The Shepherd's Week* and *Trivia,*" *Studies in English Literature* 23 (1983): 413–23, suggests that the "frank identification" at the end of the "Proeme" is itself "part of [Gay's] game of deception" (419).

14 This final movement, of course, raises the Marvellian possibility that the simple, the natural, and the naive are merely latter-day fictions created by the complexly artificial and sophisticated. A similar (if less extreme) suggestion is implicit in Gay's earlier comparison of himself and his readers to Milton's Satan visiting Paradise ("Proeme," 36–43); cf. McWhir, "The Wolf in the Fold," 417, and Wood, "Gay and the Ironies of Rustic Simplicity," 101. Wood also discusses "Gay's self-portrayal as Bowzybeus" in "Saturday" (114).

15 Wood sees Gay's ending as fundamentally similar to the conclusion of *Eclogue* 3, upon which it is modeled: *claudite iam rivos, pueri; sat prata biberunt* (111, "Shut off the streams; the fields have drunk enough"). Both endings, he asserts, serve to "limit lyricism" by calling attention to practical tasks ("Gay and the Ironies of Rustic Simplicity," 108). While this similarity does exist, the differences between the two passages are even more striking: Virgil's shepherds' songs are seen as metaphorically providing their fields with life-giving water, and are thus continuous with – as well as opposed to – their practical tasks; the songs Gay's bumpkins sing are, in direct contrast, causing their herds to die of thirst.

16 Cf. Wood, "Gay and the Ironies of Rustic Simplicity," 104–07, 115–16; see also Spacks, *John Gay,* 32–40.

17 Of the following examples, Purney is cited by Spacks in *John Gay*, 32, Shiels and Goldsmith are cited by Irving in *John Gay*, 89, and Dr. Johnson is cited by both Irving and Spacks; for further examples, see Spacks, 32–33, and Forsgren, *John Gay*, 106–07.

18 Theophilus Cibber, *The Lives of the Poets of Great Britain and Ireland, to the Time of Dean Swift*, 5 vols. (London: R. Griffiths, 1753), IV, 259.

19 Samuel Johnson, "Gay," in *Lives of the English Poets*, ed. George Birkbeck Hill, 3 vols. (Oxford: Clarendon Press, 1905), II, 269.

20 Oliver Goldsmith, ed., *The Beauties of English Poesy*, 2 vols. (London: William Griffin, 1767), I, 133.

21 Both Wood ("Gay and the Ironies of Rustic Simplicity") and Fischer ("Never On Sunday") also see Gay – for somewhat different reasons – as fundamentally "Theocritean."

Works cited

Allen, Don Cameron. *Image and Meaning: Metaphoric Traditions in Renaissance Poetry.* Enlarged edn. Baltimore: Johns Hopkins University Press, 1968.

Alpers, Paul. "Convening and Convention in Pastoral Poetry." *New Literary History* 14 (1982/83): 277–304.

"Schiller's *Naive and Sentimental Poetry* and the Modern Idea of Pastoral." In *Cabinet of the Muses: Essays on Classical and Comparative Literature in Honor of Thomas G. Rosenmeyer,* ed. Mark Griffith and Donald J. Mastronarde, 319–31. Atlanta, GA: Scholars Press, 1990.

The Singer of the Eclogues: A Study of Virgilian Pastoral. Berkeley: University of California Press, 1979.

"Theocritean Bucolic and Virgilian Pastoral." *Arethusa* 23 (1990): 19–47.

"What is Pastoral?" *Critical Inquiry* 8 (1982): 437–60.

Baruch, Elaine Hoffman. "Theme and Counterthemes in 'Damon the Mower.'" *Comparative Literature* 26 (1974): 242–59.

Berger, Harry, Jr. "Marvell's 'Upon Appleton House': An Interpretation." *Southern Review* 1 (1965): 7–26. Rpt. in *John Donne and the Seventeenth-Century Metaphysical Poets,* ed. Harold Bloom, 181–211. New York: Chelsea House, 1986.

"The Origins of Bucolic Representation: Disenchantment and Revision in Theocritus' Seventh *Idyll.*" *Classical Antiquity* 3 (1984): 1–39.

Revisionary Play: Studies in the Spenserian Dynamics. Berkeley: University of California Press, 1988.

Second World and Green World: Studies in Renaissance Fiction-Making. Berkeley: University of California Press, 1988.

"A Secret Discipline: *The Faerie Queene,* Book VI." In *Form and Convention in the Poetry of Edmund Spenser,* ed. William Nelson, 35–75. New York: Columbia University Press, 1961. Rpt. in Berger, *Revisionary Play,* 215–42.

Unpublished essay on Virgil's *Eclogues*. 1980.

Berthoff, Ann. *The Resolved Soul: A Study of Marvell's Major Poems.* Princeton: Princeton University Press, 1970.

Booth, Stephen, ed. *Shakespeare's Sonnets.* New Haven: Yale University Press, 1977.

Bredbeck, Gregory W. *Sodomy and Interpretation: Marlowe to Milton.* Ithaca: Cornell University Press, 1991.

Carey, John. "Reversals Transposed: An Aspect of Marvell's Imagination." In *Approaches to Marvell*, ed. Patrides, 136–54.

Chase, Cynthia. "A Stroke of the Scythe: Marvell's Mower Eclogues as Anamorphosis." *Enclitic* 5 (1981): 55–64.

Cherniak, Warren L. *The Poet's Time: Politics and Religion in the Works of Andrew Marvell.* Cambridge: Cambridge University Press, 1983.

Cibber, Theophilus. *The Lives of the Poets of Great Britain and Ireland, to the Time of Dean Swift.* 5 vols. London: R. Griffiths, 1753.

Coleman, Robert, ed. *Vergil: Eclogues.* Cambridge: Cambridge University Press, 1977.

Colie, Rosalie L. *"My Ecchoing Song": Andrew Marvell's Poetry of Criticism.* Princeton: Princeton University Press, 1970.

Congleton, J. E. *Theories of Pastoral Poetry in England, 1684–1798.* Gainesville: University of Florida Press, 1952.

Cullen, Patrick. *Spenser, Marvell, and Renaissance Pastoral.* Cambridge, MA: Harvard University Press, 1970.

Dana, Margaret E. "The Providential Plot of the *Old Arcadia*." *Comparative Literature* 25 (1973): 39–57.

Davis, Walter R. "A Map of Arcadia: Sidney's Romance in Its Tradition." In Davis and Lanham, *Sidney's Arcadia*, 1–179.

Davis, Walter R., and Richard A. Lanham. *Sidney's Arcadia.* Yale Studies in English, vol. 158. New Haven: Yale University Press, 1965.

Derrida, Jacques. *Dissemination.* Trans. Barbara Johnson. Chicago: University of Chicago Press, 1981.

Dipple, Elizabeth. "Harmony and Pastoral in the *Old Arcadia*." *ELH* 35 (1968): 309–28.

"Unjust Justice in the *Old Arcadia*." *Studies in English Literature* 10 (1970): 83–101.

Donno, Elizabeth Story, ed. *Andrew Marvell: The Complete Poems.* Harmondsworth: Penguin, 1972.

Dubrow, Heather. "The Country-House Poem: A Study in Generic Development." *Genre* 12 (1979): 153–79.

Edelman, Lee. "The Mirror and the Tank: AIDS, Subjectivity, and the Rhetoric of Activism." In *Homographesis: Essays in*

Gay Literary and Cultural Theory, 93–117. New York: Routledge, 1994.

Eliot, T. S. "Andrew Marvell." In *Selected Essays*, 251–63. New York: Harcourt, Brace & World, 1950. Rpt. in *Andrew Marvell*, ed. Lord, 18–28.

Ellis, William D., Jr. "Thomas D'Urfey, the Pope–Philips Quarrel, and *The Shepherd's Week*." *PMLA* 74 (1959): 203–12.

Empson, William. *Seven Types of Ambiguity*. 3rd edn. New York: New Directions, 1966.

Some Versions of Pastoral. 1935. New York: New Directions, 1974.

Fabiano, Gianfranco. "Fluctuation in Theocritus' Style." *Greek, Roman, and Byzantine Studies* 12 (1971): 517–37.

Fairclough, H. Rushton, trans. *Virgil*. 2 vols. Cambridge, MA: Harvard University Press, 1974.

Fischer, John Irwin. "Never on Sunday: John Gay's *The Shepherd's Week*." *Studies of Eighteenth Century Culture* 10 (1981): 191–203.

Fish, Stanley. "Commentary: The Young and the Restless." In *The New Historicism*, ed. Veeser, 303–16.

Doing What Comes Naturally: Change, Rhetoric, and the Practice of Theory in Literary and Legal Studies. Durham, NC: Duke University Press, 1989.

Forsgren, Adina. *John Gay: Poet "Of a Lesser Order."* Stockholm: Lagerström, 1964.

Friedman, Donald M. "Marvell's Musicks." In *Celebrated and Neglected Poems*, ed. Summers and Pebworth, 8–28.

Marvell's Pastoral Art. Berkeley: University of California Press, 1970.

Gay, John. *Poetry and Prose*. Ed. Vinton A. Dearing and Charles E. Beckwith. 2 vols. Oxford: Clarendon Press, 1974.

Goldsmith, Oliver, ed. *The Beauties of English Poesy*. 2 vols. London: William Griffin, 1767.

Gow, A. S. F., ed. *Theocritus*. 2nd edn. 2 vols. Cambridge: Cambridge University Press, 1952.

Gow, A. S. F., trans. *The Greek Bucolic Poets*. Cambridge: Cambridge University Press, 1953.

Greenblatt, Stephen. *Renaissance Self-Fashioning: From More to Shakespeare*. Chicago: University of Chicago Press, 1980.

"Sidney's *Arcadia* and the Mixed Mode." *Studies in Philology* 70 (1973): 269–78.

Greville, Sir Fulke. *The Life of the Renowned Sir Philip Sidney*. Ed. Nowell Smith. Oxford: Clarendon Press, 1907.

Grossman, Marshall. "Authoring the Boundary: Allegory, Irony, and the Rebus in 'Upon Appleton House.'" In "*The muses commonweale*": *Poetry and Politics in the Seventeenth Century*, ed. Claude J.

Summers and Ted-Larry Pebworth, 191–206. Columbia: University of Missouri Press, 1988.

"Literary Forms and Historical Consciousness in Renaissance Poetry." *Exemplaria* 1 (1989): 248–64.

Gutzwiller, Kathryn J. *Theocritus' Pastoral Analogies: The Formation of a Genre.* Madison: University of Wisconsin Press, 1991.

Halperin, David M. *Before Pastoral: Theocritus and the Ancient Tradition of Bucolic Poetry.* New Haven: Yale University Press, 1983.

Hamilton, A. C. *Sir Philip Sidney: A Study in His Life and Works.* Cambridge: Cambridge University Press, 1977.

Heliodorus. *An Aethiopian History.* Ed. Charles Whibley. Trans. Thomas Underdowne. 1895. New York: AMS Press, 1967.

Hine, Daryl, trans. *Theocritus: Idylls and Epigrams.* New York: Atheneum, 1982.

Holden, Anthony, trans. *Greek Pastoral Poetry.* Harmondsworth: Penguin, 1974.

Irving, William Henry. *John Gay: Favorite of the Wits.* New York: Russell & Russell, 1962.

Jenkyns, Richard. "Pastoral and Misprision." *Essays in Criticism* 39 (1989): 65–71.

Johnson, Samuel. *Lives of the English Poets.* Ed. George Birkbeck Hill. 3 vols. Oxford: Clarendon Press, 1905.

Johnson, W. R. *The Idea of the Lyric: Lyric Modes in Ancient and Modern Poetry.* Berkeley: University of California Press, 1982.

Kalstone, David. "Marvell and the Fictions of Pastoral." *English Literary Renaissance* 4 (1974): 174–88.

Sidney's Poetry: Contexts and Interpretations. Cambridge, MA: Harvard University Press, 1965.

Kennedy, Judith M., ed. *A Critical Edition of Yong's Translation of George of Montemayor's Diana and Gil Polo's Enamoured Diana.* Oxford: Clarendon Press, 1968.

Kennedy, William J. *Jacopo Sannazaro and the Uses of Pastoral.* Hanover, NH: University Press of New England, 1983.

Kermode, Frank, ed. *Andrew Marvell: Selected Poetry.* New York: Signet, 1967.

King, Bruce. "'The Mower Against Gardens' and the Levellers." *Huntington Library Quarterly* 33 (1970): 237–42.

Klause, John, Ann Baynes Coiro, and Michael C. Schoenfeldt. "The Achievement of Andrew Marvell: Excerpts from a Panel Discussion." In *Celebrated and Neglected Poems*, ed. Summers and Pebworth, 233–47.

Lanham, Richard A. "The *Old Arcadia.*" In Davis and Lanham, *Sidney's Arcadia*, 181–405.

Lawall, Gilbert. *Theocritus' Coan Pastorals: A Poetry Book*. Cambridge, MA: Harvard University Press, 1967.

Lawry, Jon S. *Sidney's Two Arcadias: Pattern and Proceeding*. Ithaca: Cornell University Press, 1972.

Leach, Eleanor Winsor. *Vergil's Eclogues: Landscapes of Experience*. Ithaca: Cornell University Press, 1974.

Leishman, J. B. *The Art of Marvell's Poetry*. London: Hutchinson, 1966.

Lentricchia, Frank. "Foucault's Legacy: A New Historicism?" In *The New Historicism*, ed. Veeser, 231–42.

Levao, Ronald. *Renaissance Minds and Their Fictions: Cusanus, Sidney, Shakespeare*. Berkeley: University of California Press, 1985.

Lewis, C. S. *English Literature in the Sixteenth Century Excluding Drama*. Oxford: Clarendon Press, 1954.

Lindenbaum, Peter. *Changing Landscapes: Anti-Pastoral Sentiment in the English Renaissance*. Athens, GA: University of Georgia Press, 1986.

"Sidney's *Arcadia*: The Endings of the Three Versions." *Huntington Library Quarterly* 34 (1970/71): 205–18.

Lindheim, Nancy. *The Structures of Sidney's Arcadia*. Toronto: University of Toronto Press, 1982.

Lord, George deF. "From Contemplation to Action: Marvell's Poetic Career." In *Andrew Marvell*, ed. Lord, 55–73.

Lord, George deF., ed. *Andrew Marvell: A Collection of Critical Essays*. Englewood Cliffs, NJ: Prentice-Hall, 1968.

MacCaffrey, Isabel G. "The Scope of Imagination in *Upon Appleton House*." In *Tercentenary Essays in Honor of Andrew Marvell*, ed. Kenneth Friedenreich, 224–44. Hamden, CT: Archon Books, 1977.

Marcus, Leah S. *The Politics of Mirth: Jonson, Herrick, Milton, Marvell, and the Defense of Old Holiday Pastimes*. Chicago: University of Chicago Press, 1986.

Marenco, Franco. "Double Plot in Sidney's Old 'Arcadia.'" In *Essential Articles for the Study of Sir Philip Sidney*, ed. Arthur F. Kinney, 287–310. Hamden, CT: Archon Books, 1986.

Marvell, Andrew. *The Poems and Letters of Andrew Marvell*. Ed. H. M. Margoliouth. Rev. P. Legouis and E. E. Duncan-Jones. 3rd edn. 2 vols. Oxford: Clarendon Press, 1952.

McCoy, Richard C. *Sir Philip Sidney: Rebellion in Arcadia*. New Brunswick, NJ: Rutgers University Press, 1979.

McWhir, Anne. "The Wolf in the Fold: John Gay in *The Shepherd's Week* and *Trivia*." *Studies in English Literature* 23 (1983): 413–23.

Miles, Gary. "Characterization and the Ideal of Innocence in Theocritus' *Idylls*." *Ramus* 6 (1977): 139–64.

Milton, John. *Complete Shorter Poems*. Ed. John Carey. London: Longman, 1971.

Paradise Lost. Ed. Alastair Fowler. London: Longman, 1971.

Mitchell, W. J. T., ed. *Against Theory: Literary Studies and the New Pragmatism*. Chicago: University of Chicago Press, 1985.

Molesworth, Charles. "Marvell's 'Upon Appleton House': The Persona as Historian, Philosopher, and Priest." *Studies in English Literature* 13 (1973): 149–62.

Montrose, Louis Adrian. "Celebration and Insinuation: Sir Philip Sidney and the Motives of Elizabethan Courtship." *Renaissance Drama*, n.s., 8 (1977): 3–35.

"'Eliza, Queene of shepheardes,' and the Pastoral of Power." *English Literary Renaissance* 10 (1980): 153–82.

"The Elizabethan Subject and the Spenserian Text." In *Literary Theory / Renaissance Texts*, ed. Patricia Parker and David Quint, 303–40. Baltimore: Johns Hopkins University Press, 1986.

"Of Gentlemen and Shepherds: The Politics of Elizabethan Pastoral Form." *ELH* 50 (1983): 415–59.

"'The perfecte paterne of a Poete': The Poetics of Courtship in *The Shepheardes Calendar*." *Texas Studies in Literature and Language* 21 (1979): 34–67.

"Professing the Renaissance: The Poetics and Politics of Culture." In *The New Historicism*, ed. Veeser, 15–36.

Motley, Christopher P. "Crossing the Threshold: Public Form and Private Meaning in Sidney's *Arcadia*." Unpublished essay.

Newsome, J., ed. *Pliny's Natural History: A Selection From Philemon Holland's Translation*. Oxford: Clarendon Press, 1964.

O'Loughlin, M. J. K. "This Sober Frame: A Reading of 'Upon Appleton House.'" In *Andrew Marvell*, ed. Lord, 120–42.

Otis, Brooks. *Virgil: A Study in Civilized Poetry*. Oxford: Clarendon Press, 1963.

Page, T. E., ed. *P. Vergili Maronis Bucolica et Georgica*. London: Macmillan, 1931.

Parry, Adam. "Landscape in Greek Poetry." *Yale Classical Studies* 15 (1957): 3–29.

Patrides, C. A., ed. *Approaches to Marvell: The York Tercentenary Lectures*. London: Routledge & Kegan Paul, 1978.

Patterson, Annabel. *Censorship and Interpretation: The Conditions of Writing and Reading in Early Modern England*. Madison: University of Wisconsin Press, 1984.

Marvell and the Civic Crown. Princeton: Princeton University Press, 1978.

Pastoral and Ideology: Virgil to Valéry. Berkeley: University of California Press, 1987.

Shakespeare and the Popular Voice. Cambridge: Basil Blackwell, 1989.
" 'The Very Age and Body of the Time His Form and Pressure':
Rehistoricizing Shakespeare's Theater." *New Literary History* 20
(1988): 91–95.

Poggioli, Renato. *The Oaten Flute: Essays on Pastoral Poetry and the
Pastoral Ideal.* Cambridge, MA: Harvard University Press, 1975.

Pope, Alexander. *The Correspondence of Alexander Pope.* Ed. George
Sherburn. 5 vols. Oxford: Oxford University Press, 1956.

Putnam, Michael C. J. *Virgil's Pastoral Art: Studies in the Eclogues.*
Princeton: Princeton University Press, 1970.

Quint, David. *Origin and Originality in Renaissance Literature: Versions of
the Source.* New Haven: Yale University Press, 1983.

Ricks, Christopher. "Its Own Resemblance." In *Approaches to Marvell,*
ed. Patrides, 108–35.

Tennyson. New York: Macmillan, 1972.

Rist, Anna, trans. *The Poems of Theocritus.* Chapel Hill: University of
North Carolina Press, 1978.

Rogers, John. "The Great Work of Time: Marvell's Pastoral
Historiography." In *Celebrated and Neglected Poems,* ed. Summers
and Pebworth, 207–32.

Rosenmeyer, Thomas G. *The Green Cabinet: Theocritus and the European
Pastoral Lyric.* Berkeley: University of California Press, 1969.

Røstvig, Maren-Sofie. *The Happy Man: Studies in the Metamorphosis of a
Classical Ideal 1600–1700.* Rev. edn. Oslo: Norwegian University
Press, 1962.

Rudenstine, Neil. *Sidney's Poetic Development.* Cambridge, MA: Harvard University Press, 1967.

Sannazaro, Jacopo. *Arcadia & Piscatorial Eclogues.* Trans. Ralph Nash.
Detroit: Wayne State University Press, 1966.

Opere di Iacopo Sannazaro. Ed. Enrico Carrara. Turin: Tipografia
Torinese, 1952.

Schiller, Friedrich von. *Naive and Sentimental Poetry and On the Sublime.*
Trans. Julius A. Elias. New York: Frederick Ungar, 1975.

Segal, Charles. *Poetry and Myth in Ancient Pastoral: Essays on Theocritus
and Virgil.* Princeton: Princeton University Press, 1981.

Shakespeare, William. *The Complete Works.* Ed. Alfred Harbage *et al.*
Baltimore: Penguin, 1969.

The Riverside Shakespeare. Ed. G. Blakemore Evans. Boston: Houghton Mifflin, 1974.

Sidney, Sir Philip. *An Apology for Poetry; or, The Defence of Poesy.* Ed.
Geoffrey Shepherd. London: Thomas Nelson and Sons, 1965.

The Countess of Pembroke's Arcadia (The Old Arcadia). Ed. Jean
Robertson. Oxford: Clarendon Press, 1979.

The Poems of Sir Philip Sidney. Ed. William A. Ringler, Jr. Oxford: Clarendon Press, 1962.

The Prose Works of Sir Philip Sidney. Ed. Albert Feuillerat. 4 vols. 1912. Cambridge: Cambridge University Press, 1962.

Smith, Bruce R. *Homosexual Desire in Shakespeare's England: A Cultural Poetics*. Chicago: University of Chicago Press, 1991.

Spacks, Patricia Meyer. *John Gay*. New York: Twayne, 1965.

Spenser, Edmund. *The Faerie Queene*. Ed. A. C. Hamilton. London: Longman, 1977.

Spofford, Edward W. "Theocritus and Polyphemus." *American Journal of Philology* 90 (1969): 22–35.

Stillman, Robert E. "The Politics of Sidney's Pastoral: Mystification and Mythology in *The Old Arcadia*." *ELH* 52 (1985): 795–814.

Sidney's Poetic Justice: The Old Arcadia, Its Eclogues, and Renaissance Pastoral Traditions. Lewisburg, PA: Bucknell University Press, 1986.

Summers, Claude J., and Ted-Larry Pebworth, eds. *On the Celebrated and Neglected Poems of Andrew Marvell*. Columbia: University of Missouri Press, 1992.

Swan, Jim. "At Play in the Garden of Ambivalence: Andrew Marvell and the Green World." *Criticism* 17 (1975): 295–307.

"'Betwixt Two Labyrinths': Andrew Marvell's Rational Amphibian." *Texas Studies in Language and Literature* 17 (1975): 551–72.

"History, Pastoral and Desire: Andrew Marvell's Mower Poems." *International Review of Psycho-Analysis* 3 (1976): 193–202.

Toliver, Harold. *Marvell's Ironic Vision*. New Haven: Yale University Press, 1965.

Trevelyan, R. C., trans. *The Idylls of Theocritus*. Cambridge: Cambridge University Press, 1947.

Trowbridge, Hoyt. "Pope, Gay, and *The Shepherd's Week*." *Modern Language Quarterly* 5 (1944): 79–88.

Turner, James. *The Politics of Landscape: Rural Scenery and Society in English Poetry 1630–1660*. Oxford: Basil Blackwell, 1979.

Van Sickle, John. "Epic and Bucolic." *Quaderni Urbinati di Cultura Classica* 19 (1975): 45–72.

"The Fourth Pastoral Poems of Virgil and Theocritus." *Atti e Memorie dell' Arcadia*, ser. 3a, vol. 5, fasc. 1 (1969): 129–48.

Veeser, H. Aram, ed. *The New Historicism*. New York: Routledge, 1989.

Wallace, John M. *Destiny his Choice: The Loyalism of Andrew Marvell*. Cambridge: Cambridge University Press, 1968.

Warnke, Frank J. "The Meadow-sequence in *Upon Appleton House*:

Questions of Tone and Meaning." In *Approaches to Marvell*, ed. Patrides, 234–50.

Wood, Nigel. "Gay and the Ironies of Rustic Simplicity." In *John Gay and the Scriblerians*, ed. Peter Lewis and Nigel Wood, 94–121. London: Vision Press, 1988.

Index

213